Reviews for CRAVING Part 1 Uprising

One of the most original, beautifully written and well-crafted novels I've read in a long time! I was completely drawn in from the get-go, and absolutely loved the author's use of description of the different scenery and locales, and his attention to detail. It is very romantic and literary in nature. We really feel like we are there inside the story seeing it through Noah and Nora's eyes, and feel like we are in Ireland or at the society balls of New York. Can't wait to read the next one (part 2) now! (5 stars) Laura Clarke – Indie Book Reviewers

I really loved this book and was utterly entranced at this cross-continental whirlwind romance of Noah Mason and Nora Clifford. I thought it was excellently written (a few minor editing things but nothing too major) and kept my attention from the very opening pages to the fulfilling finish… for now (the story will continue on in part 2) It is a relatively quick read, one I finished in the course of an evening. Maybe I just didn't want to put it down! This isn't some crazy action-packed over the top type novel, but more of one that examines life and love and the complications that can ensue. I was genuinely surprised at a few things that happened, and thought the narrative was great. Ready for the next one! (Craving part 2-Out of Control) (5 stars) *Essie Harmon – Goodreads; Shelfari; Barnes & Noble; Indie Book Reviewers*

This book was terrific! Once I started reading I didn't want to stop until I'd finished the whole thing. It pulls you in from the beginning, and I enjoyed the author's "voice" and his lovely style of writing. The interweaving plotlines were well-crafted and not predictable, and I enjoyed the element of the Irish background, as well as the New York High Society. The characters were all interesting and well-written. This is the first part of a 'duology" (2 book set) so while part of the story wraps up with Noah and Nora, it is clearly just getting started and will continue on in part 2. Recommend for older readers as there are some intense love scenes (not too graphic though). (4-5 stars) *Stacy Decker – Goodreads; Shelfari; Barnes & Noble; Indie Book Reviewers*

A compelling read, and one that will definitely appeal to fans of romantic/drama/literary fiction novels. It is set in the 60's, but I wouldn't consider it 'historical', although the world-building and descriptive detailing for the era is done quite nicely. Brings back some memories… I appreciated Don Fullington's writing style, and it created a very atmospheric experience that pulls us in emotionally. The story flowed well and kept my interest throughout. Curious to see what is in store for our leads in the next book. (4 stars). *Jenna Brewster– Goodreads; Shelfari; Barnes & Noble; Indie Book Reviewers*

I loved the plot line, as it was really original and unlike anything I've read before, and thought the conversations and dialogue with the characters was really well done and very authentic-feeling. I really connected with Noah and Nora, and I was really invested in their fates. I can tell that this book is more of a set up for events in the next one, so I'm eager to read on! (3 stars) *Claire Middleton– Goodreads; Shelfari; Barnes & Noble; Indie Book Reviewers*

This was the first book I've read by this author Don Fullington, but it definitely will not the last! He has a gift for writing descriptive and life-like scenes that make us feel like we are really there inside the story, as opposed to it all just being "told" to us, as so many rookie authors make the mistake of doing. I like that this book didn't feel stale or derivative of others that I've read, but instead like a new niche of literary style romance-drama. The entire novel was one that I thought was well-crafted and delivered an emotional win. Ready for part 2 now! Recommend for fans of Nicholas Sparks, Pat Conroy, etc… (4 stars) *Sam Ryan – Goodreads; Shelfari; Barnes & Noble; Indie Book Reviewers*

From the opening pages of "Craving, part 1" I knew it would be different from the books I've been reading lately and I was right! Fullington does an *amazing* job of setting the scene and creating characterizations in such a skillful way that not only sucks us in, but creates great visualizations and elicits genuine emotional investments. I truly cared about the characters' fates, and am really curious to see what the next book has in store for them. An interesting and diverse cast of characters, along with several intriguing plotlines interwoven against unique and dynamic setting makes this a memorable read for me. Highly recommend. (5 stars) *Kaylee Stevens– Goodreads; Shelfari; Barnes & Noble; Indie Book Reviewers*

I was hooked from the opening pages of "Craving" and my interest never wavered for a moment! I loved the creative and strong characters and plots that continued to build and grow more interesting and complex Although there are some familiar themes and tropes at play, the author brings a fresh voice and makes it all his own. I've read a ton of literary fiction over the years so I'm familiar with the genre, but I felt that this book stood out in terms of the quality of writing, and the fact that it wasn't boring! Ha, I'm only half joking there… I appreciated the passion and the descriptive details that really brought the story to life. Will be interested in seeing where this series and our leads go to in the next one. Recommend for anyone (adults) who enjoy an engrossing well-written novel that will take you to another time and place(s). (4-5 stars) *Anabella Johnson – Goodreads; Shelfari; Barnes & Noble; Indie Book Reviewers*

Interesting, diverse, dynamic, emotionally-engaging and creative, " Craving" (Book 1 Uprising) from Don Fullington is a must read for fans of lit fiction who want a real escape for a while. This book takes you back in time and to another country and back.. He's from US, she's from Ireland. They are from different world but cannot deny their love. But it's the life they lead, the challenges, the murky ups- and downs of the turbulent 60's that help shape this novel into something special. Overall an engrossing story and I'm ready for the next one! (4 stars) *Layla Messing – Goodreads; Shelfari; Barnes & Noble; Indie Book Reviewers*

CRAVING

a novel

Don Fullington

PART ONE--UPRISING

Contentment Books*New York

For Marie

and

My deepest thanks to all those others who one way or another made this journey possible. My father and mother; my children Stephen, Kevin and Dr. Nora (no relation to the book's major character—except that I love her name); and my grandchildren Julia, Claire and Quinn. My helpers—Mollie Conkey Fullington who escaped from Connecticut to the furthest reaches of the Adirondack high peaks so she could have a clear vision first read of the manuscript; Katie Winkowski; Dr Karim Sayad; Peggy King; Father Mark Nowel of Providence College. And a very special shout to Father Kevin Malick of the New York Catholic Archiocese who while altruistically laboring to improve his parish moved his congregants of all ages through humor and rare astute simplicity to the true vision of the Trinity. Unbeknownst to him, his homilies brought hope during the darkest of hours as my finish line approached.

Non qui parum, sed qui plus cupit, pauper est.

--Seneca the younger

Epistutae Morales

It is not the man who has too little, but the man who craves more who is poor.

--early AD Latin translation

one

1966

TWELVE MONTHS, Noah thought as his taxi sped along the Grand Central zipping in and out of lanes heading for the Van Wyck and JFK on this glorious end of July afternoon. Twelve months seeming more like twelve years. Still they had made it happen despite all the negatives, and the prospect was exhilarating.

Where was she now, he wondered. Somewhere over Boston quite likely, if the Aer Lingus flight remained on schedule. That close after so long. His heart leapt at the realization and tingling ripples spread through his body. How had he been so fortunate? Such a magnificent fluke, one that utterly dazed him from the first rush of lightheadedness.

Pictures came back to him now as they had so often since then. His stormy crossing on the old cattle boat *Naomh Eanna* from Galway to Inishmore--the largest of the three craggy, black-gray limestone reaches known as the Aran Islands. They swept up from the raging currents to loom above the merciless waves thirty miles out in the North Atlantic.

From the dock he had taken a horse-drawn jaunting cart up through the tiny Gaelic-speaking village of Kilronan and out across a rocky storm-lashed landscape of ancient Celtic-cross graveyards and scattered snow-painted fishing cottages etched against a steel sky. Several miles out in a great gray-stone box of a Georgian manor, one totally alien to the rest of the island's simplicity, a door had opened on a period sitting room, and there amongst a scattering of travelers he saw her. A girl with long silky brown hair and a deeply flushed face. She looked up from her book and smiled at him. Oh god it was so all encompassing that it rendered him breathless as he stared at her soft blue eyes. Oh so soft and oh so blue. Swift waves of pleasure swept over him. A door had opened and his life was changing.

Later he caught sight of her through the fine lines of vision drawn by broad chips of rain, gale-hurled against his steamy bedroom windowpane. She stood below facing the full brunt of the storm, there in a brown hooded slicker with her face glowing all the more and exuding a tenderness and longing that made him ache. Yet at the same time, the high cheekbones and firm full lips bespoke another facet of her being--a determination he had never seen in someone so young. Such resolution combined with a hint of passion fired him. It was as if some unknown force had seized his heart causing it to burst and flood his entire being with love. He could still remember Joyce's words as they rushed him that afternoon. *A girl stood before him in midstream, alone and still, gazing out to sea. She seemed like one whom magic had changed into the likeness of a strange and beautiful seabird.*

Then during tea that evening, as he sat with the other guests at the long massive mahogany dining table, he held his breath in anticipation of their first warmth of union. Sitting directly across from him, initially she paid him no mind but instead chattered away with the others. Then suddenly and quite abruptly she turned to him, closing out the rest and asked: "What in god's name drove you to seek a place as far distant and desperate as this for your holidays. Don't tell me it was some sudden burnin' ardor that was after seizin' you."

He laughed to cover the embarrassment of her truth. "No. Not at all," he replied finding himself slipping right into her accent. "But if I might want to be asking you the same."

"Would you now?" And she grinned from the tease of it but then quickly retreated by stuffing a forkful of seafood salad into her mouth.

"To be sure, if I knew your name." And by now he was totally taken by the blue of her eyes.

She swallowed and stifled her embarrassment. "Why it's Nora. Sure you must have heard it said here by now." Then she licked her luscious full lips and dabbed them with her serviette. And surely if it weren't for the distance, he in that moment of dazed rapture would have leaned across the table and kissed them.

He sighed to compose himself and shrugged his shoulders. "Well I wanted to be polite."

"Polite is it, Noah."

"Ah so you know mine."

"Well I wasn't after being born yesterday."

"I guess you weren't." And he laughed some more.

"I think I kind of fancy it."

"What?" he asked bewildered.

"Noah! It does evoke a certain unusual aura to be sure. A grandness of sorts. Oh I don't mean in the Biblical sense. Although there's that there as well. But when you go thrashin' it about in your mind for a spell, well it all comes out soundin' like twins."

"What?" Now he was completely baffled.

"Noah and Nora."

"Oh!" he beamed with delight. "I hadn't thought of that before."

"Well sure how could you, if you didn't even know me name?" she blushed.

"Noah and Nora, indeed. Sounds like a team. Like-- Like a perfect match," he chanced.

"Well I don't know if I'd be professin' anything as far-fetched as that mind you, but--"

"But?"

"It's grand all the same." After she'd thought on it for a moment, she went on. "But still you haven't answered my question, don't you know?"

"Nor you mine. And since I'm a stranger in your country, it's only right that you go first. Or would you say fittin'?"

"Ah," she smiled and sighed as she used her knife European-style to collect the remains of the salad for her fork. During that pause she became quite serious and put the utensils down. "I've been coming here a good few times now to be alone with myself."

"Well that sounds pretty severe."

"Not when you come from a family you couldn't cull from a horde of rips and rousers. Once you'd be chocked into the lot of them you'd see right enough."

"That bad?"

"Oh god yes. I mean they're not terrible, mind ya. But there's times when you'd have to be spot on your bean or they'd tramp right over ya for sure. And trampin' it is."

"Trampin, heh." And he giggled a bit. "I'm sorry. I'm enjoying your words, and I guess I shouldn't be."

"Ah it's all right. Trampin' of the spirit is what I mean. It doesn't sound as flat-out brutal that way, I suppose. But it does seem to snatch every screed of perspective from me all the same. So I come here and after a few days the old spirit is only pulsin' again, leapin' for life as they'd say. I suppose it is a bit looney right enough. Trudgin' clear across the country from Dublin so as I can be after reclaimin' me psyche as it were. But you coming all the way from America and not looking as if you'd been thrashed about that much. I'd say you'd never lost touch with that psyche of yours. So why did you come if I may be finally asking?"

"Ah I guess it needed some refurbishing too. But mainly I suppose because of Synge's *Riders To The Sea* and Flaherty's *Man of Aran*. The thrill of it all. I just couldn't resist." Then smiling softly at her for a few seconds, he dared the tease. "Now I'm glad I didn't." Her face reddened all the more as she blushed profusely and sent his own blood racing.

SHE WAS EQUALLY RADIANT in the next morning's sun when they lay on their stomachs at the brink of the rocky cliffs on the distant western side of the island amid the wild rock rose and mountain avens. As she spoke, he noticed her eyes were the same abundant blue as the deepening sky. "Isn't it only magical how the colors all interweave and shift so swiftly? If you just blink now, you'll be after missing dozens of only the most exquisitely formed visions."

"God!" he gasped as he leaned over. "God the creator." This view would always remain with him. A sheer three hundred feet or more below was the foaming white sea. It swirled furiously as it pounded against giant rock beds and swept up to batter the cliffs with enough power to send full clouds of pink and soft purple mist rising high over the southwestern part of the island.

"Look, but it's even grander over there," she said, pointing down the coastline to sections where waves crashed through water-carved hollows and caves in the cliff walls and then were expelled with such force that they traveled several hundred yards through the air forming giant vermilion plumes that disintegrated in heavy downpours across the sea.

"All the god-given gradations of color--the reds,

the pinks, the indigos, the greens. All vying for a place in the mind's eye, all trying to secure that much of your soul. Even if I were to have the keenest sight now and a mind doubly the size of me own, I would never be able to capture the wanderin' ways of this beauty, to realize it fully. It's all such a grand heavenly jumble. Like a throng of rainbows gone half mad."

He smiled with the joy. The essence of her words and the husky lightness of her voice in the sea-scented air swept through him conceiving the most seductive trance. He was ablaze with incredible warmth as he turned to look at her. I really am in love, he remembered thinking then. This is what it is. And surely she must be in love as well. Fueled by such extraordinary visions, they were caught by the same rapture, fused as one by the wonder. Wonder that roused her tears, tears that slaked his parched heart. "Oh," he sighed and reached out to touch the crown of her head. Then stroking the angel softness of her hair turned auburn by the sun, his lips brushed, then kissed her silken cheek. He could feel the wild pulse of her heart as he went on to stroke her neck. He spoke, yet it was as if the words hadn't formed in his mind but had come from his now free-floating spirit. "I would have hated to discover this place alone."

"And how could you say that?"

"It would hurt so much. I-- I mean all of this and to be without someone. It would be such a painful blow-- how alone, how empty you were."

"Well there's usually at least a few others here

mind you. This is a good bit unusual this day. I'd say there'd--"

"No. No. No." He silenced her and looked directly into her eyes. "I don't mean others." Then to emphasize the preciseness of his words he paused. "I mean someone, really someone."

She smiled at him, a lingering loving smile and this time without the slightest hint of a blush. "Someday I'm going to have this in my life all the time not just on me holidays. Or if not just this, at least a good fair bit of something similar somewhere in the world. Yes, even if it does sound madly impractical at present." As she spoke an indomitable verve visibly rose through her being and fired her.

"I think you will," he assured her. "And I think that's brilliant. It's the new direction today."

"What, being madly impractical?" And she laughed.

"No," he chuckled along with her. "Going after real values. That's what life is all about. People in the States are beginning to call it the new freedom. It's the only way you can touch on the energy and individuality of life."

"And you believe that, do you?" she asked anxiously.

"I'm coming around to it again."

"WHICH TERMINAL IS IT? Excuse me mister, which terminal do you want? I need to know sometime today."

"What?" Noah jumped to the sound of the shrill New York voice. Realizing where he was, he shook his head and quickly looked out to note the taxi had already reached Kennedy. "Oh--International Arrivals. Sorry, I was lost in my thoughts."

"Some pretty strong thoughts there, man," he quipped after he'd released a cloud of cigarette smoke.

"Right." But they wouldn't be thoughts much longer, he delighted as he looked at his watch. The plane should be almost here, and the thoughts will be real. How beautiful not to have to part, to be able to honor our feelings, to give them free reign to go on and on. His heart leapt and trembled as the poet Dante's had for his angelic Beatrice . He should be so thankful for this chance. It might never have happened had they not valiantly persisted in keeping their love alive at such a long distance. Together they had devised a plan that, as devout Catholics, alternately one of them would go to Mass each day and pray for their continued togetherness. Between them he didn't think they'd missed a single day.

"*How many loved your moments of glad grace*, he remembered whispering as they sat in Bewley's tea room on Dublin's Grafton Street the day before he left. Then he touched her face and ran his fingers along its beautiful contours. "*And loved the sorrows of your changing face*," he continued. "*But one man loved the pilgrim soul in you.* You have a pilgrim's soul, Nora."

She smiled. "And so do you. But you know how Yeats ends that verse?"

"I-- I guess I've forgotten. I just remembered what was most important to me."

"Ah but you have to remember it all."

"So?"

"*Murmur, a little sadly, how love fled and paced upon the mountains overhead and hid his face among a crowd of stars.*"

For them it hadn't fled, he sighed now as he thought of the plane landing. Then suddenly he felt a little quiver of panic as he pulled himself up in the taxi seat. Would she still think the same of him?

GOD, WHAT WILL HE BE THINKING OF ME, she wondered. The flight had just passed over Boston and would be landing at JFK in approximately forty minutes the pilot had announced. I must look desperate after sitting in that bloody cramped seat for the last seven hours and collectin' the smell of smoke from a crowd of these eejits. "Mother of devine *Jaysus*," she gasped aloud when the light came on in the loo and she saw herself. There was little she could do about her now very wrinkled blue tweed suit that she'd purchased at Cleary's January sale for the purpose of looking her finest when she arrived. But she could do something about her hair, which she brushed with great zeal to restore its previous early morning sheen. And her face--she soaked paper towels with hot water and began cleaning it. As she did her complexion lost its oily paleness and began to redden.

In a flash she imagined Noah standing there gazing at her in the mirror. She felt her skin go ablaze as once again she was caught by his handsomeness. The long lean plains of his youthful face, the slightly muscular yet lithe neck and strong classic jaw. How familiar they still seemed. But the eyes even more so. Pale brown eyes that dazzled with their clarity and lightness, hypnotized with their mellow longing. It was a face that was virile and yet spiritual in the way Botticelli had seen the faces of young men.

She kept his vision in her mind's eye when she returned to her seat and let herself remember the night on Aran when they were making their way back to Breda Hernon's manor house from a nearby smoky gas-lit pub. He had taken her hand as they walked along a lonely horseshoe strand on the eastern side of the island under a wash of stars. When they stopped to look at the clear night spray of lights shooting the sea from Galway and Salthill, he turned and softly kissed her with his warm moist lips. She had forced herself to talk above the fierce pounding of her heart hoping he wouldn't notice how gone she was on him. "What were you meaning this morning on the cliffs when you said you were coming around to it again?"

"Ever since I've been in Ireland, but especially since I came to Aran, I've been remembering. No, that's not right. I've been reliving the feelings I had when I was in college. Even though we had to work our way through those years, we were lit by the wonder of living as we chose. Swept up by the possibilities. Carried forth by an inner assurance that we could achieve anything we yearned for. We were exalted by it, really." Then he paused again as if to relish the memories.

"What happened?" She'd asked enchanted by the beauty of his words and not wanting him to stop.

"Oh, what people in the Fifties used to refer to as the nitty-gritty of Monday morning."

"I suppose it does have its way of banjaxing things all right."

Noah giggled and then laughed heartily. But she had been startled by this, and he had immediately stopped himself. "Oh, I'm not jeering you," he'd said and she'd loved the way he'd picked up on the Irish vernacular. Then she remembered he'd squeezed her around the waist and she'd reeled from the sensation. "It's just that you have such a happy way of making sense. And I like it. I love-- love it." Then he leaned forward and, resting his arms on her shoulders, kissed her forehead, her cheek and then gave a slow lingering kiss to her lips. Afterwards, they walked down closer to the water and sat on the strand."

"I feel so light. As light as these grains of sand," he said, letting the fine granules slip through his fingers. "Coming here is the most important thing I've ever done." When she shook her head in amazement, he insisted: "Well it is you know. I've never felt so alive. Not even during those college years. There's such clarity here, such vision. It proves that one major rule of grammar can be broken. Scene after scene is the ultimate. Who says there can only be one?" Then he gestured to the sea and the vast heavens. "You can feel it. It's like a pull. A force that lifts you up, takes you with it. You're a part of all that is, and knowing that you're at the same time distanced from it. It's as if you can see into eternity. And there is no time. Neither past nor future nor present." He lay back on the strand with his arms behind his head as if intoxicated. "Just a whirling dazzling beauty of stars. And a music so tender, so gentle, yet so compelling that it uproots your soul and sets it free to drift. Adrift among the heavens." After a time he drifted back to her. "That way and only that way can you truly know existence."

"Have you ever felt all of this before?" she remembered asking him after she too had let herself drift with the sheer wonder of his thoughts.

"Once or twice. But only fleetingly. This is the longest I've felt it."

"You should come here to write your books."

"Books?" he said, sitting up abruptly. "Who said anything about writing books?"

"Oh, I know." She smiled. "You're naturally suited to that."

"Not so." He shook his head and looked away. She could feel his spirit dip. "I tried that once."

"Did you finish one?"

"Oh yeah. I always finish what I start."

"Well, so that's grand."

"Not so," he sighed. "It was rejected all to hell."

"What are you going to do about it?"

"Oh," he shrugged. "I just put it away and went on being a newspaper reporter. I'd almost forgotten it."

"Forgotten it? That's bleedin' mad. You mustn't forget it. I can tell."

"Maybe I should show it to you sometime for a laugh or two."

"Don't be an eejit. I'd be honored to read it."

"An eejit." He roared laughing. "Nobody's ever called me an eejit before."

"Well, you are one if you feel that way."

"And what about you, Nora?"

"Are you trying to bamboozle me into calling meself an eejit?"

"Ah that's me nailed. The great bamboozler."

Then she remembered how they'd both laughed and hugged each other. And after that he looked at her, studied her. "You write poems? No. You paint. That's it. You're an artist."

"Ah sure, you could hardly be saying that of me when I spend my days working in the office of a building developer. But I do like to paint, mind you. Suppose it helps me to run away to myself. Puts things right. But how did you--"

"Ah the old Mason savvy--don't ya know," he

kidded. "Have you done many?"

"A few. I'm taking some courses at U.C.D."

"How's it going?"

"Oh, I don't know. A couple of professors seem to like my work right enough. But sure it's all too soon to tell."

"I'm not so sure about that," he said, looking into her eyes with confidence. Then as if he'd made another, more startling discovery there, he looked so darkly that she shivered.

"What?" she asked with trepidation.

"I always thought-- this was something shadowy," he said carefully. "Something-- Something that almost never happened. Well--that you should never even try for it. Because-- Because if you did you'd never find it. But it's not so. It's a lie."

"What? Whatever--"

He put his fingers to her lips. "Love," he whispered. "I mean real love. I only imagined what that must be like until now. But even then I was way off the mark. Way off anything as-- as incredible as this." His whispers seemed to be coming from the stars and stroking her heart. She wanted to reach out and draw him close, to smooth his ruffled hair, to soothe and lighten his darkness. Then she remembered him kissing her again. Tenderly at first, then more urgently. For the first time, he let his tongue go into her mouth and soon they were giving and taking breath until they were breathing as one.

BREATHING AS ONE. As she went about reattaching her seat belt, she held the thought, clung to it fretting that somehow it might escape her. She even blocked the stewardess's voice announcing landing details for JFK. After a time of convincing herself, as always before, she felt herself go all warm with the prospect. It was as if he had come to her on Aran and magically swept away all the loneliness that had haunted her from childhood. Today they'd be together again. This time not to part. Then soon, one grand and glorious day they'd be living in the Irish countryside by the sap green sea, and he'd be writing his books, beautiful books just like the one he'd let her read. What a passionate writer, gorgeous really, with such range and power for portraying all the hues of existence. He just needed more courage and conviction. But sure that will happen when he can devote himself to his real work. Brilliant work. That's what it will be.

She sighed as she thought about it. Then she remembered the letter he had written her just after his return to America. Even though she'd memorized it the moment she read it, she took it out of her handbag to look at the lovely handsome strokes of his handwriting.

Let nothing impede this. Let it be someday. I carry this thrill, this upward surge from Aran, and how wonderful it feels. I set my mind adrift. Our cottage, if not on Aran, will be somewhere in the west of Ireland, high on a wind-lashed hill where our acreage will sweep through verdant grasses and garnishes of purple and white heather down to the shore of a rolling frothy sea. And beside the cottage we will have two fine gardens. One with radiant flowers to nourish our souls. The other with many vegetables to satiate the hunger borne of seaside air. I will write seven hours a day, and you will paint gorgeous landscapes. Each day we will take time to swim in the sea, and such will fuel our spirits. Then at night, we will sit beside the hearth, sipping strong tea and dreaming the dreams of lovers. And on our mantle will be flowers. Always flowers-- Words come at me in such a rush when I think of this. They form a beautiful vision, an indelible imprint.

> *Yes, we will build a cottage in Ireland*
> *Beside the sea.*
> *Fine and proud and whitewashed be.*
> *And it will rise strong, this cottage beside the sea*
>
> *Strong to take all gales, this lee.*
> *And stand it will till judgement's due*
> *Love's covenant that we both drew.*

She sighed again from the utter thrill of the thought as the plane began its descent. Someday soon they would have this. And only each other.

NOAH GLIMPSED HIS IMAGE in the restroom mirror and wondered if he'd worn the right clothes. He wanted to look his handsomest for her, but he hadn't been able to decide whether this would be achieved with one of his dapper new summer suits or his lightweight navy blazer and white duck trousers. As he mused over his selection an image of his mother, tall and slim and quite youthful came to him from distant years and with it a scene played out. They had just watched Joan Crawford and John Garfield in Warner Brothers *Humoresque*. In those days his mother was the ticket seller and his father the projectionist in their small town movie house--The Ritz. "Oh wouldn't I just love to be able to have glad rags like hers," his mother, who looked quite like Joan, sighed as she peered so longingly into the window of the New Yorker dress shop on Main Street. "Of course there's nothing Joan Crawford would even consider wearing in this dump of a town. But at least it would make me feel good if I could buy something out of this window."

"Why mama, I'll buy you something better than this stuff when I get big," Noah insisted. "And you'll be able to have houses just like she did and filled with all those grand things."

"Oh how swell that would be. The money to have it all," she said as hope loomed. But then she quickly quelled it and retreated to her somber nature. "Don't be making promises you can't keep, Noah. That's what your father did. Once you make them, it just about eats your heart up if you can't keep them."

Noah shooed the image and went on to delight that he had chosen the blazer and white ducks. After all it was the latest fashion and put forth a far more dashing image than his pale summer seersuckers would have. He laughed to himself. A few weeks ago he would have had little choice of apparel. But so much had happened in his career since then. Certainly at first he had found the changes painful. Then he had made the adjustment. A much larger paycheck will help do that. Now he was quite pleased that he was advancing moneywise toward the time in the not-too-distant future when with Nora's encouragement he would write the books he so longed to do--through the money he so longed to have. It would be just as Nora had written him. *Someday soon please god, you'll be here in Ireland bursting with the confidence, writing away and it will all come round with only the most captivating of stories tumbling down onto your fine pages.*

Not only was he in love with her, but he was in love with her words as well. Swept away by them. How could he help but be? To him, she was just like Jennie in Selznick's *Portrait of Jennie.* A film he had seen six times during its three-day run at the Ritz back in the Forties when he was only twelve. He could hear the Debussy themes playing over the love scenes. Jennifer Jones and Joseph Cotton. She the embodiment of a spirit returned to earth. He the disillusioned artist. They fall in love, and she inspires him to do his finest work. So often he had returned to the conclusion that this was nothing but a put-on. Particularly after watching the strange sorrow of his mother and father. Now as he waited for Nora's arrival, he disbanded all the negative thoughts. This would be.

THE PLANE TOUCHED DOWN then coasted along the runway. As it turned toward the terminals, dazzling sunlight flooded her. She glanced at her cuticles and began wringing her hands. She'd forgotten about them. Fizzin' hell, they're like the bleedin' dukes of a farmer, she thought. Before she left she had scrubbed them raw with Sunlight soap to remove the last traces of viridian and burnt umber oils. Even though she'd used loads of her mother's precious Nivea cream, the softness hadn't returned and the redness hadn't disappeared. Now she was even more tense and fearful that he would be overly disappointed, so she crossed herself. God, I hope he's not. And after letting meself come all this way with no proper means of shirkin' the rigors of fate. I'd be right banjaxed all the same. Joinin' the ragman, to be sure. And her tension began to shift to panic. I can liken this fair enough to the jittery way I felt in Dublin the day he came to call on me parents for the first time. The jitthers were only hoppin' in me heart. She remembered she and her da racing about dodging nieces and nephews in a mad anxious attempt to tidy the house and vainly give the shock of life to the cushions on their dilapidated sofas and chairs.

"I don't know what Margaret and Mick will be

thinking let alone you're American lad by the cut of this place," daddy fretted away.

"Oh always Margaret and Mick. Always what they might be after thinking. Never what I might be feeling," Nora could still hear herself giving out that day.

"Ah Nora, don't be daft thinking such thoughts."

Then in the midst of the madness, Noah arrived at the door. "Good god almighty, what must you be thinking?"

"Something very nice." And he had such a loving smile. Dear lord it was only gorgeous. Then he'd kissed her. "Now stop all this apologizing, you'll make me out to be a snob," he had whispered, calming her fears while at the same time rousing her body.

"Are you joking me?" she asked as the da continued to hustle about. "I told them you're a writer from New York and already they think you're only brilliant."

"Brilliant is it?" he teased.

"Yes, so you can relax and be enjoying all this ditherin' around."

Just then mammy called out from her kitchen duties: "Davy, don't be foostering in there like an eejit. Stop that bloomin' tidying. You don't want that bloody Yank knowing we're quaverin' over what he's after thinking do you?"

Daddy's face blanched in horror as mammy scurried in to meet Noah. "Kathleen," he gasped. "What a thing to be blitherin' in front of Nora's gentleman caller."

Mammy laughed heartily. "So you're here are you?

Well I'll tell you what I've always told my own. It's the people that count and not the cut of their fizzin' reception rooms. If they're not worth a tinker's damn even a classy mews house wouldn't cover their effin tracks. So what are they worth? Bugger all! I'll tell you."

"Kathleen!" Daddy gasped again as Noah laughed.

Still she kept on. "But if they're only the salt of the earth--as we are of course, don't ya know--we could be domiciled in the middle of a bloody loo and the halos of the saints would be glitterin' off us like those northwren lights. As of course they are and why wouldn't they be."

"Kathleen!! And a loo yet. Would you be plaverin' on like this forever?"

NOW AS SHE WAITED for the plane to roll to a stop. Nora shuddered. She was remembering how when they were only after ridding themselves of the grandchildren to the pictures and having their first jar that her granny had rushed over for a good spy of Noah. "Oh I didn't think anyone was here," she said in a bright cheery voice as she burst into the room, smoothing her winter white hair. "Well I won't stay at all, at all, sure I won't."

"Oh no, of course you won't stay," mammy snapped at her. "You didn't think anyone was here. You just got all dressed up in your fanciest clothes only to be after crossing the road. And I suppose you didn't see Nora's friend arriving either?"

"Oh so he's the American," nanny feigned surprise.

Then her eyes moved across every inch of Noah's face with a cautious scrutiny that appeared to shift to horror. As Noah said later, it was as if she were confronting *The Creature From The Black Lagoon*. Then suddenly she sat down and professed to all: "He doesn't look like one."

"One what?" mammy asked sharply.

"A Yank! He doesn't look like most Yanks do. All cock of the walk, struttin' about with their snoots in the air higher than the Nelson's Pillar. Sure he's not that bad looking a lad, given a bit of a chance. Not as fine as our own, mind ya. No. Not at all. Not like our Irish lads. Sure you could do better finding a lad in your own country, Nora. Sure you could."

To this day Nora remembered turning purple with embarrassment and anger.

"Mam, will you give over for the love of god. Quick Davy, get her a jar."

Daddy rushed to the kitchen and poured her a tall Cork gin and tonic. "Oh no, I wouldn't be able for it," she waved her hand when he returned. But before he had a chance to retreat, she grabbed hold of his jumper. "Well seeing as you're here." With that she snatched the drink from him and without the slightest hesitation took a huge swallow and abruptly turned her attention right back to Noah. "Suppose you only favor the odd bit of jizz. Sure that's all the Yanks are after. Sure it is rightly so. Roisterin' about lookin' after the girls with the garters sure."

"N-o-o-o," Noah said with obvious hurt and such earnest intensity that once again he roused her passion for him. "I mean I feel so deeply about--"

"Ah we know, we know Noah," mammy said, taking pity on his awkwardness.

"N-o-a-h!? That's a Jewish name, isn't it?" nanny chided. "Jew man, right enough. Well laudy-daw."

"Nanny!" roared daddy. "Would you ever send that tongue of yours tongue on a holiday?"

With that, mammy immediately jumped up from the sofa and went to sit on the arm of Noah's chair. She stroked his head, smoothing a bit of ruffled hair. "Pay no mind to her ballyragin', Noah. If it's meant to be, all of this, it will be, please god." Then she hugged him as if he were her own.

Nora could still recall the riot of emotions she felt at that moment. That Noah had professed his love in the company of her parents thrilled her with a consuming rush. And that her parents had taken so kindly to him was a great relief, because it would have been only brutal to see him hurt. But still she could feel the first wounds of jealousy, as if they were delivered by a well-honed cutlery knife. One was foolish. Surely she realized that. She'd be envious of anyone other than herself touching Noah with affection. But the other did her daggers and to this day there was no escaping the piercing pain of the truth. There had never been a time in memory when her mam had stroked her in such a loving manner, let alone hugged her.

Meanwhile nanny continued her slagging: "Truth be told, I've never seen the likes of a dacent Yank. They're all a crowd of messers and thricksters. Reprobates all. And maddenin' it is. Why look what they're doin' to the poor Vietnamese people now."

"Quick," mammy roared. "Get me mam another drink, lashins of it Davy , before she only starts delivering whole soliloquies on the fate of the world. Get us all another. Bring in the whole bleedin' bottle we're only desperate for it now."

"Kathleen, you'll have Nora's friend thinking we do nothing but take to the drink in this house."

"Sure what else would we be doing? And mam driving us only bonkers. Poor Noah." And she patted him on the head again. "He'd be parchin' for another jar most of all to escape this lunacy."

"Oh no, I won't have any more," Noah said.

"Ah you will. You poor Yankee creature you," nanny insisted in a kinder tone but then with a crocodile's snap delivered the crowning blow. "Sure you may as well be drunk as the way you are."

GOD HOW DID HE have anything to do with me after that day, Nora wondered as she collected her hand baggage and prepared to disembark. And what a darlin' man as well. After all that, he had insisted on staying to see my work. "If you don't let me see it, I won't let you see my novel." As mortified as she was she had to let him have his way because she so longed to read his book. She also longed to have him alone, away from the whole family who had gathered later that day to meet him over the dinner.

"Even though I love them dearly, it's always the same," she remembered saying as she led him up the creaking stairs to the small windowless room. "They leave nothing for me. They know you're only here for a short time and look at the way they rush in hoverin' and fawnin' over you as though you belonged to them."

"Why I was rather flattered."

"Well, I wasn't!" And to this day she still fumed over it.

AFTER HE'D HAD a long silent look at her work, she recalled him reciting some poetry:

"Exultation is the going

Of an inland soul to sea,

Past the houses, past the headlands,

Into deep eternity!"

"Those are your words?" Her mind clouded.

"No," he was quick to answer. "Don't I wish they were. They're from Emily Dickinson. She must have written them with something like these paintings in mind."

Now she couldn't wait to be off the plane and with him. The rush was so intense she felt dizzy. God, I'm only dying for him now.

EXULTATION IS THE GOING of an inland soul

to sea. Past the houses, past the headlands, into deep eternity! He remembered those words as he waited in the crowd at International Arrivals. He had come to think of her in the same way he had thought of her paintings. He recalled having gone into this small, gloomy room, and there amongst the scattering of palettes, tins of oily water and clay pots of brushes and twigs and bits of straggly paint-hardened rope, there amongst the rich earthy scents of oils, he felt a sudden sharp tingle of energy envelop him, as if the room were instantly electrified. Then as he was captured by sheaves and stacks of paintings leaning against the walls, the breath literally left him.

"Are you all right there?" she had asked.

"Yes," he whispered. "May I look?"

"Go ahead," she said and stepped back.

One by one, he went through dozens of them. He would never have thought it possible that such beauty could be captured so many times and in so many different ways. It reached right through to his soul and made it ache. These were no mere picture postcard oils and watercolors of rural and urban Ireland. Rather each shimmered with iridescent light capturing every nuance of spirit. There was nothing precise about them, because preciseness would have robbed their beauty. Just the moods rendered by the constantly changing drama of Irish light. The mist blown valleys, the smoky sunsets, the diffused fields of soft-scented heather and pungent turf, the glittering seas, the lonely rain-swept country roads and bustling city streets. Each painting a vision ephemeral as a dream yet profound with lasting truths. And each with a poetic intensity that was at once seizing and hypnotic. But those that were peopled seemed fired with the shock of life. Figures alone and lost, caught in bursts of fury or melancholy; others brimmed with joy, fraught with sorrow. Then mixed in with these were the pen-and-ink and charcoal drawings composed during her trips to poverty pockets not only of Dublin but Belfast and Derry as well. Powerfully disturbing studies that captured the utter frustration and despair of those caught in the fast fading light of life.

"Words," he whispered finally, unable to look away from the incredible feast.

"What?" she asked.

"Brilliant, timeless. You can hear them." Heavenly god, he thought as chills engulfed him. There they were as if recorded by some divine instrument, portrayals of his most intricate feelings of beauty, of love and life, loss and hope, heaven and hell, of light and the dark, bleakness and exhilaration. God any moment she would walk out of customs and be his.

2

WHEN SHE FINALLY ENTERED the vast International Arrivals waiting hall wheeling a trolley that supported her sprawling case, his spirit soared once more.

"Nora," he struggled to call out over the crowd. When she didn't respond, he slipped up behind her and crushed her in his arms. Overcome with joy, he pulled her around to face him. Then they were kissing and he was saying something to the effect: "I didn't think you'd come. I didn't believe this would ever happen." After she regained a semblance of control, she whispered a soothing "S-h-h-h", then touched his lips and stroked his face. Holding each other, feeling the same chemistry as they had when they first met, they began to cry with relief and joy. "God," she said wiping her tears. "I had the fierce worry come over me that that bleedin' blaggard of an immigration officer wouldn't let me pass. A genuine rotter to be sure. The cold stare of him was only merciless. I expected to be all but pandied by him. Course I would have given him a boot in the bollix. But then to my out and out amazement, he waved me on, no bother." Noah burst into laughter and shook his head.

Now that she'd been let through into the new world, now that Noah's strong arms had come around her, all the fears lifted. Right off she felt adorned with a special grace. It could only be coming from their sheer sense of shared love. She was utterly taken by its radiant glow, cocooned in its blissful peace. Surely he was setting her true life in motion. So with god's blessing she had done the right thing. And she was only over the moon.

Finally she struggled from his grip. "Let's see what

I'm gettin' meself here with all this time that's after passing." And she pushed him away from her. "God," she gasped as she stared at his mode of dress. "You're the real article now." He seemed so completely changed from the rough- hewn, down-to-earth way her mind's eye had captured him on Aran in his fisherman knit and jeans.

"It's still me, the same bill of fare." And he laughed.

But what does that make of me, she wondered as some of the panic returned when she quickly glanced about to see what other women in the hall were wearing. God help us, I look like something escaped from Dublin zoo. All around her were young women in gorgeous breezy silk summer frocks. Why did I not have the fizzin' cop on? As they moved out of the air-conditioned building, she felt all the more the *oinseach*. The sun was only screaming out of the heavens, and she wondered if it mightn't be hurtling itself to earth. "Jaynee Mac, the heat is only diabolical."

He laughed some more. It was both joyous and endearing to hear her turn of phrase once again. "Well summer is summer here," he assured as he parked her enormous, ton-weight case and took off his blazer.

"I must look like a right *culchie* dressed like this," she went on as she immediately peeled away her tweed jacket that she was just now realizing reeked of plane smoke. Thanks be to god for the excuse, she thought. Even though her periwinkle blue silk blouse was very wrinkled, it was by far a better look on its own. But if truth be known she'd only kill to pitch the entire ensemble into the nearest dustbin. Then suddenly she burst into laughter at the folly.

"What is so funny?" he asked in shock but only loving the sound of her laughter.

"I'd be a far sight more classy walkin' around in me slip than this bleedin' outift. What in be *jaysus* was I thinking of at all, at all buying such a fizzin' article to wear over here in July?"

With that Noah had to drop her case again as he too exploded into laughter. Then they were both doubled over convulsing. When finally he was able to catch enough breath, he blurted: "Well I don't mind if you want to take it all off and go round in your pretty little slip. It could be quite trendsetting you know."

"Oh god what a right eejit," she said as her laughter faded.

"Ah Nora, you're just lovely," he insisted putting his arms around her and squeezing her tightly. "What was I ever doing without you all this time? Don't think anything of your clothes. I'm the one at fault here for not writing you about the heat."

WHEN THEY WERE FINALLY in a taxi, he said: "Oh god, I forgot this, Nora." And he pulled a rosebud from his blazer pocket. "It was broken from its stem and the only one they had like it at the flower stand here. The man wouldn't even let me pay for it. He just winked."

She took it and held it in her palms. "You remembered," she said. And Noah said yes that it was the

Fenian dreamer man John Boyle O'Reilly:"*I send you a cream-white rosebud with a flush on its petal tips. For the love that is purest and sweetest has the kiss of desire on its lips.*"

"God would you ever silence that husky voice of yours and come over here to me." Then they were holding each other and kissing once more.

When they noticed the taxi driver having a long gawk through his rear view, they pushed apart, and she began blushing madly. "Now let's have another look," she said moving further away. "Why have you gone all highfalutin on me since I last saw you?"

"Ah I just spiffied meself up a bit for you me luv," he teased.

"Now you're actin' the maggot."

"Only in part. You know I got a different job on a different paper just of late so I sort of have to keep up with fashions and all that nonsense. That's why the clothes."

"Oh really," she said with surprise.

"Yeah. It's called *Fashion Connoisseur Daily*. It's like a trade rag and a consumer paper combined."

"A rag?"

"No," he chuckled. "I mean it covers all the new fashions and the garment business news along with the social whirl. You couldn't believe society is such a big circulation booster today."

"But do you like it?"

"Yeah well-- I don't have much choice," he

answered feeling her disappointment. "I know its way off base from the *Herald Tribune* slice of life stuff that I loved."

"Some of those were only brilliant now. Especially the one you did on the mob restaurants of Little Italy. It was so real. To be sure, my family believed as I did that we were right there in the restaurants with those shysters."

"Yeah. I know," he said with obvious longing. "I loved that piece. I loved a lot of them. My heart was really in them, you know."

"I do know."

"But unfortunately the *Trib* is nearly out of business while *Fashion Connoisseur* is soaring. And they offered me a lot more money."

"That's terrible. Tragic all the same," she said and then realized she was hurting him. "Oh I mean, it's wonderful you've got a good solid position now."

"Yeah," he sighed. "Money talks in this town." Then he shrugged off the bad thoughts. "And so I grabbed for it thinking of the good life I'm going to make for us."

"Sure we'd be all right under any circumstance, Noah. We don't need any grand extravagance. The important thing is that we'd be together and you'd be writing. How's it coming might I ask?"

"Well-- It's kind of waiting."

"Waiting for what?"

"For you."

She smiled. "Now you'll have no more excuses. I'll be making certain of that, mind you."

"I think you will," he said with a thrill.

"Excuse me sir," the taxi driver interrupted. "What was that address again?"

"Forty-eighth Avenue and Forty-sixth Street," he told the driver and then turned back to Nora. "You know I figured you'd be too tired after that long trip to want to go out to a restaurant. So I thought if it's okay, we'd have a bite to eat at the apartment."

"Sounds grand."

"Then we can play it from there."

"Noah, now I don't mean to sound bold and pushy mind you--but you were able to get me me own flat or a bedsitter?"

"Oh yes. I did indeed. And it's just a couple of blocks from me in Sunnyside. It's safe. And it's only forty-five bucks a month."

"Smashin'. And only two roads over from you. Oh that's grand all the same. Course I'll have to be getting work right off to pay for it."

"Don't worry. We certainly will manage."

AS MUCH AS NOAH DESPISED his dreary Queens walk-up in the midst of dive bars and dingy stores, it became precious once Nora entered it. "I like your taste in art," she said, nodding to a small oil painting she had sent him, one he'd framed and displayed prominently on the living room wall. It was that of a young couple embracing on rain-swept Dun Laoghaire Pier outside Dublin at the height of a storm, a couple that could have been the two of them. "Only the best, the very best, will do for Noah Mason. I'll tell you. Now if I could only dump the dump surrounding it," he replied as he switched on his hi-fi and music from *The Umbrellas Of Cherbourg* enveloped the three drab rooms and drowned the sound of the rattling old a/c.

After they exchanged a long impassioned kiss, she showered and changed into a somewhat cooler flowery pastel dress of a softer cotton fabric. Then they sat on the sofa, nibbled various pates and toasted each other with a light Beaujolais. They talked a little of Nora's family and how sad it had been leaving that morning. "I went all weepy because for the first time I can remember they actually seemed sorry they were going to see the back of me, which only amazed me. And wouldn't you just know me granny'd rush over at the last possible moment and warn me yet again about the evils of America."

"About the evils of me, don't you mean? *The Creature From The Black Lagoon.*"

"Oh will you ever forget that?" And they both laughed. "God help her. She even gave me money you know. Crushed it into me hand and all but brusin' it. Then as the taxi was about to depart she carried on only thunderously hooshin' and proddin' me to hide it away from you and not let you know of its existence. And right there in front of the ould biddy neighbors with their ears all cocked me way, she roared: 'And you make yourself mindful once you're over there that that young lad of yours isn't *shinannicken* after all the Shelias while he's plaumausin' ya.' God I could have only died. But mammy finally shooed her away so we could after be saying our goodbyes in peace. "

"Shinannicken after all the Shelias?" he repeated. "While I'm plaumausin' ya? W-h-a-t?"

And for ages they couldn't stop laughing. When they did, he hugged her and they drifted into silence, each mellowing in the pleasure. She felt so safe as the warmth of his body crept over her that she closed her eyes and sighed. There was a greater security here than she had ever felt in the familiarity of Dublin. The reality that someone really cared for her for the first time in her life, someone found her worthy, overwhelmed her with happiness.

Noah watched her as the last bits of evening sun made their way through cracks in the crumby window blind and fell across the softness of her forehead and the creamy rose of her cheek while at the same time turning her hair a golden bronze. With her in his arms, he closed his eyes and let his inner voice whisper—*thank you for this, god.* And he realized what he had felt for so long was true. New York was a soulless place without a woman to love. A memory of the days when he and his college buddy Tim Anderson courted the old Cedar Bar along with crowds of other writers and artists in hope of catching some moments of blissful passion flashed through his mind along with the gloom that surrounded it. Then after he met Nora a year ago came Max's Kansas City, the *le dernier cri* of both the Establishment and the underground where he went for drinks with Tim who failed to accept his celibacy for an Irish *bird* who wasn't even in the country yet.

-I've got some great Acapulco Gold that'll loosen you up, Noah. Then it's onto full frolic again, buddy. Lusting with the licentious. Ah to *volupte.*"

-Put that stuff away, Tim. All you have to do is inhale in this place."

-You've got to get with it pal. Just look at those two babes over there. Slinky black minis and see-right-throughs. Va-va-va-voom! I think they're ogling us. O-h-h *License my roving hands, and let them go. Behind, before, above, between, below.*"

-You idiot, Anderson You're completely out of control."

-Not so. No more than John Donne. Remember the emphasis on all that stuff at Ithaca and how we took it for real? *Full nakedness all joys are due thee. As souls unbodied, bodies unclothed must be. To taste whole joys.*"

Thank god, those days are over, Noah thought. And now as he stroked her arms he felt the most wondrous peace sweep over them and lift them up and out of the darkening apartment until they seemed to be floating above the scented flowering trees of his beloved Brooklyn Botanical Gardens caressed by the tender breezes of the summer twilight. And in this rapturous moment he possessed all the beauty of the world and all the dark lonely hours were gone.

When he opened his eyes again, he watched the shadowy rise and fall of her breasts as she slept. So beautiful were they that he let his whole body slide down so he could rest his face against them. He gasped with the wonder as he did so. How deeply he had fallen in love with her. Was there ever anything that could equal this moment? It brought his entire body alive and he knew he would have to restrain himself. When would they make love for the first time, he wondered. If only he could flash forward and know. What would her face look like as they did? He tried to imagine it while she continued to sleep. This only fired him all the more, so he forced himself to stop thinking and just be so thankful for this.

"Heavenly god, what hour is it?" she gasped when they both finally awakened together. It was pitch-dark.

"Very late," Noah said checking his watch after he turned on a small table light.

"But what about me new abode? I'd best be making me way," she said pulling up and righting herself.

"It's too late, love. Stay here and you'll go tomorrow."

"But I can't."

"Why not. Who's to know? I'm not going to rape you, you know."

She laughed and stroked his face. "I know that, pet. It's just--"

"It's just that already you feel guilty, and it's only your first night away. Well do not. There's no reason for it.

You take my bed, and I'll sleep out here. That way I'll be able to fix you a piping hot breakfast in the morning with all those sausages and rashers you're after bringing me. Then we can go off to Mass together and give our thanks for being so blessed."

"Well-- I guess I am pretty knackered. So I'll stay, but only if you let me sleep here and you take your own bed. It's only fair."

"No. Well lean back and take it easy. There's time for that. Besides I just want to hold you a little longer. We've waited so long."

"I know, poor man."

She didn't awaken again until dawn, and when she did, he was still holding her.

"I couldn't bear for us to be apart on your first night here," he said. "I guess I can never bear to be apart from you."

"Never."

3

"NEVER EVER, do we want to be apart. And that's the way it's going to be. Forever," spouted a young black-haired reporter as he darted across the newsroom at *Fashion Connoisseur Daily* clutching a clipping. Scarcely able to contain himself, he continued on to a gathering of editorial heads. "See it's verbatim what she said outside St.

Barts on her wedding day almost exactly two years ago."
He waved the article at them and a stocky much older
balding man with a salt-and-pepper moustache snatched
the piece away and avidly eyed it. "Now look at this," the
reporter exalted as he flashed an eight by ten. "Looks like
Miranda Ramsey is saying the same thing again but to
someone else now."

"Wow!" gasped the balding man as his eyes
devoured the photo of a couple in passionate embrace. "Who
would have expected our guys to get a shot like this at the
Saratoga races."

"Back of the grandstand yet where they thought
nobody could possibly see them," the reporter beamed as the
rest of the crowd poured over the shot. "The guys drove half
the night to get the raw film back to us in time. And there's
a contact sheet on the way with even more angles."

"Well no mere dalliance this. It's certainly febrile.
What will young husband Clayton have to say--and do? Ah
the spectacle of it all," the baldy man went on.

"Pity we won't be able to run it in tomorrow's
paper," a wiry cohort advised. "We're all locked in on
deadline with the advance scoop on the St. Laurent
sketches."

"Are you mad. We have to get this in. The Ramseys
are the hottest young jetsetters today. Couples don't come
any more beautiful than they. And with all those grand
family roots--and money. Undying love disintegrates as
Miranda takes a lover. Can you just imagine what Oliver

would say if someone like Suzy or Charlotte Curtis scooped us? It runs tomorrow without question," baldy insisted.

As Noah stood watching the scene grow more heated, he felt the anxiety rising in him. "Don't let it scare you. Stuff like this happens every day around here. You'll have to get used to it because you're going to be in the thick of it very soon," insisted Kathy Murphy or Murphs as she was oddly called. She was one of the paper's chief style writers who had just returned from her summer vacation. Earlier that day she had introduced herself to Noah who was still very much the novice here. Now they were gazing across the seas of smoky paper-strewn desks and the vast assemblage of frantically busy people who made up the newsroom of fifth-floor editorial. The paper was the star in the crown of the Wilton Press trade newspaper empire, an empire whose publications swept the range from fashion and interior design to architecture, antiques and collectibles only to most recently touch down in the travel arena.

Presided over by its incorrigible young manipulator-publisher Oliver Wilton, *Fashion Connoisseur Daily*, or *FCD* as it was now widely known, was fast becoming not only the fashion trendsetter for the entire garment industry but the barometer of high society as well. Oliver had managed to merge the two elements beautifully under his cocky fresh philosophy--*always lead the dance.*

"A few years ago this empire was dying. The only people they could get to work here were those who came in to get out of the rain," Murphs went on over the clamor of pounding Underwoods as she tossed a long mane of blazing hair across the shoulder of her striking rust mini-skirted linen suit. "But as soon as Oliver finished Yale, he talked all his old-folks-home relatives into retiring and he really cleaned this creaking house and its musty publications. New blood and far-out ideas. Way ahead-of-its-time stuff."

"Like they say, he set forth a new journalistic arena for the Sixties," Noah agreed.

"And it worked. Now that the company's soaring again, everybody's heard about *FCD*. It's the in-place to be now. And it's really such a lot of fun. Even though I'm far from being fatuous or vain, I love fashion and worship writing about it."

"Well I was quite surprised when they sought me out for society coverage."

"Why I'm not. They loved your *Herald Tribune* stuff. And you're a young dapper looking guy. A perfect live wire. And you'll have a fresh new approach. It's quite a job." Then she hesitated. "I hope that's what you want."

Noah noted the warning tone. "I guess. I'm just playing catch up so far. Trying to shed the shyness, because I've never done this sort of thing before. I've only been here a few days and I'm already off to all these grand lunch-bunch places. Struggling to fast track my way to suaveness."

"But that's just the beginning. Once Oliver gets back from his Tuscan villa holidays, the word is he's going to work the tail off his newly prized acquisition. That means sending you to every she-she evening event he can think of. I mean all this lunch business is just your break-in period. Society acquaintances of his taking you under their wings so to speak. But at least that way you'll really get to see the whites of their eyes early on."

"What does that suggest, that I'm going to want to shoot them?" And he laughed.

"Well don't laugh. Your predecessor was on the verge. He couldn't stick them in the end. It takes a very special person with a unique quality to deal with those people. Thank god I'm strictly fashion. I know that I couldn't take them on a full-time basis."

"Why do I feel you're scaring me, Murphs?"

"Oh god, I don't mean to. You just have to know the playing field, and the guy before you didn't. You notice I referred to them as Oliver Wilton's society acquaintances. I didn't say friends. That's because Oliver Wilton doesn't have any friends in society, except they say for some of his Skull and Bones buddies. He's aloof. He wants it that way so he can play the grand puppeteer. Maneuvering them around that glorious field. And you're his wordsmith."

"You mean he's going to take away my mind and dictate?"

"No. Never. He won't form your words. He loves your writing. He'd be mad to do that. It's more like he'll form a mood as it were, and you'll have to play off of it. Oh he does it in fashion too. But you Noah have to be out there dealing with all these people. Some nice. Some not so nice. I think the technique is to never make them look like your crossing them even though you'll often have to."

"Well so far they seem all right, even kind to me for all their money."

"Of course they are. They're most likely scared to death you won't like them. I mean now they live for mentions in *FCD*. Even if only a line in the *Zoom-In* column. It's de rigueur. And quite fatal to them if they're left out--or spoken of unfavorably."

"Maybe I'm being too wide-eyed not to be troubled."

"No," she assured and for the first time wound down. As she looked at him, her glowing school-girlish face seemed to be at odds with her hazel eyes that now so swiftly, knowingly scrutinized him. "You know I think you're just right. The other guy became far too sarcastic. That's why Oliver let him go. He was too crude. But you I can see have a certain air of innocence that's appealing. I think it's going to work." But then she added abruptly: "Just be careful. Watchful really. Not to let yourself start taking it too seriously."

"What's that supposed to mean?

Before she could answer, that stocky baldy man, who Noah had met only in passing, suddenly appeared. He was Jack Warren, the city editor. "You know Murphs, I just heard Oliver's coming back next week and he's hell bent on a full staff meeting on Zhivago. So I hope we're all prepared," he pronounced with raised eyebrows.

"What's Zhivago? A nightclub?" Noah asked innocently.

"Is he kidding? Clue him in if he doesn't want to be out," he thundered ominously causing Noah to shudder.

As he rushed off blaring a warning to the rest of the staff, Murphs made a sneering face to his back. "Don't let that grumpy fossil upset you. He's always the same. Zhivago refers to *Doctor Zhivago*. Ever since Oliver saw the film he's mad about all those full-length fashions. He's determined that come hell or high water, he's going to make the world buy into it. And he wants all the ideas he can get to put it across editorially."

"God I don't know what to say about that."

"Don't worry. You're society. And you're the hot new property. The light in Oliver's eyes. The sun shines on you right now. So you can do no wrong. But it would be especially enterprising if you could come up with something. Hey, I know. Just think of lavish old movies and gorgeous gowns. I don't know if you've ever heard of the Adrian wardrobes. Well of course you have with all those movies you must have grown up with."

"How did you know that?" Noah asked in amazement.

"Oh well--" Murphs replied and suddenly became jittery. "I—I don't know. I-- guess everybody our age grew up in the movies."

"Well that is true of me. And my mother longed for

all those gowns and dresses."

"So mention them by all means," she quickly added losing her tension and returning to her bubbly self. "So far we've only talked about coats, so dresses would be a whole new angle. I'll give you the nod when I think it's the best time to chime in, don't worry."

"But that's not fair to you."

"Oh I've given them plenty of ideas. And I'll come up with something else. But besides this, we need to get together so I can give you some fashion counseling. I mean you're going to have to at least briefly describe what these society grande dames are wearing when you're writing about them."

"God, you're so good. How can I ever thank you?"

"You don't have to. I think I've just found a great new friend. And believe me that's rare around here. There's plenty of backbiting I can tell you."

"Well, I can't say how grateful I am. And even more grateful to have such a rare new friend."

4

EVEN THOUGH HE WAS NEW to Wilton Press, Noah had arranged to take a few days off to be with Nora when she wasn't scouting job prospects, which she had insisted on doing immediately and on her own. After he had convinced her that the streets weren't on fire, that what she thought to be giant rolling clouds of ivory and ashen smoke coming from the manhole covers were actually composed of steam, she began to tolerate the impersonal *quareness* of New York.

To calm herself during spare moments when Noah's arm wasn't around her, she would concentrate on the furor of the city from an artistic point of view. Every moment here was like a sea change creating an immense circus of startling colors. And as they shifted in kaleidoscopic fashion, all the shades of life swept past her from only the most brilliant to the ugliest of hues. She began wondering how she might capture on canvas this madness of a people moving at such a stupefying pace it snitched most of the values of life.

But all this daftness quickly faded from the foreground when they were strolling through the quaint areas of the Village or the ambient lanes of Central Park where a youthful unfettered spirit rose and handsome lovers courted so openly. She found that it roused her spot on because she had never seen such likes at home. Well only rarely when on moon bright nights she happened to be passing the darkest of lover's lanes. Then she could see very little, just enough to fire her mind with wonder. Here it was on outright display like a rich erotic canvas.

A LIGHT BROKE upon my brain. It was a carol of a bird. A lovely bird with azure wings. And a song that said a thousand things. And seemed to say them all for me—

As Byron's words reverberated through his mind so

often during those days, Noah began to think of the world as his. "It's a great symbol of hope," he told Nora on her first visit to the Metropolitan Museum. There in one of the second floor European galleries among the Monets was *Le Debacle (The Thaw)*. "I never noticed that about it before. All I saw was a canvas of frost and ice on the Seine." They had moved up close to where the icy vapor appeared to lift from the river. And behind it at its center, in the very faintest of strokes, were the hints of life. A trace of soft green, a glimpse of orange, a minute brush of purple.

"They're barely there mind you. But there nonetheless piercing that fierce freeze."

"Those colors have all the iridescent promise of a new world," Noah went on with his arm around her. "It's like a beginning of the wonder of what's to come."

"And why would you only be noticing that now?"

He turned to look at her and stroked her hair. "Because you weren't here before."

"DO YOU LIKE MY COOKING?" he asked anxiously on a special Saturday night he had planned for them at his apartment.

"Ummm. It's delicious beef."

Early that morning he'd gone to Walter's, a small neighborhood butcher in the West Village who had been strongly recommended by Murphs, and had selected a special roast for the occasion. But now he noticed Nora was striving unsuccessfully to stifle a grin.

"What's wrong?"

"There's enough--" she said and then broke up. "There's enough-- Enough meat here to doubly feed all of Dublin and then some." It was true that it was a huge roast that took up more than half the table. "No wonder it took so long in the cookin'. Is it the whole animal that's here?" she roared, making him burst out laughing as well. When they'd regained control, she asked: "Why in god's name did you get so much?"

"I wanted to impress you," he replied smiling through his seriousness.

"You don't need to impress me."

"Yes I do," he said gravely, instantly making her feel a surge of passion.

They were sitting at Noah's kitchen table, an ugly chipped enamel affair, which he had covered with a new white tablecloth. He had turned off the glaring fluorescent light and had lit candles in an attempt to achieve a little romance in his dreary untidy hovel. They ate a little but couldn't take their eyes or their minds from one another. Utterly seized, Noah put down his utensils and touched her hand. Without a word, they took their candles and their red wine into the living room without turning on the lights. This made the place actually seem warm and alluring. God this is incredible, Noah thought. As they kissed, a wave of pure enchantment descended, and as if by some joint heavenly plan, they slowly undressed one another.

The light was perfect. It spilled over Nora's body

lifting it out of the shadows and accentuating its deepening creamy flush. God, he sucked his breath at the luscious swell of her young full breasts and the sensuous curve of her hips. Such radiant beauty caused his mind to reel from its splendor. And when he drew her into his arms and felt her softness, he realized at long last that his imagination hadn't deceived him and he went feverish with desire.

She too was instantly aware. Noah's face was ecstatic, his eyes shimmering. As she pressed herself against the strong curvature of his chest, she felt her nipples go all hard and her head go light. She stroked his face. Then still gazing into his eyes, she dared run her hands over the strength of his smooth broad shoulders and then down the muscles of his back to his taut buttocks. Pulling him closer, she could feel the thickness of his swollen penis growing between them.

Noah reached up to draw his fingers through the sheen of her hair as he brought her lips to his and kissed her passionately. When his other hand began caressing her breasts, she gasped. Then his lips and tongue were alternately tracing a delicate line down her velvety hot skin causing her to shiver and tremble. When he finally drew a nipple into his mouth and sucked on it, she shuddered and her belly immediately convulsed in orgasm.

Noah held her tightly for support. When she was calm again, he continued the journey with his tongue down over her smooth stomach. When he was on his knees, he let his cheek rub back and forth across the downy softness of her hair. She held him there and felt the heat that was rising so rapidly from her being. After a time, he firmly took hold of her shapely long legs and with a slight tug made her spread them. Then pulling her buttocks towards him, he buried his fervid face. She had never heard of a man doing such a thing to a woman. But the pure tenderness of it was exciting her to the point where she was gasping her pleasure. She hadn't dreamed of anything so lovely, even when she had spent long hours imagining the magnificence of their lovemaking. Oh let him keep on forever I'm only possessed by him, she thought as she felt his lovely fingers spreading her lips there. But when his tongue touched her, touched the wetness and then drew a line from the bottom to the top of her lips, she could hear herself crying out from the overwhelming pleasure that sent her into a purple haze. Then she felt herself going, collapsing.

Holding her up with his arms, he stood and lifted her onto the sofa. His eyes gleamed as he bent to kiss her then kissed his way back down her body. When he was there again, his fingers gently touched the wetness then tenderly rubbed at it with the back of his hand until her entire body was suffused with rippling sensations that intensified and signaled the next spasms of rapture. "Oh god," she sighed as her mind drifted off to relish this new onrush. With that, he touched her erect bud, rolled it and gently built the pleasure. This time when ecstasy reverberated through her, it was so intense that she screamed and nearly lost consciousness. "Jesus," Noah gasped in joyous amazement.

Her orgasm was so strong and ongoing, her face so utterly beautiful in its splendid agony, that it was pitching him over the edge, quickening his already surging, aching penis, setting off one of the most powerful orgasms he'd ever had.

As she revived, she moved around and slowly covered the fine hairs of his stomach with little kisses. "I never knew," she whispered. And he smiled dreamily. Then she reached out with the tips of her fingers and touched his penis and felt an immediate sadness sweeping her. "I'm sorry."

"Are you mad? Don't be sorry," he insisted. "It was fantastic for me."

"But sure, I didn't do anything."

"S-h-h-h. You did so much. So much. There's time for more."

Purposely, he didn't go any further that evening. He wanted to move in stages so that their love would grow, so that there would be no sense of rushing things, no sense of regret. He loved and cared for her more than anyone or anything in the world. He wanted her to know this. And he never wanted to come away from the feeling of this moment, not for an instant.

5   EARLY SATURDAY EVENING, August 20 at Quintessence, John and Carole Dawson's simple little summer cottage in Newport. The Rolls, the Mercedes, the BMWs were rolling up in a never-ending parade. Dozens of guests invited: twenty dozen to be exact. They spilled through the mansion, out its rear doors and onto the four soon-to-be lantern-lit terraces, sipping Dom Perignon from fiery sunset-caught crystal and nibbling on tiny heart shapes of toasted bread dolloped with Beluga. Somewhere inside a small orchestra was already striking up the silvery music of romance.

There among the swirls of people were Noah and his photographer. They had driven up the previous day in a rented Bentley Continental with Noah agonizing over having to leave Nora alone in the city for the first time. The purpose of the journey was to cover the fashionable opening of the 86th Invitational Lawn Tennis Tournament and the many glamorous social events that surrounded it. As a weekend houseguest of his new acquaintances the Dawsons, Noah felt honored. The splendor of Quintessence had enveloped him, both instantly and completely. He had never known such sumptuousness, such gorgeous visions. He wondered if he weren't visiting this in some extravagant dream as he drove through the open gated roadway and up the long winding drive flanked by ancient beech trees and banks of scented sea foam roses then around the staggering circular fountain as it spilled its sun struck waters over a statue of Bacchus in front of the grand entry. There they were greeted by Benjamin the stalwart master attendant who since they were early arrivals had time to fill them in on the history.

Built in the 1890s for a Vanderbilt, Quintessence was patterned after an exquisite French chateau. Somewhat smaller than its more famous neighboring cottages and unlike most of the others still thriving as a private domain, it contained fifty-five rooms and an enormous pale yellow Siena marble entry hall that stretched all the way across the house to end in a spectacular array of windows and French doors overlooking lawns, gardens and ocean.

As for the furnishings, this mansion was a treasure trove including representations from the Ming, Medieval, Gothic, Renaissance, Baroque, Neoclassic eras. This galaxy of styles, which could have easily occasioned utter folly, instead flowed with such artistic panache as to bring Quintessence to breathtaking life. Lavish was too modest a descriptive for the pargeted ceilings with their grandiose celestial murals, the carved mahogany walls, the golden chandeliers and the looming red alabaster columns with their gilt reliefs. What greater wonderment, Noah delighted to himself because he had an acquired knowledge of all this. Shortly after he'd come to New York he had attended countless lectures at the Metropolitan Museum on the grand architecture and decor of the western world and was drawn back time and again. He had thought it was just a fascination with history until now when he was actually confronting it, when marveling was turning into pure covetousness.

After he gave his photographer free early reign to shoot, Noah roamed the vastness of the mansion, up and down the sweeping lustrous marble staircases, along the distance of halls with their breathtaking original paintings and through its endless succession of cavernous rooms. As he did he became intoxicated by the enchantment and so wished Nora were there to share it with him. Even as droves more arrived to the accompaniment of the orchestra's *Shadow Of Your Smile* and *Taste Of Honey* in the ballroom, he continued to revel in such splendid delight.

"You seem so young to be a society reporter," a voice called out snatching him from the clouds. It was Gloria Hamilton Collins. He recognized her as one of *FCD*'s favorite photo targets. Tall, willowy blond and stunning in a vivid yellow peau-de-soie mini—thank god he thought for Murphs fashion counseling-- that accented her deep tan, she was an airline heiress who had recently married the leading American race car driver Bruce Collins, the man who had won the Indy two years in a row. "Isn't it past your bedtime?" she went on as she caressed the naked shoulders of an imposing obviously aroused male angel, a telamon that upheld one side of a towering white Caen stone fireplace.

"No, I think I can manage to stay up a little longer," Noah replied awkwardly and began to look around.

"What's the matter?" she persisted. "You look as if you'd lost something. Did someone steal your favorite GI Joe?"

"No. I'm just looking for a bar. I'm thirsty."

"Well, don't be shy." And with that she called across the way: "Oh maid, get this boy a glass of milk and some brownies please."

Noah blushed and laughed but felt quite intimidated as he waved away the maid.

"Don't mind me, darling," she said as she came over to him. "I'm always my audacious self. I'm the one who adds the color to these little soirees." Then she began to adjust his black tie. "You know it's only criminal to be as young and divinely handsome as you are. Why you're not with someone is beyond the beyonds. You're not gay, are you?"

"No. I'm working here," he replied with a slight snap.

"You can work on more than one thing at a time, can't you?" she asked stroking his face. "And as far as I'm concerned, you can work on me any time you want."

Noah laughed then blushed some more. "But you're a married woman," he nervously replied and awkwardly backed away.

"You call this a marriage? Boy, are you green. You know something, you remind me of my first husband. I loved him, only I didn't know it. He was kind and gentle. A little stupid. But absolutely beautiful and a great lover. What a fool I was. Maybe I've been given a second chance."

"I think you're too late," Noah said without hesitation as he spied a bar and began to head off.

"It's never too late," Gloria called out as she wafted over to a neighboring bronze lion crouching atop a massive marble column and began stroking its mane. "You'll see. I'll remember you. I'll just bet you can be quite the impetuous savage under all that nervous youth." From the way she said it, Noah knew she more than meant it. Impetuous savage, he thought and grinned from ear to ear.

This was his first major weekend assignment for *FCD*, and he had no idea it would include a proposition. Nor had he any idea that this evening's party would be so enormous. All Oliver Wilton had said in his drawling uppity accent when he phoned him from Antibes was: "*Ah* know little events up *they-ah* in Newport can be quite the *boah*. P-l-e-a-s-e don't make this one a *boah* for *ouwah* paper." Now for purposes of the story and layout, he was going to have to introduce himself to scores more whom he still didn't know and then guide his photographer through this mélange while scribbling surreptitious notes as well.

Well there was nothing to do but have a drink and begin. Then hopefully he'd coast through it like Carole Dawson, whose black-tie party not only honored the Lawn Tennis Tournament but the successful launching of her designer apparel firm, a fun yet charitable enterprise devised to generate some extra excitement in her life--or so she said. So with drink in hand, he wandered nervously down to one of the terraces where he found Carole holding court. Sensing his tension, she came over and took him by the hand. "Come Noah darling, I'll introduce you. E-v-e-r-y-b-o-d-y's here," she marveled. And so they were. Burdens, Vanderbilts, the Revsons, Babe Paley and Bill, the Rothschilds, Sculls, Newhouses, Kennedys, Rockefellers, along with a host of the newest and as such very lively nouveau riche whom Noah had been told were not generally a part of the staid Newport scene. "Oh, there's Baby Jane Holzer. Hi darling, you look simply m-a-r-v-e-l-o-u-s," Carole trilled merrily on to the hot nouveau model/celebrity. "Dior, is it?"

Noah figured Carole to be in her mid-to-late forties, but she wore the years well. The long, shiny black hair, sparking eyes and firm lips generated glamour. That, along with her rather daring, pink silk handkerchief St. Laurent gown, made her unquestionably the star of the evening. Taking his hand again, she led him across the terrace and through the mansion. As they went, Noah marveled: "It's a staggeringly beautiful place, Carole."

Carole laughed. "I think that's probably a very good way to describe it." Then in a mocking tone she went on: "I'm almost certain every possible style from the early Tang Dynasty onward is represented here. I haven't even had the time to discover it all myself. Nor quite frankly do I want to. But John, who has every item catalogued, thinks it's perfectly de rigueur. Even the gaudier aspects. So here we are in the midst of it all." When she noticed Noah was a bit embarrassed and taken back, she quickly added: "Oh never mistaken, I have a passion for the bits of true elegance. But do we need a whole museum? And one that rivals the Metropolitan yet?"

Noah chuckled. "I suppose it is pretty far out there. But still I think I could easily adapt." And he could feel the electric charge streaking through him. "But I'll tell you. I think it's a terrible waste," Carole insisted. "We have to have a staff here year round you know and the upkeep is incredible. I think we could put the money where it could be much more beneficial to the needs of others. The guilt complex that accompanies having these places is quite incredible. But certainly John doesn't feel that way any longer," she continued as they finally reached the grand entrance hall where Carole proceeded to introduce him to throngs more and his scribbled notes turned into shorthand.

"Darling, you've outdone yourself. This is super," cheered the Duchess de Cordova. "And I'm thrilled about you're going into the fashion business. You spend so much time and money on all those charities. You need to be doing something exciting just for yourself for a change."

"Well it is a bit of a thrill, but it's not for me. I'd have to have more of a purpose than that to justify it. Everything's to be divided between cancer research and the Henry Street Settlement."

"Oh never mind such details. It's all too complicated, I say. I'm just happy you're happy," the Duchess rattled away twisting at her pearl necklace. This along with a short hairdo only emphasized her wrinkles. "But did you hear the latest?"

"Of what?" Carole asked bemused.

"Of Jackie, of course. Oh come now, you do know."

"Don't be ridiculous, Charlotte. Who is he?"

"I don't know. Lee wouldn't tell me," the Duchess mourned but then perked up. "She's not here is she?"

"No. No. Antigua I hear."

"Pity that. You might have encouraged her to shed some light." Then as she began to sadden once more at the loss of a possible source, she suddenly rallied and gasped: "Antigua--in A-u-g-u-s-t?"

Just then industrialist Wellingford Ashley moped over from the crowd, and the Duchess instantly squeezed his arm and gushed the news: "Isn't it marvelous, Wellie? Jackie's romantically entwined again."

"I guess so," he pouted.

"Why she's your dear friend. Aren't you excited for her?"

"Don't be absurd. There are more serious things," he puffed in true old Wasp fashion as he smoothed his thinning dark hair to the right across his forehead.

"Is something wrong, Wellie?" Carole asked with genuine concern.

"Young people today. I don't know what's happening to this generation. Where is the fiber of responsibility? After all the finest education at Princeton, I've got one son who wants to join the peace corps and another who without a moment's hesitation has become involved in Viet Nam protests. Two fools burn themselves to death in front of the UN, and my son takes up the gauntlet. And you know what he wants to do with the rest of his life? He wants to go off to the mountains somewhere to run a ski lodge no less."

"Well at least they've got some thoughts of the future in their heads," Carole admonished. "Look around you here, do you see any young person of lineage with even a half a brain. And Wellie quite frankly you don't know how lucky you are. You still have your boys." Then she suddenly and quite dramatically turned stern with the warning: "Don't you ever for one moment forget that."

Wellie flinched at her bite. "Oh, I don't mean to be malevolent, Carole. I just want the best for them. But they won't have anything to do with solid corporations. Suddenly that's declasse. It doesn't groove. And you can't tell them to forget this do-your-own-thing business. Why they're iconoclastic beyond belief. What they really need is to get themselves haircuts and some respectable Brooks suits--and go to work. They'll find out. Another year or so and all this craziness will blow over. But then where will they be? That's the big question."

"I don't think it's going to blow over," Noah said abruptly, and a vision of a whitewashed Irish cottage with himself and Nora standing beside it leapt into his mind followed now by a flux of far-flung gorgeous chateaux. "I think it's just the beginning."

"Of what? The end?" Wellington snapped.

"No, of people doing the things that are important to them."

"What's more important than advancing to a superior position and making money?"

"Getting something of substance out of life."

"Try it without money," Wellington sneered and shook his head.

"Oh money's important. Well it's vital. But surely they can do both. There must be a balance," Noah insisted, because he truly felt they could find it if they put their minds to it.

"You can't do both. It's an utter impossibility," Wellington demanded. "Why it's frivolous beyond belief."

"Not so," Noah instantly replied with equal fervor. "Can't do both? Why of course you can. That and so much more." When Wellington growled at the thought, Noah realized it was pointless to continue. In the rarefied world of such privileged family icons, corporate power was oxygen.

As Wellington shook his head in disgust and moved on, Noah said: "I'm sorry. I didn't mean to come on so strongly. I hope I didn't cause a scene."

"Darling, you were perfect," Carole said in amazement. "I was dumbfounded."

"Like a breath of fresh air," the Duchess added with verve.

"I just think there's so much more," Noah stressed. Just then a maid walked by offering hors d'oeuvres. As he took some and thanked her, the Duchess whispered to Carole: "Oh he is s-o-o charming and innocent. So divinely refreshing and *gallant*. What a discovery. I can't wait to have him to my next party. He's going to be the sensation of the season."

As Noah fought to defeat another grin of delight before he turned back to them, he heard Carole say: "Yes, it's true. He is a darling. A treasure really." Yet when he glimpsed her looking at him, she had gone sadly pensive and totally out of character for the scene. "But enough of this," she finally said, more to herself than anyone else. Then with great gusto, she burst forth again: "Let's celebrate." And so they did.

Guests clustered like clouds and drifted through the flamboyance of that evening. This was their food, and they were never satiated. Uprisings of delight and transitory splendor were spontaneous and echoed through the house and gardens so that it was difficult to tell where one began and the other ended.

Through it all, Carole continued to effervesce, while bestowing hugs and kisses, that is until her husband John, who had arrived late for the party, furtively tried to squelch her. "What do you think you're doing? And dressed like that," he whispered, but Noah was close enough to hear.

"Enjoying myself."

"Well that's obvious." He forced a smile that instantly froze. "Don't you realize we're not in

Southampton? This sort of tacky behavior doesn't play here."

"Oh really," she snapped casting an impudent wave to an arriving Andy Warhol.

"And why did you invite along so many nouveau strays? It's like oil and water."

"Oh don't be such a colossal fossil. Get with the times. It's the Sixties, remember? Monies are mixing today. Even here."

"Hardly to this extent unless you'd invited those jazz festival freaks."

"So what did you want? Just another stagnant old blueblood party?"

"I can't imagine what they must be thinking of all this."

"Well they all seem to be enjoying themselves."

"Because they're too reserved to reveal their horror over such boorishness."

"So you think we'll be the disgrace of Ocean Drive and Bellevue Avenue."

"Hah!" he spouted and couldn't prevent himself from blanching. "Word of such vulgarity travels far further and very swiftly, I fear."

"Oh I'll just bet you fear."

"Well there's a time and place for everything. You know we have an invitation to Wakehurst for tea tomorrow. I'm certainly not going over to Mrs. Bruguière if we've disgraced ourselves here tonight."

"Don't then. Or better still, you go along with the rest of the old-folks home, and leave me here, since I'm only contaminating your blood stock." Then she swept across the hall to the nearest bar, collected a glass of champagne, nodded a mock toast to her husband and heaved down the entire drink.

Somewhat older than Carole, John had descended from a long line of Wasp sovereigns dating back to the beginning of America. Now he owned one of the country's leading architectural firms, among so many other properties, including a scattering of houses around the world. He had long since reached the billionaire status and stayed there even after the purchase of such properties. With curly gray and white hair and distinguished good looks, he exuded an air, albeit stuffy, of masculine cool. But the fury in his eyes was beginning to betray such demeanor.

What a shame, Noah thought. To be surrounded by such elegance and still not be happy. To avoid being considered an eavesdropper he slipped over to consult with his photographer, after which he decided to go outdoors to relish the thought of the grandeur. The orchestra's mellow version of *Blue Champagne* followed him out past the silly giggles and haughty vain voices of a crowd of terrace bound young men and women. Lacking all the high flying spirit and shrewdness of their nouveau contemporaries, inexplicably they had become the mindless descendants of sagacious patrician Wasps. It was as if all their rich blood had drained away. And without family lifeline support, Noah could imagine them instantly falling by the wayside.

"He's obviously a Westsider," one of the languid men surreptitiously drawled in a disdaining voice but it carried to Noah.

"Definitely one," another concurred.

"Definitely not one," insisted another. "I don't think he's past being a Queens Baysider."

And they all tittered away over their syrupy green daiquiris casting glazed fleeting glances over Noah's way.

"Oh I wouldn't laugh," one of the arrogant young women who was slightly more tipsy than the rest proclaimed. "Guys like that can show us preppie aristocrats a thing or two."

"Like what?" one of the men said with obvious shock.

"Like an orgasm for one thing," another harder young woman who scarcely could have finished her teens spouted. "And I speak from experience."

"How could you say that after being with me?" And crushed looks prevailed.

"Because you don't know my love button from my Cartier tank. Although I must confess I didn't even know what one was myself until a new world guy like that so roundly showed me. Since then I'm just one throbbing clitoris in waiting--for more. Dressed in Valentino couture of course."

As Noah moved quickly to put more distance between himself and such utter imbecility, he thought it truly was the end of a powerful breed that had produced the most moronic examples of gilded youth. God what I wouldn't do to be able to gather the crumbs from all they're heedlessly letting elude them. They're totally oblivious of their chances. But then he forced himself to push such fruitless envy, or maybe it was anger, from his mind as he crossed the darkling lawn.

Suddenly a lustrous near full moon burst from a bank of fleeing clouds and flooded the palace behind him. As the distance grew, he turned and watched the facade become tinged with a pale blue luminescence that transmuted it into a resplendent emblem of all the riches and wondrous romance the world had to offer.

Even though he was aware of the first caress of tender dew, the evening was warm and clear and suffused with the scent of pine. He could hear the soft continuous breakers rush from the far end of the starry sky. For a moment he thought of his parents, of how overwhelmed they would have been with all of this. There wouldn't be a word in their vocabulary for it. Long ago they had stopped at *ritzy*--as if that were the ultimate dream. The trappings of an old Joan Crawford movie. God how proud they would be that he had come so far as to touch down here. And what of Nora? What would she think? Surely she would have to marvel. How could anyone fail to be but utterly entranced?

If only it were always to be like this. Nights of star wash and whispering seas and shimmering castles when at any moment golden meteors might streak across the heavens and cascade their glittering ore at his feet. Before he could turn the thought into a disenchantment, some vivid voice, most certainly Nora's, came to him soothing his disquiet. *It will be. It will be. It will be.*

"I think you heard what John had to say," Carole worried as she came up behind Noah, causing him to jump. "Don't pay any attention," she said, taking a sip of a tinkling, whisky-looking drink and appearing in manner and tone to be a completely different person. "He's become paranoid trying to keep his precious old money separate from the new. It started as a hobby to occupy his mind. Now, other than his architectural dynasty, it's become his single lifetime ambition."

"Doesn't that trouble you?" he ventured but then wondered if he weren't being too nervy.

"Oh yes, it used to a lot more than it does now. But I think it was Edna Millay who wrote: *In a year or two, you can get accustomed to anything.*" And she laughed and this time took a more than lady-like swallow of her drink.

"And you don't tire of it?"

"Oh we probably couldn't exist anymore without it. We've become accustomed to these scenes, because we can't think of anything better to do. Of course we pretend to change. That way it seems we're leading such thrilling lives. Come September, we'll rush back to New York--the theater season. How that cleanses and refreshes us. Then it's on to Paris, and London--s-o-o Dickensian at Christmas. The Alps, so vivifying. Vienna. And as the year drifts on the Cote d'Azur and the dazzling tans. Palm Beach. Southampton. Capri. Well you name it; we've got it. Oh, one location would never do us." She sighed and smiling bittersweetly revealed for an instant a dark chasm of spirit. "But in the end, they're all the same. And so are the people."

"But that's so wrong."

"How wise you are. Wiser still if you remember my words. Don't do anything more than observe these scenes. Because once you become involved, it changes you."

Noah shook his head, a little fearful of her warning.

"We weren't always a part of this, you know. Even with John's lineage and fortune, he was once the polar opposite. He abhorred it. So we stayed pretty much to ourselves. You can you know."

"But you weren't happy?"

"Oh yes. Very."

"Well then why would you change?"

She shrugged causing the ice in her glass to rattle. "Suddenly one day we didn't have a reason not to."

"I don't understand?"

"Well suddenly it became necessary to be occupied. So we joined up. We had the name. We had the money. The houses. Why not take advantage. It wasn't long before we forgot there could be any other way." And with that she lost her edge and became plaintive. "But then--we didn't want to remember."

"It seems very dismal to say the least." And he shivered at the threshold of what, during the course of this weekend, he had come to think of as some of the world's greatest glories.

"Oh no." And she bounced right back. "No. No. It's all very cheery you see. And the glamour is thrilling. You just forget everything that's missing and forever ride the jet stream."

"THIS PIECE IS FABULOUS." "Marvelous." "Remarkable." Three Wilton powers chimed almost in unison at a morning editorial post mortem, and another raved: "Oliver Wilton just phoned from Antibes and is completely, I mean absolutely swept away by your Newport. Noah, it not only reads--it *s-i-n-g-s* as Oliver loves to be able to say. Those people come alive. They lift right off the page and speak with a story to tell. Why the whole event is like something out of a comic opera. Biting but on the safe side of offensive. Somehow you sort of deliciously castigate without castigating. I can't imagine what you'd do if you really let loose."

"Now if we could only come up with a way to have the women in such a splendid feature suddenly start wearing long elegant clothing," pined one of the spruce powers.

"We have," Murphs chimed. "Well at least Noah has. And it's perfect. Take pictures of all the Fashion Idealists and superimpose images of truly chic *longueur* looks over them."

"Why that's sensational, Noah," rhapsodized *FCD*'s svelte fashion director. "It would conceptualize and forecast the whole trend through the leading ladies of society. Why they'd be our paper dolls. That's it. A sort of *What If* piece. Oh Noah, this is perfect. Brilliantly insightful."

"Well wait. Murphs here formulated that idea" Noah insisted.

"Oh come now, you're being modest," Murphs countered. "It was solely your idea. You should be proud of it, Noah. You're doing a fantastic job."

Noah was thrilled to hear all this praise. Suddenly he was the hero of *Fashion Connoisseur Daily*, and it felt so good. It felt even better when after the meeting he was advised by one of the powers that he'd be receiving a fifty-dollar-a-week raise."

"DON'T BE SILLY. We're sympatico you know. And it's a happy compulsion of mine to help," Murphs enthused after the meeting.

"But why give me all the credit?" he pressed.

"Because I don't need it. Our dear fashion director just selected me as one of the *fashionistas* to cover the Paris couture this fall? Puts me right up there."

"Well I couldn't be any higher at the moment myself," Noah delighted. "With all that praise and my new raise. Wow!"

But it was only a few days later when he was to receive even more good news. It seemed that Oliver Wilton had just returned from his European travels that morning and now one of his secretaries was on the phone. "Mr. Wilton would like to have a meeting with you as soon as possible."

"Do you want me to come up to his office?"

"No, he'll be right down. That is if it's okay with you."

"Well—well yes."

This would be the first time Noah would actually meet him. So he quickly pulled on his Brooks suit coat and rushed into the men's room for a quick inspection. He was no more than back at his desk when he recognized the man he had only seen in photos until now emerging from the bank of elevators. Tall and thin with a rich thick mop of blond hair, he darted across the editorial floor exuding all the youthful bravura of a dynamic frat man rather than the powerhouse behind a hot publishing company. Immediately Noah felt the dullard since Oliver wore a maroon and white striped oxford cloth shirt with sleeves rolled to the elbows along with tan poplin trousers held in place by matching maroon suspenders that also complemented his loosened grosgrain tie.

"Noah," he called out from the distance as he gave passing waves to various staff members. Then when he reached him he forcefully gripped his hand and upper arm and beaming looked him directly in the eyes. But when he began to speak, out came a stream of words all studded with that rarefied accent he must have inherited from his stately ancestry and never lost at Yale. "*Ah* cannot tell you how happy *ah* am to meet you at long last. *Ah* was such an *admahrah* of *youah* work when you were at the *Trib* that *ah* cannot say what a *purfect* delight this is to have you working with us. Now let us *ratire* to the conference room." Noah followed him thinking that close up he looked to be in his late thirties but his speech pattern conflicted with his dynamism making him seem older. Perhaps that was the way he wanted it because it gave him the edge of being the boss.

Once inside he closed the door. "We won't bother to sit because *ah* want to take you to lunch very soon. But what *ah* wanted to do in private was offer you *ma* sincerest apologies for not having been here in person to greet you sooner. *Ma* travels wouldn't permit it but still that's no excuse."

"Oh it's perfectly understandable. There's no need to do that."

"Well *ah* feel as such. *Regahdless ah* wanted to deliver this exciting news to you in person. We're all so delighted with your work that we need to place more emphasis on it, so starting next week *youah* to become *FCD*'s reigning society columnist. And *ah've* decided the column will bear your picture and be called--" Gesturing broadly: "*NOAH SEES*. That's with an extra fifty onto that raise of *cause.*"

"Well that sounds pretty thrilling. Thank you so much sir."

"No *sir*! You're to call me Oliver. Now we must get back to work." And he shook Noah's hand fervently and darted off while Noah stood stunned thinking no adverse signs of Skull and Bones here.

SOME DAY SOON we'll be very rich. So elated was Noah with the thought that later that day he went to Brooks Brothers and inhaled deeply as he gazed about.

"Sir, may I suggest a little finer quality wool in the made-to-measure?"

"Fine."

"It would be more apropos to your taste level."

And so it was. So much so that he decided on two. One a black pinstripe and another--a gray flannel. By the time the fitting was over, he felt like a millionaire. Soon he would be graduating to bespoke suits. On the way out-- thinking on the way up, he paused to select a half-dozen luxurious sea isle cotton dress shirts. Some with stripes to match Oliver's mode and all charged with his recently acquired Brooks Brothers plate. As he left, he decided to drop by J. Press and then Paul Stuart to relish their handsome offerings. How sumptuous. How absolutely sumptuous.

During the next days, he drifted into the stratosphere with the thoughts of making all that money. His salary would be almost five hundred a week. While it was nothing compared to what his college buddy Tim Anderson was making as chief ad agency creative, it was more than Noah had dreamed would be rolling his way for a very long time to come. And he was so proud.

6

"THE NEXT THING they'll be genuflecting," Nora whispered after Noah had checked them into Boston's Ritz on an unexpectedly cold September day with an air so heavy laden it foreshadowed snow. For him the thrill spawned by the combination of breaking in his new American Express card and signing as Mr. and Mrs. Mason was engulfing and nearly left him breathless. In that instant he thought of himself as having all the power in the world. Nora's immediate reaction was to recoil while no less than two porters carried on as though they were escorting the Queen and Prince Phillip to their quarters.

When the porters threw open the massive double doors and gave sweeping arm gestures for their entry, Nora gasped. It was a suite the size of a palace. As the men proceeded to arrange their luggage on polished mahogany stands in front of a giant four-poster bed, she whispered: "Now I can see why you insisted on packin' me clothes in your bags. Can you just imagine me bringing that yoke of mine in here?"

"This is what you should always have, Nora," he insisted squeezing her around the waist and kissing her on the cheek. Before she had a chance to reply, he went over to dismiss the porters. She couldn't believe they were only that much away from kissing his hand as he lavished their mitts with dollars.

"Well you know this goes hand in hand with the territory. I mean if I'm up here to do features on the connoisseur world of the Cabots and the Lowells, I have to enter something approaching that world. And Wilton is paying for it." True he fibbed a little. They would pay for the Ritz room rate but not the difference required for the lavish suite he craved for his love.

As Nora remained in dismayed shock, Noah was in the clouds totally absorbed by the surroundings. "You know when I first came to New York I'd come up here on the weekends sometimes. I'd stand down there under those willow trees and dream of what it would be like to stay up here." He went on as if enchanted.

"Funny that, I used to walk by the Shelbourne in Dublin when I was little and imagine having me afternoon tea in that fancy front sitting room under those glittery chandeliers. Then it came to me that it was only a bit of childish snobbery. Because why would I be after going in there when I could be off to the likes of a Bewley's and for a quarter of the price now I could be tuckin' into a grand fine mixed grill. Why it would be only more than enough to fill me guts and do me the day."

Noah laughed heartily and reached around her to hand her a glass of champagne. "Here, fill your guts with this."

"What?" she gasped and then realized the source of the muffled pop.

"I had it arranged in advance. It's Dom Perignon."

"Dom what?"

"Never mind. Enjoy it." And he laughed some more. Then he clicked her glass with his. "This is to you and your first job in America."

She took a sip as she came back to reality. "Thanks be to god for that. I was blessed really. If it hadn't been for those *dacent* people at Aer Lingus arranging for my working visa and a job to boot, I'd be packing me bag and using the return part of me ticket to go home approaching beggary."

"Never! Don't say such things."

And he sat his glass down along with hers, slipped his arms around her from behind and kissed the milky softness of her neck. "I'd never let that happen." And he whispered words of love that were doing a slow sultry dance through her being as she felt her blood rising. Ahead of them the swollen dark clouds suddenly exploded sending cascades of snow falling across the Gardens and the Commons muting the early autumnal hues to pale orange embers.

When he finally pulled away, the snow ceased and the clouds were back again. "I'd guess it's only freezin' cold out there now," she said and shivered.

"Well we'll just have to be going after some coats then. Who'd have ever thought?"

"Not at all, we won't be going after some coats then. We'll do with what we've got. I've me toasty warm blue jumper and a suit jacket to put over it. And you've that handsome maroon vest that's pure virgin wool along with your blazer."

"I suppose. But you could use some warmer clothes going towards winter. And there's a Bonwit's just down the road on Newbury Street."

"We will not be going down the road--" And then she caught sight of his face and noticed his air of persistence. "Oh I see. So you're telling me the articles I've got aren't good enough."

"No," he said gentling down a good bit. "Well-- Well I do wish you'd told me when you were going off to Alexanders. I mean I could have helped you do a lot better. And I could have given you more money."

"It's not the money, Noah. Well it is. But it isn't. What I've bought is the type of clothes I'd wear. They're practical, the way I am. I'm not a Bonwit girl, you know."

THAT AFTERNOON with the sun glimpsing out, they did make do. Noah sensed an annoyance there so he backed off. Instead of pushing the shopping, they spent their Saturday afternoon hugging away the cold while strolling the dreamy expanses of the Gardens, then proceeding to the wealth of Colonial structures on the Freedom Trail where pine smoke still curled from the chimneys into the frosty air.

By that evening when they arrived at Anthony's Pier Four all had been sidelined in the light of rustic romanticism. The normally booming restaurant was quiet, probably because of the continued threat of a storm and the heavy fall of flurries that came again with the nightfall. They were able to snatch one of the window tables facing Boston Harbor. These were usually reserved for larger parties, Noah said as they delighted to the glimmer of lights across the water. "But they should always be for lovers only," he added and then watched her blue eyes glisten.

They ordered bowls of sauteed lobster and a bottle of Chevalier-Montrachet. "When I'm having lobster, I feel I should be celebrating something."

"You seem to be celebrating something every time we meet," she teased.

But in all seriousness he insisted: "And I always will. I want us to be together forever."

She could feel his electricity. "And would you be proposing to me now, you cheeky lad?"

"What do you think I've been doing all this time?"

"You won't be disappointed? I mean there's lots better out there than me, don't you know?"

"No! I don't know."

"Just look around you. All those fancy ones. I've been hearing those words, well reading them in your paper as well--*slick, chic.* Would you not want--"

"No! I would not want. My wanting days are over. You ended those, don't you know. Now I want to propose a toast," he said lifting his glass and glancing out to the harbor. "To the beauty of snow as it softly fell across our engagement eve, blessing our hearts with their newly found unity in love."

"Ah you're lovely all the same," she whispered, then leaned over and kissed his lips.

"Lovely am I?"

Once again she was lost in his cloudy eyes, his beautiful words and the gentle force of his maleness that came behind them. As they fell into dreamy silence, the refracted light from the harbor on falling snow set her brimming with inspiration. "Oh Noah, it's going to be so grand for us. Someday we'll have our house in Ireland. And it will be just us. All alone and so happy in our aloneness."

"It'll be a grand fine house, Nora. All you could ever imagine. Everything."

"Right. Then we'll have children. But they'll be like extensions of ourselves. Bringing us even closer."

"Children?" Both his voice and his demeanor jumped from its groove.

"Yes. Yes, of course. You do want them?"

"Well-- Well, yes."

"You don't sound certain."

It was a jolt, one he'd never considered. Children didn't exactly fit with all the grandeur, he was anticipating. Grandeur he now realized was advancing by the day. With the silence came the coldness. The second such rift of the day. He couldn't bear it. He was so in love. So he looked over at her and grinned: "Of course we're going to have children, Nora. How could we not?" As he brought the light back into her eyes, he told them both: "We're going to have everything. Our lives are going to be the fullest you can imagine. Only as you'd say Nora--doubly that."

LATER IN A TAXI under the continuing fall of snow, Nora said: "I think we should give each other a gift for this night."

"I'm sorry. I should have thought."

"Poor pet," she said, stroking his face. "I didn't mean that."

"I know, but I should have something. And not just something but something really exquisite for you."

"You do," she whispered.

He looked at her with puzzlement until he saw in her eyes the release of a flood of longing.

THEY WERE NOT in their true senses. A cloud, fashioned of all the vapors of passion and love that had been forming since that ecstatic night in his apartment, drifted across their minds. It screened out everything except the concept of beauty, that tender radiant light that burned around them. This time it was going to happen. Their bodies were so acutely sensual that every touch summoned a little orgasm. And they touched each other everywhere. Then as their passion welled, Noah forced himself to stop. "I better get a--" "No. No. My period's due." And she pulled him back. Then he was moving between her silken thighs, and she felt the hardness of his aching penis brush over her engorged labia, which were throbbing with such force she thought her heart must have gone down to beat there. Back and forth he moved until she felt she would cry out. "Oh please," she moaned. Still he held back. The tension built to an unbearable state. Then suddenly he nudged in a little, stopped then nudged a little further into the welcoming wetness. She could feel the pulse of the broad smooth head now as its ridge pushed past the inner folds of her skin. "O-o-o-h"-- her vagina contracted with all the strength of its longing and drew at his velvety hardness, bringing it further, deeper within. He trembled, then moaned at the thrill.

He could no longer linger from this ecstasy. But when he tried to push further, the membrane blocked him. He increased the pressure. "I'm afraid I'm going to hurt you," his voice rasped. "Oh you're not. You're not," she insisted and anxiously reached to pull his shoulders down as she arched up to meet his force, to bring him through the obstacle. This time he felt a slight giving. Instinctively she slid her hands down to his tense buttocks and pulled on them with all her strength forcing his penis to stretch her tissue, stretch until mercifully it gave way. Slowly, carefully he edged into the enveloping fervor, stretching the walls of her vagina. From the white city light that seeped through the split in the drapes, she could see his worry and gripped his buttocks again. This time it caused him to thrust through the tightness to the hilt and her vagina to spasm in a continuous spontaneity around his hardness. "O-o-o-o-h Noah," she gasped as a great wave of warmth washed through her body to her mind.

She was caught utterly in her own rapture, until he began to move. As his rhythm built, she felt the electric energy of his strength, then the sudden sharp charges that penetrated her so deeply they made her whole body quiver with a vibrancy it had never known.

There was nothing in his experience to compare with the magnificence of this union. This is life. This is what it's all about, he thought. At once infinitely tender, at once rapturously rousing. It was so vital he wondered how he'd ever lived without it. His heart pounded, and he began losing control of his rasping breath.

Then as her hands tightened their grip on his buttocks, she seemed to stop breathing for a few seconds before her back arched and he felt her start to tremble. Her cries, soft at first, grew louder and louder. He adored her for this, for letting him tenderly ravish her. He could feel nothing but sheer love. Moving faster and faster, he heard her cry out again, and this broke something in him.

Seconds later, dozens of thundering waves released deeply within him and roared over his brain. And he came and came as he had never come before, and holding her fast sailed away on an enchanted sea.

Later Noah opened the drapes, and they lay in bed watching the snow softly falling over the fuzzy glow of city lights. It lulled them into dreaminess and he fell asleep holding her with his face pressed against her feverish breasts and his warm breath caressing her. She would protect him while he slept--this man who had kindled a new life in her, a woman's life. It wasn't long before she felt the growing silky hardness of his penis once more. And it amazed her with delight that still in sleep he moved around until he covered her body and slowly, drowsily entered her again. Awakening only slightly, he began the moves that led to a gentle sleep-laden climax. So sensuous was it that she came too, in soft little ripples of splendor. Then with the embers of their lovemaking still burning deeply within her, she let herself drift to sleep among the heavens.

In the early morning light of a warmer day, they made their way through the lingering snow into the Commons, where they were isolated from the city, from all but each other. Realizing this, they were in each other's arms again, kissing and feeling the intense reverberations of all their orgasms. "Oh god Noah, I want you there always."

He stroked her face to soothe her. Then he sighed. "Forget always. I gotta go to work today."

"Ah no. I'm after forgetting."

"Yeap. After Mass, I've got to get all duded up in my gray flannel suit and my black wingtips and go off to the Somerset Club for lunch. Sherry in the drawing room and all that sort of thing. I think it's going to be pretty stuffy stuff, but still I wish I dared take you along."

"Well you can't do that with only one invitation. And besides I wouldn't quite think I looked the part in me woolen jumper." And she laughed.

"Don't be going back into that now. Not after the hot night we've had." With that he looked around to see that they were still alone then proceeded to lift the front of her bulky sweater and run his hand down under her slacks and panties to the drenching wetness. "O-o-o-h," she sighed as another orgasm was imminent. "What are you after doing to me, you wild rogue you?"

7

"I DIDN'T THINK I'd ever start writing seriously again," Noah said a few Saturday mornings later over breakfast in his apartment. So joyous was he with his turn of fortune that he'd started working on some short stories. He was so pleased with their development that he planned to send them to *The New Yorker* when he was finished.

"Of course you'd start again," Nora insisted. "You had to."

"I wouldn't have without you."

"Regardless of me. You were born with that. It's god's will."

"Well speaking of that, you have to send to Dublin for those paintings."

"They embarrass me, Noah."

"Let others be the judge," he warned, pointing his finger at her. "Just as you said to me--you have to."

"Ah, it's hardly the same thing."

"Now!"

"Oh, all right. Give over will you."

8

"WE'VE GOT TO GET more names before anyone else gets them," city editor Jack Warren exclaimed as he skirted the newsroom hounding the *FCD* staff. When he reached Noah's desk, he snipped: "Mason, can't you come up with more than five definites? You are supposed to be such a hot shot columnist, aren't you?" He had seethed with jealousy ever since Noah had been promoted.

"I don't think Oliver's too worried about my performance," Noah snapped right back. "So I wouldn't sweat it Jack."

This was near Thanksgiving that year and just before Truman Capote's black and white masked ball. It was to be held at the Plaza to celebrate the recent success of his *In Cold Blood*. The entire *Fashion Connoisseur* staff was working itself into a tizzy over who was going to be on

Capote's secret 500 "closest friends" guest list. Some claimed this would be the party of the century, but certainly by any standards it was destined to be the party of the Sixties.

Yet Noah was subduing his panic after trying so many sources and coming up with so little. He had met Capote on a number of occasions and had brief conversations. But all he could glean from him now was: "You can only be certain of yourself being there, dear one. Yourself and of course your lovely friend Nora whom I've yet to meet." Even Noah's now close acquaintance Carole Dawson, who knew everybody and everything, wasn't privy to many more names, since they were so closely guarded. Of course it was Capote's way of drawing more attention to the event.

"Stay cool, Noah," Murphs whispered. "Don't let all this blow your mind. I called my source for you. Here." And she handed him a sheet of copy paper. "You see we will beat all the competition."

Noah looked at the sheet and gasped. "Is this for real? How did your source come by all these names? Why there must be more than fifty here."

"I have no idea. All I can say is that in all the time I've worked here, the guy's never been wrong about one thing he's told me. He knows everything about society and fashion."

"Well, you turn these in."

"Absolutely not. Society's your beat. Consider me your source this time."

"Are you crazy? That's not remotely fair. I already owe you so much."

"Oh no. Just the opposite. I owe you more than you know."

"Huh?"

"AH NOAH, I DON'T want to go to that bloomin' thing," Nora panicked when he told her they had an invitation to the Capote affair.

"But I want you there. Don't you want to be with me, too?"

"Well not at the likes of that do."

"Do! Nora, do you realize important people are leaving town on the pretext that they have urgent business, just so no one will realize they weren't invited?"

"Sure that's all the more reason I shouldn't be going. I'm nobody."

"That's not so. Don't ever say that." She could see the hurt in his eyes as he drew her to him. "You're the woman I love. I'm proud of you, and I want you there. Truman would like you to come too. He specifically asked that I bring you."

"What am I going to wear for the love of god?"

"I took care of that," he thrilled with great pride and presented her with a stack of boxes he pulled from his closet. Two magnificent chiffon evening gowns, one pale orchid, the other ice blue, slipped from the tissues of the Bonwit Teller box.

"Noah, have you taken leave of your senses altogether?"

"No, I'm being sense-ible. You need these clothes."

From the Bergdorf Goodman box came a black and white silk crepe dress with high-padded shoulders and a short swirling skirt. "That's for the Capote *do*, as you called it," he said. "You have to wear black and white. You also have to wear a mask. I didn't get that yet."

"A m-a-s-k? Are you having me on?"

"No. It's a masked ball. Well I have to wear one, too."

She shook her head in complete amazement. By the time she had gone through the rest of the boxes, including matching shoes, bags, wraps, jewelry, even lingerie, she was completely speechless. "The money!" she managed to gasp.

"Don't worry. I have charge plates. Besides it was worth every penny."

"But there's only one dance. Why in god's name did you get so many things?"

"Oh there'll be many more events. This is only the start for us. And they're going to look gorgeous on you."

Although she never dreamed of wearing such clothes, it was true. They made her look only fabulous, and oh how grand she suddenly felt. The lad has exquisite taste, she thought. He's like some sort of Prince Charming lavishing me for the first time in my life. Any girl would do her nut to have him. But at the same time she was uncomfortable about the whole situation. She could compare it to the feeling of disquietude she had experienced those brief moments at the Ritz in Boston. But now it became even clearer that he might be trying to make her over to fit the ways of high society. She refrained from saying anything because she thought it might be a bit unfair considering his thoughtful extravagance. Still it caused her a bit of a fright all the same.

ON THE NIGHT OF THE BALL, they attended one of the many prefatory dinners being held by prominent members of the social set. This one was at John and Carole Dawson's overwhelmingly elegant Fifth Avenue apartment. Overlooking the park and with ceilings attempting to reach the stars, it seemed a city version of their Newport mansion. Well he later learned that indeed it did consist of eighteen rooms, including ten bed chambers, a library, and two enormous reception areas.

"Noah dear, I'm so delighted you could come," Carole called out across the entry hall when her maid opened the door. Then she swept over in her white satin Channel shift, hugged Noah and kissed his cheek. "And this must be Nora. Oh how charming, how perfectly charming," she went on as she took a long look at her. Then she clutched her welcome and kissed her on the cheek. "I can see everything Noah told us about you is true. Oh, I'm so happy for the both of you. I can't wait to be the first to introduce you to everyone. Come." As she ushered them over to the bar where about ten social stars were clustered, she asked: "How do you like New York?"

"Oh, it's grand, grand," Nora just managed, trembling, blushing from nervous embarrassment and wishing she could only disappear.

"Noah," called a woman from the gathering.

"Brooke, it's so good to see you again." And then acknowledging the rest, which by now he knew on a first name basis, Noah responded gleefully. "Charlotte and CZ. Winston. Leland and Pamela."

"I'd like you all to meet Nora Clifford from Dublin," Carole cheered.

"Marvelous." "Delighted." "Charmed." "Thrilled." One after the other enthused as more clutching and kissing ensued. After they had collected what Noah considered a truly sumptuous glass of 1951 Georges de Latour Cabernet, they moved on to another cluster and did the whole thing all over again. Nora had never been hauled about and kissed so much in her life. At first, she was shocked and intimidated. But by now she was ready to say: Give over, ya bloody bunch of shytes.

In this second group, she met Carole's husband John. "How lovely. What a beautiful young woman you are. And what a welcome addition to New York." Nora could tell from the way he looked her over he had more on his mind than merely welcoming her to New York. Dirty old geezer, she thought and was disgusted.

"We've got so much to catch up on," one of the society matrons trilled to Noah after bubbling over Nora. "Let's do lunch early next week. Maybe Cote Basque."

"Fine," said Noah. "I must say you look dynamic in that de la Renta. I never see you in anything but his clothes." Then he laughed. "People are beginning to rumor a little."

"Oh Noah, you scoundrel, what nonsense. Rumor a little. Don't you dare print that in your column." But from the way she said it, Noah wondered if secretly she didn't want him to do that very thing.

By now Nora was amazed. Noah knew all these people and on such intimate terms. It seemed only baffling. She had expected him to be removed, far removed. Instead he was behaving as if he were one of them. At once it was equally embarrassing and annoying to her. But she'd have to be thwarting such thoughts. It was part of his work, she told herself. His technique for getting good material. She had to expect this. But she didn't have to like it.

"You know Carole, Nora is a truly fine artist," Noah interceded at one point, causing Nora to jump with the panic.

"So you told me. I'd love to see your work, my dear. Exquisite Irish landscapes, I believe."

"I'm afraid Noah's a little premature on that. I do some painting right enough, but I don't consider--"

"Now, now, now. You artists are all the same. You must show me. I know quite a few people in the downtown galleries. I support them, and they're always looking for new people."

"As soon as they arrive from Dublin, we'll show them to you," Noah piped before Nora could say a word. She didn't even know what she thought of this. For the moment, she felt put upon, as though something personal had been ripped from her and flung on display. She wanted nothing more than to slag him for it.

"Come dear," Carole said to Nora. "I must show you my early Renoir sketches before dinner. I picked them up at Sotheby's for a steal, a mere steal. Can you imagine?"

Noah watched as the two crossed to the other side of the room. Nora looked quite radiant in her grand gown with her hair pulled back with an onyx headband and falling so beautifully across her shoulders. Somehow this atmosphere suited her more. For to him it heightened her beauty. It also heightened his spirits. Just putting on his new Paul Stuart tux had triggered the surge earlier. Instantaneously it had produced the hardest hard of his life. They'd had to carefully strip away their fashions so they could ravage each other right there on the floor of his living room. Now being here at Carole's was supreme. How easy it was to imagine them in their own rooms filled with similar Louis XV and very rare French Renaissance furniture as they peered at their original Renoirs.

"Wouldn't you just die for these things?" he whispered to Nora as the guests were being ushered into the dining room.

"Well they're nice enough all right," she replied. "But I can think of better uses to put me money to be sure."

"*Nice enough?* They're magnificent."

Nora looked at him, realized he meant what he said, and her heart missed a few beats.

AFTER A MARVELOUS DINNER consisting of bouchee of fruits de mer and noisette de veau along with an exquisite 1961 Chateau Trotanoy Pomerol, they all began trooping down from Sixty-sixth Street through the light mist to the Plaza. Along the way gossipy bits bubbled from the ladies turning them into even more vain creatures than Nora could have ever imagined. "You know Augusta was absolutely in a hissy tissy over her hair. Straggly roots or something. Anyway to calm her, Babe sent her over to Kenneth this morning. And she usurped so much of his time fussing that his top clients waiting to be coifed went berserk. I hear she even grabbed his crotch when he tried to dismiss her. A lot of good that would do with Kenneth. But can you imagine after all that and now the mist is dampening her curls."

Nora roared laughing. Purposely she had kept Noah at the back of this gathering wishing they could just run away. "Are they serious? I think they're bloomin' retarded imbeciles," she snapped in full voice.

"Sh-h-h-h," Noah replied but couldn't help but chuckle when he realized she hadn't been heard.

At ten as they entered the Plaza, they all donned their masks for Truman's ball. "Actually this mask isn't half bad," Nora said as they exited the elevator and wove through the tight security engendered because of the crowds of sightseers. "At least this way no one will be able to see me."

"Will you stop," Noah said. "Everybody loves you. Now enjoy it."

"I can't relax around the likes of these people. I feel like I'm on exhibition." It was a thought that only compounded itself when all were forced to queue at the ballroom entryway to have their names boldly pronounced by an announcer.

Mr. Noah Mason and Miss Nora Clifford

The voice loudly reverberated over the proceedings. "It's a bleedin' nightmare to me Noah," Nora fussed on through clenched teeth just before she was presented to Truman and the guest of honor Kay Graham owner of *The Washington Post*.

And as such they entered the gold and white candlelit ballroom with its scarlet tables and its fast arriving 500-plus black-and-white attired tycoons, artists, film and theater stars, social matrons, designers et al--a potpourri of the very famous and then some. After Truman emitted a high-pitched southern squeal over the array professing—"We're going to have fun", Peter Duchin's orchestra set the whole spectacle ablaze with the likes of *I Could Have Danced All Night* and *Camelot*. While this ensued, guests cheered and steered their way about the room first detecting then fervently greeting their elite friends and acquaintances in the lustrous splendor of the occasion.

Noah was so excited by the sweep of the event his skin began to tingle. He took deep breaths as if to draw in and savor the scent of all the money that enveloped the scene. He felt taller somehow. Loftier. The perfect match. Everybody seemed to know him now, right through his mask. They called out, waved, shook his hand, clutched him. Even the dippy young bluebloods who once mocked him for being even less than a Westsider, now were courting the man whose column in social circles was growing more powerful by the day. And all of this made him feel as luxuriously monied as they. Now if only he could loosen the binding ties of Nora's shyness, she would feel the same for she too would be riding his power wave.

Once he'd instructed his photographer, who along with all the other cameramen, was required to remain outside the ballroom and shoot from there, he quickly collected champagne flutes for himself and Nora hoping to calm her. After they'd downed them, she did lighten. Relieved he swept her around the dance floor to *On A Clear Day You Can See Forever* and became so elated it was as if the whole ball had been arranged in his honor.

"You're the prince and princess of the evening," Truman proclaimed with a giggle as he took hold of their arms when they'd finished their dance.

"Sure," said Noah sarcastically.

"No. I'm serious. Look around you. So much *joie de vive* wilting on the vine as it were. Pity. I had no idea until I put them all together. But you two have an innocent--well it's blinding--*je ne sais quoi*. It reminds me a little of all that electricity when young Monty Clift danced with Elizabeth Taylor in *A Place In The Sun*."

"Monty Clift!" Nora exclaimed as they left the dance floor. "Ah there'll be no stoppin' ya now."

"I don't know about that. He's dead, isn't he? But Elizabeth. Wow. How do you like those apples?"

"God, would you ever believe that?" And she let herself go and roared laughing. Unfortunately her tension returned as soon as they sat at the table assigned to them, a table shared with a variety of suave, haughty, conceited types. And she the only ignoble amongst them. For the love of god, what was she doing here? Noah, who once again seemed well acquainted, introduced her around not only compelling her to extend her now icy hand but to chat idly while he often dashed to other tables gathering material for his column.

By midnight, after everyone had de-masked, twist music began to predominate and drowned the bubbly conversation. No one seemed to mind however since most of the guests were bubbling internally from all the vintage

Taittinger--a factor that greatly relieved Nora's sense of conspicuousness. Noah delighted in her apparent relaxation.

Once she excused herself to go to the ladies room, he quickly took another opportunity to scamper about gathering quotes for his column. As he did he spied Oliver Wilton and his equally waspish wife Martha bidding adieu to Carter and Amanda Burden while others minced and winced about them--most likely fearing for their lives that Oliver would take sudden displeasure with them and prove such in print. "*Ah* think we've seen enough of these *ahdent* spirits for one night," he told Noah as he and Martha were leaving for their old Greenwich estate.

"Well I wouldn't mind seeing a bit more of them, Oliver," his strikingly attractive wife almost implored.

"That would be quite impossible for the publisher of *ahwa* paper to be over displaying himself at such an event," he snapped rather harshly taking her by the arm. And as he turned back to Noah, he thought this was the first time he had seen a sharper colder side of his boss. "*Ah* do feel that you will do a *mahvelous* portraiture of this *halaquinade*. *Ah* wouldn't think any of the other papers, or magazines for that matter, would come close to leading this dance when you *ah* around. You must remember you *ah* our *stah* now." Noah shivered a little when they were gone. He'd have to pull together this whole zany madness the next day, including the beautiful-people repartee and fashions along with a good few zingers to gently skewer some of those who had faltered. Above all he'd have to make certain the piece was the lodestar—that no other press coverage came close. But he could—and would.

When Nora returned from the loo and couldn't find Noah, she collected another glass of champagne, stood by herself away from the throngs and gazed about this come-all-ya of the American super rich. In an instant the ballroom froze into fresco formation in her mind's eye. Then as she focused on various tableaux, she began thinking of the British Rococo painter William Hogarth who had plumbed the morality of 1700s society, particularly the aristocracy of Georgian England. The caustic feelings of his work easily translated to this ballroom--vivid scenes of bejeweled pomposity, giddy folly and omnipotence with not the least screed of true virtue to be seen. And always the mad waste of it. But by far the most shocking thread coursing through this tapestry was that of self-adoration.

"Having fun?" a voice called out from behind. She turned to find it was John Dawson who'd come over to her.

"Yes. It's quite a spectacle," Nora said, biting her tongue and trying her best to be personable.

"Well Truman wanted to outdo everyone. And he certainly has. He got everyone."

As she felt him watching her, she nervously finished her champagne and set the glass aside on a nearby rail hoping to make an escape. "I guess everyone's here right enough. It's beyond comprehension."

But then as she started to move on, he continued. "Yes, and somehow it's all rather lonely. The goal for so many of these people is to outshine everyone else. Imagine, they have so much and see so little. Someday if they have to confront real losses, maybe they'll realize there are more important things than pure frivolity." Then he tossed back the remains of what appeared to be a whisky and sat the glass on the rail alongside hers.

"It's a desperate pity," Nora exclaimed with sudden great fervor. Even though she harbored an instinctive dislike and mistrust of John, a certain truthful passion in his thoughts had ignited her. "Just think of what all this expenditure on opulence could do for the needy. Why what it could do in my country alone for the poor Catholics in the North. It's shocking all the same. And bloody sinful. I'd like to rub their noses in it." For the moment she had forgotten that she wasn't just thinking but was thinking aloud, very aloud.

"Well you certainly have fire," John said, smiling at her. "I thought that of you. And I was right."

"Too much so I'm afraid," she added as she quelled her anger and prepared to move on once more.

"You know who the most remarkable person here is?" he asked, stopping her with his voice again. "The one with the most beauty, the most brilliance. Well let's face it, there is no beauty without brilliance. But unquestionably that person--is you. I've been watching and I know."

"Oh please. Thank you. But that's not necessary."

As she began to shift away, he cautiously looked around and surreptitiously took hold of her hand. "My dear, you're positively vibrant."

"And you're positively married," she whispered sharply not giving a moment's hesitation as she tried to retrieve her hand. But he only tightened his grip when he realized they were still safe from the awareness of almost everyone.

"Even so, I really need someone like you to talk with. I appreciate what you have, which is more than all these people put together. It's such a perfect perspective. Young and yet so mature."

"Please let me go," she continued in a whisper, hoping no one was noticing.

"I'd just like to talk with you. No one has to know." And he smiled as if to comfort.

"Stop this. I'm with Noah."

"Look, why don't we just get out of here for a few minutes," he continued, gesturing to a nearby entryway and still gripping her hand even more tightly. "I've already told Carole I have some business to attend to. And Noah will find someone else for the time being. Half the women here are hot for him you know." With that he attempted to lead her toward the exit. As she struggled as secretly as possible, he pressed on: "We'll just go for a quiet drink downstairs in the Palm Court. We'll be safe there, and we'll come back in a half-hour. No one will know we're missing. You'll see. Our secret." And he winked at her.

"Stop it, you bloody blackguard. You're half pissed," she finally hissed under her breath, barely able to restrain her mounting fury. But thanks be to god it was enough she noted as she watched the scoundrel recoil in horror. It was as if the penny finally dropped and he knew she was about to expose his true nature to others of his lineage. And by now many of those had begun to sense the discord. Mortified, John quickly headed back across the ballroom to his wife, as Noah rushed to Nora.

"What's wrong?" he asked.

"I want to leave," she replied.

"Nora, calm down. Just calm down."

"I just want to get out of this looney bin. Now."

"What did he say to you?" Noah was speaking in as low a voice as possible in an attempt to quell her vehemence. Thank god Oliver had left. He almost sighed his relief.

"He propositioned me as though I were a common whoore."

Noah glanced around to see if anyone was still watching. "S-h-h-h," he said as he led her over to a quiet corner. "It's my fault. I shouldn't have left you. Rumor has it he can be really lewd when he has a few drinks. Just forget him."

"The only way I can do that is to get out of here before I lose me temper all together." The more she talked the more incensed she became. And even though her tone remained low, people still had an eye on them. Mercifully the orchestra struck up at that point with *If Ever I Would*

Leave You. He would have laughed at the perfect timing if it hadn't been so serious. "Ah love, please let's stay a little while longer. I need to get more material. You'll see. It'll be all right."

Even though she stayed, her rage shifted back to disdain for the duration.

THEY ARRIVED BACK at Noah's very late and collapsed on the sofa.

He sighed. "I'm not angry with you. Will you stop saying that?"

"Well then you're disappointed in me."

"Disappointed that you didn't like it more. I mean it wasn't just an ordinary night."

"Well thanks be to god. It would be a shockin' shame if they were all to be like that now."

"But you know, all that elegance. Just the feeling of being around it. Now John Dawson aside. Don't you think it's exhilarating? I mean coming from our backgrounds."

"Backgrounds!" she riled.

"Well I just meant--"

"I can't speak for you, but I'll have you to know that I'd take my background any day over the whole effen' lot of their's"

"Oh I didn't mean-- I mean I just thought all the surroundings. The romance--I-- Well I guess I thought you'd be entranced by it."

"Entranced by what? Those bloody gobshytes, those morons, those bleedin' arseholes throwing their money away."

"Nora, will you calm down. I love you too much to see you like this."

"I can't calm down. All that wasted money. And we were a part of that waste."

"Well it's Truman's money. I guess he can spend it any way that suits him." And he laughed.

"That's not the point. It's the whole general attitude--or lack of attitude behind it. And the worst of the lunacy was to see all those people pawin' ya. How do you manage that?"

"It's part of the scene. It doesn't mean anything."

"But you enjoy it."

"As part of my work, I do. Enjoy getting the story."

"I can't bear to see you give so much of yourself to them. And how after all we've had together you could even begin thinking of equating that with romance." And tears sprang in her eyes.

"You really are serious. That amazes me. It's all surface. You'll see. And after a while you'll see it's not so bad. Far from it. You just learn to ignore the pretentious and the distasteful. There are good things there. And besides these people are going to be very helpful. Even if her husband is pretty strange, Carole Dawson is a powerful woman. A moving force. And kind. She'll get you exhibited someday. Just you wait and see."

"I don't want to be exhibited. That's another thing. Why do I feel you're putting me up for show without even asking?"

"Not you, you goose. Your paintings. Those beautiful paintings. I'm proud of them, and I'm proud of you."

"Yes, but how long will that be for? That bloody bollix said half the women there were hot for you. *Monty Clift.* I keep thinking of what my granny used to say—you can't make a silk purse out of a sow's ear."

"Oh don't be ridiculous, Nora. I can assure you there wasn't one woman there who even approached being as beautiful as you. *Elizabeth*," he said, putting his arm around her. "Now stop talking about this. I want to do something else." His eyes were twinkling.

"What?"

"I want to take your clothes off-- and slowly come into you-- until I've filled you," he whispered, stirring her. "And then-- I want us to ravish one another-- until-- it's pure ecstasy. Then I want to stay like that-- inside you for the rest of the night. Doing it over and over again."

"But aren't you after forgetting you're going to have to be firing off that story tomorrow?"

"There's no better ammunition. Believe me." Then he drew her towards the bedroom.

9

EVEN THOUGH HIS COVERAGE of the ball did become the lodestar, culminating with Oliver lunching him at La Grenouille, Noah was left with a gnawing feeling over Nora. After he'd averted the crisis that night he decided that he would have to soft pedal the whole society situation and ease her into it until she was more comfortable and would be able to accept it for what it was. Since Christmas was on the doorstep that year, he thought it might provide the perfect aid.

"Oh your father would be so happy, if he could see you with Nora. Well no happier than I am. I just can't get over how lovely she is," Noah's mother went on after they arrived in the small rural town of Yearnington in upstate New York for the holidays.

"I know. I'm one lucky man, mama," Noah said.

"I only wish you didn't have to see this horrid house with this crummy furniture. But social security doesn't afford very much, you know."

"Will you give over, Mrs. Mason? It's far from a mansion I was reared," Nora insisted not having a clue as to why she was continually apologizing for her cozy little home.

"Don't worry, mama. Someday this is all going to change for you."

"Do you think there's some aging prince out there

waiting just for me?"

They were sitting in the Mason living room having after dinner highballs of whiskey and ginger ale as Noah began to flick through a box of old pictures he'd taken down from the closet of his boyhood room, pictures of his father to show Nora.

"Oh he was a fine cut of a man. Lovely," Nora said.

"Yes-- he was---once," Mrs. Mason responded and her voice trailed off betraying her disappointment. Yet when Noah handed her a few snapshots as a reminder she suddenly brightened. "Oh, now I see what you were looking at. Oh yes. He was some man back in the days when these were taken. Why he was the handsomest man in town, Nora. He'd just come back from New York to visit his ailing mother. He'd been working with Walt Disney on his first sound cartoon *Steamboat Willie*. And Walt wanted him to come right back."

"That was a real tragedy," Noah said.

"Yes, because Mildred got worse and lingered some months before she died, so he being her only child couldn't leave her. But as sad as it was for him, I guess that was a strange kind of good fortune for me. If he had gone back right away, I never would have met him. But instead he went to work here in the movie house showing the pictures. That's when he swept me right off my feet."

Nora looked at Noah and caught his devilish glint as Mrs. Mason went on: "I was the envy of every girl in town. Why your father being the smooth talker he was persuaded the priest here at St. Paul's to marry us within just a few months. Oh we were so happy then. We were going to go everywhere and do everything. We had such plans."

Mrs. Mason suddenly stopped. She sighed and began to frown as she handed the pictures back to Noah. The room fell silent, and Nora realized he should be alone with his mother. Although she was most reluctant to leave him, she excused herself to take a bath and retire.

After she'd gone, Noah and his mother went to the kitchen where he made them another highball. There they sat at the table, and after she'd mellowed a little, he tried to reinstate her earlier delight. "Mama, you never did tell me much about the days after you were first married."

She thought for a moment, letting her mind play back. "Oh I don't know, all I can remember are parts of it now. It's been so long."

"Well there was that old photo of you in a breezy Twenties dress and dad in those sporty plus-fours standing beside the running board of his old Ford. And you both were glowing with such happiness."

"Oh I remember that all right. It was just a few months after his mother passed away and just before we left to drive to New York. We were to meet up with Disney there. He was about to move his operations back to California, and your dad was certain he would offer him a big sound job out there because that's when the talkies were really taking hold." The fact that she was letting go would have been a rarity at almost any time but especially now after the four years she had lived alone since his father died. Even her eyes began to brighten. "We were so excited, I can tell you, just thinking of going all the way to sunny California to live, with orange trees growing in our yard. And of course the movies!" With that she paused as if she had returned to the glory of the moment.

"Oh tell me more, mama," he finally urged.

"Well we left here and drove to Pennsylvania. We decided to stop in the Pocono Mountains for the honeymoon we hadn't had. It was Shawnee-on-Delaware where we stayed. Oh it was so fancy. Why they even had this dinner dance. And I had a ball gown. A beaded ball gown. *Oh my.* It was ivory silk with silvery pearl drops. And a shawl of Chantilly lace. Why it was the finest dress I ever had. It shimmered in the moonlight." And she stopped as if she were remembering every detail, as if she could reach out and touch it, caress it once more. "And your father, why he looked just like a matinee idol in his new tuxedo. We'd spent a fortune on those things in some ritzy resort shop in Stroudsburg. But what if we did? We were soon to be making fortunes in Hollywood. We were certain we could tell that just from looking at the nighttime skies. Oh lord they were so bright. I've never seen them like that. Not before or since. Your father said that the moon was our lucky silver horseshoe, and the stars were all the diamonds that were headed our way."

Once again, she stopped to bask in the wonder and

recapture it all the more. "Fred Waring's orchestra with the Pennsylvanians was playing there. And now I remember. They had one of those best-dancing-couple contests one night. And movie stars! Ramon Novarro and Mae Murray were there among the judges. Imagine that. Well nobody could do the Lindy and the black bottom like your father. So we won the contest." She clapped one of her delicate hands over her mouth as her face exploded with joy. "Afterwards Ramon Novarro came right over to our table. And he said to your father: Sir, you are sitting in the presence of the prettiest woman in this room. Then he asked me to dance. And even though I thought I was going to swoon at the time, I did. Of course, your father got to dance with Mae Murray. Oh did we think we were something that night. Imagine me dancing with Ramon Novarro?"

His mother's face was truly radiant now as if she were still dancing in Ramon Novarro's arms. Noah just sat there watching her, thrilled that she once had this moment. "Ah it must have been some night, mama. How come you never told me about it before?"

"Oh, I guess I'd forgotten about it. I guess it's the drinks that are making me remember so much. Too much. I shouldn't be having them and going on so."

"It means so much to me to hear about it."

"Oh well-- That was long, long ago."

"What happened, mama? What went wrong? Can you tell me?"

"I don't know, Noah. I don't know--that I want to."

"Did dad once ask you not to?"

"No. We never talked about it again. Never once." Tears came to her eyes, and Noah took her hand and stroked it.

"I'm sorry, mama. I should never have asked. It wasn't my business to."

"Oh yes, you have a right to know. Someday, I'll tell you. But I can't tonight."

THAT NIGHT AFTER his mother went to bed, Noah turned out all the downstairs lights, except those on the Christmas tree. Then he sat listening to the howl of westerly wind. It carried the drunken voice of his father from another Christmastide. One when Noah was very young.

--None of us Masons are ever going to amount to a hill of beans. We're all jinxed. The Mason curse. Just look at the family. The whole rotten barrel of us. Far back as you can trace. One failure after another. Look at my father. He wanted to be a concert pianist. Can you just imagine that? Best he ever got to play was the fiddle at a bunch of broken down carnivals. Lost one responsible job after the other, because of all that foolishness."

--Why was it foolish, dad, if that's what he wanted?"

--Because he wasn't good enough for that dream. Because in the end, he hanged himself. Hanged himself from a tree up Dutch Flats way in broad daylight."

Noah could feel the shock of that revelation and the chill from its implications to this day. Was the Mason business true? Was there some fateful flaw? As far back as he could remember, he wondered and feared.

"NOAH, ARE YOU SURE you should?" Nora whispered when he crept into her room later that night.

"Do you mind?" The howling winds swept the eerie shadows of pine tree limbs across the walls bringing back ghostly images of lonely often scary childhood nights. "I don't want to sleep in another room tonight. I need you now. She won't find out."

"Well I want you here. God save us, I thought we'd never be alone again."

"I know," he said as he quickly stripped and slipped naked into the squawky old three-quarter bed. He immediately pushed up her flannel nightdress and proceeded.

"No," she gasped. "I didn't mean to make love. I just wanted you alone. I know I'm terrible all the same. But all I could think of all day was not wanting to share you. I can't bear that. You've made me so selfish I'm ashamed."

She heard him giggle.

"It's not funny."

"I know. It just makes me feel so great that I have that effect on you. No that's wrong. It makes me feel so-- so *lascivious*." With that he began to slide her body under his.

"Stop! Are you mad?"

"Why? You're soaking wet."

"I know. But she'll hear us with the noise of this bloody yoke."

"Not over those wailing winds. Her hearing isn't that good anyway."

And with that the sounds of the bed intensified until she panicked that the whole of Forest Street would hear. But panic gave way to ecstasy, ecstasy so profound that when they reached orgasm she was certain the very foundations of the house were crumbling.

When they finally spoke, he whispered: "I've never felt so good in this house. You take away all that was ever bad in it." Then as he began to drift off to sleep, he finished faintly: "And you bring back all the wonderful dreams that were only possible in the movies."

"OH NOAH YOU WERE WAY MORE FORTUNATE being an only child and never having to have the feeling that you were forever being left somewhere down the lane."

"Well you don't have that anymore. You've me now." And he hugged her.

"Thanks be to god," she beamed as they strolled into Yearington town to do some last bits of Christmas shopping after they'd visited Noah's grandmother at the local nursing home. A hush had fallen over the village as a gentle fall of snow came with the dusk.

"But being an only child was no wonderment, you know. Money always seemed to get in the way."

"How did it come around to being so important? I'd say without the slightest doubt it's a desperate concern in this country."

"Well I couldn't say with any certainty. But up here I'd guess it had something to do with the Depression. Remember what Grandma Gibson just said—there isn't a living soul that doesn't have dreams but money can come along and be a fierce enemy. It can rob you blind, break your heart and swipe the very faith from you."

"Poor soul, you could only see how it was to leave a terrible strain on her for all these many years. But in Ireland being poor was to come natural as the rain. Course it was only a struggle from day to day to keep food making its appearance at the table. But we did make do with little fuss or bother. Just thanked god for the day that was in it."

BY THE TIME they'd finished their shopping, a strong north wind had blustered the gentle snowfall into a near blizzard. It was under the marquee of the now permanently closed Ritz, where Noah had seen *Portrait of Jennie* and so many other Forties love stories, that they paused to brush the snow from their hair and bundle up a little more.

Without the slightest hesitation, Noah took her into his arms and kissed her passionately on the lips and neck. "I love you, Nora," his breath rushed from him. "Here,

I have something for you." And he whipped out a small wrapped box from his ski jacket.

"Oh no," she gasped.

"Well, open it."

After she peeled off her gloves and stripped away the wrapping, she gasped again seeing the pale blue box with its thin blue ribbon. "It's from Tiffany's. Heavenly god." After she opened it she was stunned to silence.

"Don't you like it?"

"Why it's only gorgeous. Oh Noah, I love it. But so big. And from Tiffany's. You eejit." Tears were streaming down her cheeks as he removed the ring for its box and slipped it on her finger. Then he took a tissue from his pocket and gently dabbed the tears. "Will you for god's sake stop your crying. It'll all freeze to your lovely face."

"But it must have cost a fizzin' fortune," she managed as he burst out laughing. "I'd say you're far more than worth it, woman."

"MAMA, WE HAVE SOMETHING TO TELL YOU," Noah said after they'd changed from their wet clothes. "We're officially engaged." And Nora held up her ring hand.

"Oh my god, that's so wonderful," mama cried out as she first hugged Nora then her son. After that she stood back to look at the two. "How I've prayed every week at Mass for all these years that you'd find someone so wonderful, Noah. Oh and let me see that beautiful ring,

Nora."

"It's from Tiffany's, mama," Noah interjected.

"O-o-o-o, Tiffany's," she gasped, took hold of Nora's hand and gazed at the ring. "I'm so glad you got it there, Noah. I can't wait to tell all my friends. They'll be green with envy that I have a son who buys his fiancé gifts from Tiffany's. Oh Noah," she went on as she hugged him again. The color in her ordinarily pale face was approaching the level of her bright red woolen sweater. "This is the most wonderful moment of my life. It makes amends seeing the two of you so happy. Your father would be so proud of you."

"Would he?" Noah's eyes grew even brighter. She couldn't have said anything more wonderful. "Would he really, mama?"

"Oh yes. O-o-h yes."

Then he was truly beaming. He knew now it was the answer to one of his greatest longings.

OH WHAT PLEASURE IN THE PATHLESS WOODS, Noah thought, remembering the Byron as he took Nora for a walk in the forest behind his mother's house. The lovely silence was broken only by the lonely whistle of an Erie train from the hills above. He recalled how that used to send his blood racing as he spun daydreams that carried him along the rim of Great Lakes through the sunlit-morning towns of Ohio and Indiana to glistening, cavernous Chicago then on under the midnight star sweep of Great Plains to the frosty Rockies and the deep crimson sheen of twilight Pacific. He'd see it all. But in the manner of great success. He'd prove his father wrong—and reverse direction. As he saw the world, he would become the writer who would change the family fortune. And all would be his.

As Nora walked beside him with her hand in his, she could feel his writer's dreams pulsing through her. How perfect a landscape. It was truly an artist's paradise, she realized. Then she was recalling the snowscape visions of American painters, especially the haunting poetry of the Andrew Wyeth watercolors and temperas. For reason she could only think of as torture, her mind suddenly snapped, and she was seeing all the unattractiveness of the New York world they had left behind. The Capote ball and all that was false and consuming.

"It's good to have a place like this to come to," he said, interrupting her thoughts. "I used to come here to escape."

"Oh god, it's one of the loveliest, softest places I've ever seen."

He slipped his arm around her waist and kissed her forehead before they continued over the snowy trail that led along a wide creek with its exquisite tiers of silvery frozen waterfalls. The only footprints were theirs. She captured this vision as one of her mind's crown jewels while she savored the bliss of being with the man she loved, here where there were no people.

"I love being alone in the world with you," she

whispered as they stood beside one of the petrified waterfalls. And what she said stirred him. She saw the intensity come into his pale brown eyes and hoped she had won him over forever.

"We never did make love outdoors. And not in the snow," he whispered softly smiling.

"You must be mad."

"N-o-o-o." And he guided her hand to his raging erection.

A burst of warmth and excitement sped through her as he unbuttoned the lower half of her coat and drew down her jeans and panties. Heavenly god, how much I need him this way. Crave him. Her mind raced with the realization as he lifted and leaned her against the snow-dusted trunk of one of the last surviving ancient oak trees and let his penis push between her legs. It was hot, as feverish as it would have been in bed. To her amazement, she was wet and wildly fervent. Quickly he drove into her and her whole body was aflame. Her vision clouded and was lost in the softly falling flurries. His movements were so rapid, so deft that immediately she felt her whole body convulse with orgasms as they both cried out releasing the steamy vapor of their breaths. Finally she collapsed in his arms. Then they were quiet and toasty warm for a long time, both drawing in the beauty of one another.

As they watched the pink light of late afternoon slip through the trees and fall in broad shafts across the white forest floor, Noah continued to hold her and follow her spirit as softly he spoke her words. "I love being alone in the world with you, too."

10

"WE'RE GOING TO WEAR OUT this bloody bed if you keep going away and coming home like this, you horny devil," Nora said when he'd returned from one of his many out-of-town assignments during the weeks after the holidays. Assignments he welcomed since it kept emphasis off the New York social scene and left more time for him to figure a way to ease Nora into that world.

"You want me to stop, do you?

"Are you daft? That would be the last thing I'd ever want."

"Well at least it's a bit easier for us now. I hope you don't have any regrets."

"No. Absolutely not. Once I realized just how much we love one another, I came to me own terms instead of my family's and my country's. And if that weren't enough by far, there's the whole lot of side benefits. The money we'll save from the cost of those daft rooms and being here all the time I'll be able to help you work that much harder."

"Oh you mean to greater perfect our performance?" He grinned as she felt his penis rising.

"N-o-o-o, you bloody eejit. I mean to perfect your writing," she replied shoving him out of the bed so he landed starkers on the icy floor.

"I'll get you for that, I will." And he leapt up and bounded onto the bed with his rearing penis flapping in the cold air as he reached for the condom box. "Oh fizz, it's empty. And there's no more."

"For the love of god, don't tell me you've gone through all those yokes. You're just after buying a whole lorry load of them. Just think of all the babies we could have had."

"Would you think it's safe enough yet?"

He saw the dreamy drift of her eyes. "Ah I'd love to feel you naked in me all the same. Especially after you've been away. From *me* loneliness, I only want to devour ya."

"So it's not. But god you're tempting me. Oh well— hello Genovese's," he sighed as he got up and fought his cock into his briefs.

"Do you think it will always scare you? To have children. I mean in the future."

"No, of course not," he said trying to hide his fear.

BUT HE DID TAKE TO HEART what she had said about the work. Every free moment over the next weeks, except for a few whirlwind trips to cover some of the trendy European ski resorts, Noah pursued his writing. More often than not, he would ride it out past midnight.

It had been during one stopover on that trip that he'd met a top literary agent skiing at St. Moritz. And just like that he expressed interest in reading his novel. So encouraged was Noah that he began interweaving time between finishing his short stories and revising the novel. But this was so overly time consuming, he could feel the drift of Nora's loneliness.

It helped relieve some of his guilt when Aer Lingus became so pleased with Nora's work that they promoted her with a thirty dollar a week raise and insisted on having her attend all their major strategy conferences. This helped to occupy some of her lonely moments as she worked to develop a series of new promotional tactics.

To busy her even more, he urged her to purchase some rudimentary art supplies hoping to restart her painting career. With that she set up a small working area by an alley window in the corner of his living room. There she neatly spread a canvas drop and established an easel. Next to it were two small folding tables she had salvaged from a Salvation Army shop in Queens. On them she placed her well-seasoned wooden palate—the one item she'd carefully wrapped and brought from Ireland—along with tubes of oils, jars of brushes and charcoal pencils, palate knives, tortillons.

Noah loved the smell of the paints mixed with the pungency of linseed oil and turpentine. He swore the commingled scents helped him write better, and he knew without question they fired his body. This led to more than one spontaneous orgasmic brushing session on the floor as they drove each other's naked bodies crazy with pointy round sables, blue squirrel quills, cat tongues, badger hair fans and mongoose filberts.

Unbeknownst to Noah as he worked at his typewriter, Nora had started one of her few portraits, his portrait. It was the perfect opportunity to catch all the tenderness and sensitivity, the nuances that radiated so beautifully as they went into his writing. His eyes were the color of barely steeped first flush Darjeeling against a snow white cup. Always in the past when she'd painted brown eyes she had used a mixture of the sienna, burnt umber and ochre hues. But they alone couldn't accomplish the task here. She found she had to dash in a minute touch of titanium white to portray the liquidity of their dreamy paleness and the translucent longing that seemed to beckon from the soul. What amazed her most was that even in the depths of his work when she could read his most cognizant thoughts, he never completely lost touch with the underlying innocence of his being. As certain as the milky reddened complexion of his youth, the fountainhead of purity remained constant and once the writing ended, rose in his eyes to exude once more. If she could but capture this—this rising, this mixture of wisdom and innocence, this would turn what was certain to be a good portrait into something far more. It would extend her reach way beyond anything she could have ever imagined.

She couldn't help but wonder what he would think of it. But by no means did she want him to see it before it was finished. So whenever she sensed he was coming out of one of his sessions, she would quickly cover it over with a seascape of a storm off Cape Clear that she was developing from memory. She had rigged her easel with a small block to prevent smearing his precious portrait.

It was during this time as well that her paintings arrived at the Port of New York U.S. Customs. Fortunately she had signed the canvases, since the custom officers refused to release them at first. "How could we know you're not importing stolen rare artwork from Ireland?" She had to produce three forms of identification. Bothersome as it was, requiring a second trip to the docks with seemingly hours of wait, Nora was quite thrilled that the officers would consider them rare pieces of art.

"See I told you," Noah said and immediately called Carole Dawson.

"There here?" she thrilled. "Oh I must see them right away. I just have this feeling."

Yet as they prepared a sampling to take to her the next day, Nora insisted she couldn't be abandoning her job to go along. But the truth was she was only that embarrassed.

TWO DAYS LATER after he'd seen an ecstatic Carole, a rather dour-looking man probably in his later fifties greeted them at the door of Winsor de Caine on East Fifty-Seventh Street. It was one if the city's more prestigious upper eastside galleries. "I hear from Carole your work is quite remarkable. She has such a keen eye, so I'm most anxious to see them," he went on with at least spirit in his eyes as he ushered them struggling with piles of rolled up canvases through the gallery proper and to the offices at the back.

After they plopped them down on what appeared to be an endlessly long antique oak library table, Julian took each of several at random, unrolled and anchored them with heavy brass blocks. In time, he finally said: "Hmmm. Interesting." As he did his eyes grew even brighter. After he'd finished with those, he went on to unroll a dozen or more. This time without anchoring them. Then he went back to look at the anchored ones again. "They have been a little mistreated rolled up so tightly. But— Well Miss Clifford--"

Why isn't he after saying they look like piss and just f-off, she wondered.

"Well—These are quite good. Very good as a matter of fact. These particular ones seem to just rush right out at one—of their own accord." He chuckled to himself as he thought some more and continued staring at them, then went on to look at a dozen or so more. "Yes. Somehow they go beyond the limits of color, even the laws of perspective."

What in god's name he was palavering on about she hadn't a clue. But still she loved it all the same and even more so when he continued. "Above all-- Yes. It's the wide emotional range they evoke, even in the landscapes, that really make them true accomplishments."

Nora sighed with such a great gush that it was as if she had been holding her breath since she'd arrived. There hadn't been a screed of doubt that he would all but throw her out.

"I want to show them. But this is a problem."

"Oh," Nora said. Sure, here it comes. The *th*rickster-- Most likely he had just been polite to appease that one—Carole Dawson.

"I'm so impressed. Just as Carole said I'd be. But I'm too impressed. And I'm sure I'll be even more so by the time I go through all of these. I think most likely your work is deserving of a show."

"Ah you must be havin' me on," Nora gasped as Noah secretly kicked her in the foot. "A whole show? I can scarcely believe it."

"Well yes. You seem to have so much superb material right here, But we would certainly want you to continue to be prolific. I assume you're still working on more."

"Oh indeed I am," she insisted.

"Well that's very exciting to hear. Unfortunately that still leaves us with scheduling problems right through the season and into next fall. Unless something comes up, it could be October but I would think no later than that."

"That sounds grand to me." Suddenly and for the first time she felt this lovely surge of delight over her work, that it might actually possess something of value.

"I'm really sorry it can't be sooner, I'm that thrilled about it. But I'm just thinking, what we could do for now is take a few of them, and we'll properly stretch them and mount them for display here. But of course they won't be nearly as effective as when we have a full showing."

"Now how do you feel about that?" Noah said afterwards, imagining how sensational he'd feel if some big publisher were saying to him—we love your novel, but the next season is fully fleshed out, and we'll have to wait till fall. He didn't have to wait for her reply, she was only beaming.

SPURRED ON by the mesmerizing thrill that was symptomatic of the initial stages of Nora's success, determined it be repeated forthwith as a result of his own work, Noah put the finishing touches on his *New Yorker* short stories in late February. With a silent prayer they would prove him worthy of his confidence, he slung them into the darkness of the mail cute and crossed himself.

"They're very good to be sure. I'd be certain you stand only the grandest of chances with them," Nora reassured afterwards as she hugged him in the street. And rightly so, she told herself. She treasured the one of upstate New York where money worries always stood in the way of relationships. But the one about New York society was so scathing that she could scarcely believe he'd written it. Then she realized that by fictionalizing the names and events he'd been able to fire away with no restraints, telling everything exactly as it was. That made her happy. But even so she wondered if he saw it as a scathing portrait of a crowd of *lousers* or if in his heart somehow he still didn't find these people and their lives attractive. Regardless she questioned whether she really wanted to find out.

11

DISCO VERSIONS of *What Now My Love* and *Monday, Monday,* piped from a turntable, enlivened the background of Bonwit Teller on the late-February night that occasioned the preview of Carole Dawson's Place, one of New York's first fad-spawning boutiques to open within a specialty store. That along with the Dawson social esteem and Carole's philanthropic association with cancer research turned it into a winter piece de resistance for the beautiful people. Among the early-arrival luminaries were the CV Whitneys, Happy Rockefeller, Cynthia Phipps, CZ Guest, Cecil Beaton, the Joseph Lauders, Gloria Guinness, Lee and Prince Stanislaw Redziwill.

"I guess events like these are putting such bloated pomposities as the Capote ball in their rightful place perspective-wise," the always charismatic Tim Anderson, whose agency handled the Bonwit account, delighted to Noah and Nora most likely because he hadn't been invited to that ball and was seeing that proper justice was being inflicted on that sort.

"Well yes," Noah agreed. "Cancer research is one of the redeeming factors today, especially after all the recent press thrashings targeting those self-indulgent events."

"That sort of heedless behavior is begging for condemnation when you consider race riots, anti-war teach-ins, homelessness. Image-wise it's paramount now to show heart and wisdom. Noblesse oblige and all that."

"Yes and everybody's jumping on the bandwagon. But I wouldn't think *heart* has anything to do with it. And certainly not when it comes to Carole," interrupted Karen Sutton, a young shipping dynasty blueblood who seemed instantly magnetized to Noah and certainly bent on capturing his attention.

"Oh Karen, I don't feel you're right about that," Noah insisted.

"Why not? I think she's just blaring her own trumpet."

"How could you when she's going to put every cent she gets from this boutique into the American Association of Cancer Research?"

"So she may say. And so you may write. But she'll feed on all this attention she'll amass from her patrician friends and the general public alike. All under the banner of righteousness, of course." With that she cast her tight snooty snoot Nora's way and forced a smile. "Speaking of which I guess *general* is suddenly *in* these days." Then she deigned to ask: "What do you think, my dear?"

Though she had been to very few of these occasions since the Capote ball due to Noah's cautionary care, Nora decided without hesitation to put a riff in such conversations and replied with haughty stiff-upper-lip splendor: "My dear, I wouldn't have thought you knew what righteousness was. But then I wouldn't have thought you thought."

Tim turned to muffle his laughter, while Noah, surprised at Nora's turn, immediately attempted to clear the air. "Yes, I guess everything is changing today. But I do think Carole's a forerunner."

"Well that would be only brilliant if it were to be so," Nora continued. "Especially after all the eejity egotism I've seen in my days in this city." Then looking directly at Karen, she merrily added: "I wouldn't have believed most of these people courted anything but money and a mirror."

"*Veritas simplex oratio est*," Tim, who had only just met Nora, quipped while Noah's shock grew.

"Noah, she's perfectly charming. Wherever did you find her?" Karen managed through clenched teeth and a grin. "Quaintness like hers is so rare these days."

"Well I can only be gathering you've foolhardily mistaken the word for integrity."

And just like that, Karen lavishing Noah and Tim with BP kisses disappeared.

"Nora, I love you," Tim pronounced. "I couldn't have written that put down better if I'd tried."

"Well you didn't have to go quite so gladiatorial, Nora," Noah said before he had to break into laughter. Just looking at her halted any further protest. She was so delectably beautiful in that whispery silk orchid dress he'd bought her. Tantalizing really when he considered the slight swirl of the skirt that ended just above the knees and the snug fit of the top that suggested the luscious swell of her breasts.

As heady as this made him, he regretted that Tim who was his best friend had no such woman in his life. While there had been many, none had seriously attracted him since the loss of his first love way back in college days. By now he had been promoted to the top of one of the city's youngest ground-breaking ad agencies and was pulling in millions in billings a year. As such his name had recently been included in the title—Cooper, Marshall, Anderson. And on the side he'd written a full-length family drama that David Merrick had read and was chomping at the bit to see his revisal.

Looking at him at this party, there was no doubt he was among the handsomest, most eligible and certainly the trendiest. He'd let his golden red hair grow longer which was right in style with the times, and his clothes which stage-whispered money consisted of a custom-made tweed riding jacket, imported cavalry twill slacks and bespoke boots from Britain.

"It's a pretty sorry thing you're here with no one," Noah said.

"Oh don't feel sorry pal. I'm just between involvements."

"Yeah between flibbertigibbets with great asses." Noah insisted while Nora grimaced at such vulgarity. To take away her annoyance, he slipped his arm tightly around her waist and briefly caught her with the longing in his eyes. "Seriously though Tim, when are you going to bring someone of value into your life?"

"Oh we can't all be as lucky as you guys." And he smiled happily at them. " Noah told me what bliss it was for the two of you, Nora. And now I see the truth of his words. There's a Latin phrase for it you know—*sine qua non*. Being indispensable that is."

"Watch it pal, don't be romancing her. Once he starts in on the Latin, Nora--" And Noah grinned at the tease as he once again squeezed her waist.

"Ah never. I'd never infringe on that. I guess that's because I know too much of its importance. But you know something, and you'd probably appreciate this Nora since Noah told me you're quite an artist. There are these paintings I've seen at the Metropolitan by this French painter from the 1800s. Cot is his surname. They're of two young lovers. They always capture me and riddle me with envy. *Le Printemps* and *Le Tempete*. In a previous life, I think the two of you must have posed for them."

"Ah there you go with the French yet. Now listen to me buddy," Noah insisted with a few hard pats on the shoulder. "You go off and really find somebody and rid yourself of all that envy."

AFTER THEY'D LEFT Tim near the entry area, they began to make their way through swelling crowds of BP and media chiefs toward the spotlighted focal point of the evening Carole Dawson's Place, while Nora in a hushed rather fractious tone asked: "How does he know so much about us?"

"Oh he's my best friend. I had to wait all this time for you to meet him. We've both been so busy we rarely get to see one another."

"Well considering that, you certainly said enough to one another," she snipped back. That caused his mind to flash back over the Christmas Yearnington scene and her once spoken words—*I love being alone in the world with you.* Before he could consider it further, Murphs spied them and rushed to their side. She had just completed her notes as she finished chatting with Carole. "Oh you must be Nora," she cheered stuffing her note pad into the suede handbag that matched her blazing hair. Before Noah had a chance, she clutched Nora's hand and introduced herself. "I'm so happy to finally meet you. You should hear the way this guy of yours goes on about you at the office."

Nora blanched but then turned red with the embarrassment. What had he said, she wondered. But before she could even contemplate, Carole was at their side with the answer. "He has reason to. Not only is she a perfect delight, she's an enormously talented artist."

"Well I have to thank you for all you did. I was never after expecting anything of the sort with my paintings."

"It's very difficult for even the most talented, which you are, to get started here. But I was determined." As they both hugged one another, Nora thought there was something so sincere, so genuine in this revolting world chock-a-block with the highfalutin lot that she felt a growing fondness for her. And even more so as she continued with her face radiating delight: "You know there's really no way of expressing how happy I am that it's going so well for the two of you. You exude real happiness, and I don't think that's indigenous to this local."

When another crowd of well-wishers rushed over to Carole, Noah dashed after his photographer leaving Nora with Murphs. "How are you adjusting to events like this, Nora," she asked.

"Well I don't know if I'd actually dare to be saying without risking Noah all but skelpin' me." And she shook her head and laughed causing Murphs to follow suit.

"I wasn't trying to put you on the spot, I want you to know. It's just that I have such a hard time with all this sort of thing myself."

"You do? I was beginning to think I was the only one in New York who did."

"Oh no. With you I'd guess it's the slickness and phoniness."

"Would those be your reasons as well?"

She laughed. "Oh I think it's even more fundamental. It's something inherent in me. I was an adopted child, you see. It was during the Depression and my real mother felt she couldn't take proper care of me. So I ended up with this woman who thought she wasn't able to have any children. But then after a couple of years she did, and she really didn't need me anymore. I remember she used to dress her own in such beautiful clothes, while as the years passed I became Cinderella. So I grew up to abhor rich people. Or those of the supercilious sort, which heaven knows most of them are."

"Well why would you be here then? Living such a life?"

"Aspiration," she answered immediately. Then she nodded and smiled ruefully as she let her hand lightly brush her gorgeous green silk blouse and buttery suede calf-length brown skirt. "You see I didn't grow to abhor beautiful clothes. And all the beautiful things she made me so long to have. That for good or for bad registers indelibly."

WHEN NOAH RETURNED with the photographer, he arranged various shots of Carole, who wore one of her own much touted designs, a splashy patterned midi dress. It was at one point that breaking from chatting with the notables she whispered to Noah: "I must talk to you about something." Then as the crowds began to shift, she pulled him around the corner to the backside of the boutique. From her former cheery self, she went quite ashen. "I know you suspected before. But now there's real trouble afloat. I want to make sure you have this story before Suzy at the *News* or someone else prints it first."

"Is it John? I was quite surprised he isn't here."

Carole nodded in the affirmative. "There have been

other women from time to time. Always clandestine, of course. He couldn't allow his blue-blooded ilk think there were any impurities. Foolishly, I always turned a blind eye. And as such we continued on our merry way. But I simply can't handle it anymore. It's just too sickeningly degrading."

"Carole, take it easy," Noah said.

"Oh I suppose it was inevitable after what happened to us. But now it's all so ugly. Bank accounts. Stocks. Estates. We're even haggling over our jet. But who cares? It's all for spite. No matter what happens in the divorce proceedings, I'll still have fortunes. And so will he. Fortunes and that's all."

"You know, you shouldn't do this," Noah insisted, surreptitiously glancing around. "Don't give anyone the opportunity of seeing you down. Especially tonight. Carry on as if you're blissfully happy."

"Oh I just had to let go for a moment. And I wanted you to be the first to know." Then she looked at him and smiled as if she were surprised and delighted over his wisdom. "Of course you're right. And thank you for that, Noah. You know I've come to realize there are very few things that matter in this world of mine anymore. Along with the fulfillment of helping my charities, there are my truly close friends like you and Nora. Though the number is slight. I supposed you're surprised at that. But there are very few of my close acquaintances who are faithful. You can tell them very quickly--the truth and love shines from them." And she smiled fondly and hugged him. Noah was so moved he had to curb his tears as he wondered how any man could be so cruel as to hurt a woman so lovely.

As they headed back to the boutique she checked her watch and gasped. "I can't believe all these people are still here it's so late. I've got to get out of here. I'm scheduled to usher some top Federated directors to a late supper at 21. They don't know it yet but they too will open Dawson boutiques in their stores and make us lots more money."

Worried that she might need a greater return of spirit before her departure, Noah engaged her in a bit of wit. "But Carole, you do know there's rumor that the Duke and Duchess of Windsor are going to drop by?"

"Oh I'm not going to worry about those freeloaders. As long as there's plenty of vintage Dom Perignon and Petrossian caviar, they'll be blissfully happy. Why they won't even know I'm missing. And certainly they won't want to have anything to do with charitable donations." With that she shook with laughter, hugged him and then sincerely thanked him as she whisked herself out a side door leaving the Bonwit bigwigs in charge as Noah began to search about for Nora.

IT WAS SHE who caught sight of him first as she sipped a fresh glass of champagne. He was in the distance struggling through an enveloping, ingratiating crowd. They're only cajolin' him with their fizzin' waggin' tongues, she thought. But was it a struggle he was willing to lose, putting on airs the way he was. Her sick feeling was far worse than it had been at the Capote ball. She couldn't help but think of the beauty of his innocence that she'd been capturing in her portrait. And now this shower of shytes was all but robbin' it.

Meanwhile, coming over and addressing her with a distinct British accent was this woman with extremely pale makeup and a Vidal Sassoon geometric haircut. Probably in her mid-thirties, she wore a jet mini dress that while it matched her hair made her look decidedly porky. Instantly her aura of ostentatiousness left Nora edgy.

"Smashing party, isn't it my dear."

"Yes. It's pleasant right enough." Now she remembered the woman from pictures she had seen in *FCD*. She was Liz Warton, the British designer who had swept the fashion world some seasons back with her forerunners of the mini-skirt and the slip-dress.

"Oh god," gasped Liz, upon noticing the man Nora was watching. "He is s-o-o-o gorgeous in that youthful American way. If only I were down by a couple dress sizes—and a year or two. Blimey, I'd have a go at him right here on the spot."

"He happens to be my fiancé," Nora snapped.

"O-h-h-h sorr-ee," Liz softened immediately after she had a good look at Nora. "As envious as I might be, you know I could see how you two could make a beautiful couple. And I do wish you the very best. Better than I ever had."

"Oh I think things are grand all the same," Nora insisted abruptly.

"Perhaps for now. But you seem so lovely and innocent, I'd be very remiss if I didn't warn you. Watch out, as the Dylan lyrics go: *The times they are a changing.*"

"Whatever is that supposed to mean?"

"Come, come luv," she insisted with all sincerity. "I speak from the heart, and I don't do that for everyone. This is the Sixties. Nothing is permanent anymore. And certainly not when it comes to relationships."

"Well, it is with us," Nora professed more to herself than to Liz Warton.

"All I can tell you is wait till you've been around this jollified milieu for a while. Take me as an example. Why I whizzed through three men in four years and had to have three abortions as a consequence."

"Three abortions?" Nora was shocked, then sickened.

"Oh I used to feel that way too. Morbidly depressed. Filled with the greatest regret. Extending to all the rigors of remorse." Then she added quite casually: "At least for the first two."

"Three abortions!?" Nora repeated as if to convince herself.

"Well yes. Those blokes, one after the other, vowed undying love, and I believed them. So off we went—Bob's your uncle. That is until I became preggers and it was obvious all they were up to was *ride the wild mare,*" she sighed dolefully then recalled with resignation: "So when I saw what just about every other girl I knew was doing, I took a tumble. You see, it's quite simple. One could even say sensible, if you're allergic to the pill."

"Don't you have any principles?" Nora's voice and temper were rising in unison as she bypassed Liz's attempts for sympathy and prepared to bullyrag her.

"Yes. I finally forced myself to extinguish all scruples in favor of pleasure. Once done, I found pleasure is the greatest consummation. It absorbs everything else. In the end, it's the only thing that matters as it were."

"Even if you're after having to kill for it?"

"Oh dear, you're Irish aren't you. Please forgive me. I didn't mean to be rude," Liz continued expressing regret. "I'm forgetting your people haven't kept pace with the rest of the world."

"Well thank god they haven't," Nora roared. Unlike at the Capote ball, this time she lost all control and exploded into a shouting rage. "I've never heard the likes of such despicable behavior. How could you have had three abortions? How could you have had even one?" Suddenly she was so loud that shocked gatherings in all the nearby areas were rendered silent.

Even through her pallid makeup, it was obvious that Liz Warton's face had turned beet red in light of the astonished stares from everyone. "I was only trying to do right by you, luv," she managed as she fled into the crowd.

Nora remained still shaking with the fury. By the time Noah, who couldn't help but be aware of what could only be called a major altercation, reached her side, conversations had started effervescing again though in a quieter tone. As he put his arm around her and they began edging away, he whispered: "What is the problem?"

"This whole bloody scene."

"Did you have to encourage a full blown bleedin' donnybrook? And with Liz Warton, no less?"

"If you'd heard the things she said. She's the pits. A right bloody wh*oo*re, if there ever was one."

"But couldn't you have held your tongue at least for a couple of hours?" he persisted, hopelessly trying to stop her as he felt himself deflate in stature and glanced around to see who might still be watching them.

"Sure I'm supposed to stand here and listen to all this blasphemy and act happy as Larry. Well this time I'm not going to. If you stay, I'll understand. I'll just be seeing you later. That would be the truth of it, right enough." And while he stood in shock, she headed for the coat check.

"Ah don't go," Noah said, catching up. "Don't give them the pleasure. Besides if you stay, I'll be able to leave that much sooner. It's already ten o'clock."

"You're scared shyteless of being embarrassed aren't you Noah?" And once again her voice rose panicking him.

"What do you mean?" he whispered.

"If I leave, what will all these precious people be

thinking? What will they say?"

"Don't be ridiculous, Nora. Please stay."

"No. I've demeaned myself enough tonight, thank you," she insisted pulling on her coat. Then as she left, she shook her head insisting: "The absolute vulgarity of it all."

AS NOAH WAS SWALLOWED by another cluster of beautiful people, he realized what she had said was true. He was embarrassed by her. So much so that he had difficulty conversing. Regardless, he struggled through another half-hour for the sake of his column. Then convinced he had enough material, he dismissed his photographer and began to disentangle himself. Just as he retrieved his overcoat and was about to slip away, a voice called out.

"What do you say we blow this place together and go for a quiet little drink?" It was Gloria Hamilton Collins, the blonde airline heiress who often surfaced at these BP parties. Tonight she wore a chocolate crepe number, which Noah thought was probably from Balenciaga's latest collection, along with a fragrant trace of Channel. The dress did wonders for her leggy legs, and the scent was guaranteed to turn any man's head. Noah remembered her from the night she propositioned him at Carole's Newport mansion. She was still married to Bruce Collins the famed race car driver, but her interest always seemed to be in other men.

"Where do you suggest we do that drink?" Noah

teased. "In a quiet little Park Avenue penthouse?"

"You've got the idea. Come on. Let's be happy."

"I'm already happy, Gloria."

"It didn't look so a few minutes ago."

"That depends on how you define your terms." And he smiled.

"Well, I'm not into semantics," she said, caressing his face then drawing her hand lightly down over his chest, causing him to jump from the sensation and glance around to see if anyone had noticed. "But I know one thing. I can make you happy. Very happy."

"Just out of curiosity, why don't you do that for your husband?" he replied, removing her hand.

"He's already off racing, of course. And besides, this is far more intriguing. You must know, you're the hot new number now days."

"Oh you mean the catch of the day?

"So to speak."

"Well Gloria, I'm afraid your line just broke." And he started to head off.

"Don't worry. I'll catch you yet—Moby Dick."

"LOOK I JUST DON'T want to talk about it," Nora insisted as she turned her back to him. She had already gone to bed by the time Noah arrived home that night. The fact that she was wearing a nightdress, something she'd rarely done since they became lovers, sent a pretty clear message of her anger. Regardless he sat beside her stroking her cheek and whispering: "I'm sorry."

"If you're wise, you'll say no more," she said, pushing his hand away. "Just go to bed." And she crawled over to the very far side of the mattress.

"But surely Nora, you can't blame me for Liz Warton's behavior," he went on as he rose and took off his tie and shirt. "You just had the misfortune to meet up with her."

"The way she was looking at you." Unable to contain herself, she jumped up and went over to him. "She only came right out and told me she wanted to rape you. If you haven't gone and let her already."

"Come on, don't you become vulgar now. It doesn't become you."

"It certainly doesn't suit you either. I can see the way you attract these women."

"Are you joking me? You think I'm attracted to Liz Warton? Why she's downright ugly. And I didn't even know she was there. Not until you announced it to me. Correction. Make that, announced it to the whole bloody building. Why didn't you just bring along a bugle and sound it? It would have been far less taxing on your vocal cords."

Enraged, she stormed into the bathroom and slammed the door. He stormed right in after her and spun her around. "I will not have you making these accusations when there's not an ounce of truth to them."

"Well if not now, it won't be long." She snatched a

bottle of aspirin from the cabinet, opened it, popped a couple and washed them down with a swallow of tap water.

"You have no right to blame me," he defended.

She caught his image in the mirror and saw the blow she had delivered to the unconditional return of his virtuosity. "Well maybe I don't. But what I can call a true misfortune here is you in the midst of that whole menagerie courting those people and worshipping the very air they breathe." Virtuousness aside, the thought made her even angrier, so she pushed him away and left the bathroom. He followed right after her.

"Don't tell me we're going through that again."

"Well, you're the one who's after asking for it, you are. I'll tell you now Noah, I'm raging with you. If I hadn't given up that bed-sitter, I wouldn't be here now."

"Oh Nora. Now stop. Just stop," he said on the verge of tears as he followed her back into the bedroom.

"No, you stop and bloody well start taking stock of yourself."

"I don't know what in god's name I've done, but it is my work. And it's making us money. Good money."

"I know that. But when I go to an event like tonight's I start feeling I'm with a perfect stranger. And one I absolutely abhor. And I'll tell you now, it's making me go sick." With that she busied herself tidying the bed again.

"Come on. You're being overly dramatic."

"I'm being overly dramatic?" she said looking him

directly in the eyes. "Look who's after turning into the ugly American."

"That's not so. You want me to stand back and be a wallflower at these things. But I wouldn't get a dime's worth of story material out of them if I did."

"Surely you must be able to figure a better way than surrendering yourself to their values and behavior."

"I'm not surrendering anything. I'm taking advantage to get my stories. It's a bit like a sports arena out there."

"Well you're certainly playing the game," she insisted as she pitched herself back into the bed and pulled up the covers.

"You bet I am. But what you fail to see is that once the party's over the game ends. If only you could have some fun with it, instead of being so serious. Not everyone is as vulgar as you make them out to be."

"Sure that would be hard proven to me. Why even your so-called friend is quite the article with all his palavering."

"Tim? Oh god, you don't know him."

"I've eyes in me head."

"That's a front. He's one of the nicest people I know."

"That being the case, I'm sure you fashion grand company for one another. You're probably just as much a womanizer as he is."

"When have I given you cause to distrust me?"

"All the time, since I can't figure out who you are. You know I keep thinking back to that Capote party. Which one was you? The one with or without the mask?"

"Oh stop being bromidic. I'll show you who I am. I'll show you yet again that I'm the man who loves you." And he sat beside her and tried taking her in his arms.

"Not tonight," she insisted, pushing him away. "I just can't after all that. I feel so nauseous."

"You really do." And he stopped and felt the pain of it. "This is going to be the first time we've been together in this bed and haven't made love."

"I'll make it that much simpler. I'll go sleep on the couch." And quickly she started to get out of the bed.

"Don't. Please, please don't," he said as he gently took hold of her shoulders to stop her and looked into her eyes. "I'm sorry if I hurt you. The only way I can make it up is through love."

"The only way you can make it up is to be true to yourself," she countered, overpowering his glance. "I suppose the best thing would be just not to go along with you to these things. Then I wouldn't see any of this."

"I'd hate it. But---is that what you really want?"

She thought for a moment and then sighed. "No-- It's not. Because-- Because I'm afraid--" She both surprised and frightened herself as the words came. Words she did not want to hear herself say. "I'm afraid someday you'll drift off into that world, and I'll lose you forever."

"WELL, I SEE YOU WERE the life of the party," Jack Warren huffed the next day as he flipped a page of the *Daily News* gossip section on Noah's desk. Pencil-boxed by Jack was a paragraph that read: *"One of the more spectacular and unexpected moments of the evening was contributed by a friend? consort? of Fashion Connoisseur Daily's society supreme Noah Mason. As such, fiery Dubliner, Nora Clifford of Aer Lingus was more than overheard in face-to-face combat vehemently denouncing British fashion wiz Liz Warton over her wildly flamboyant lifestyle. Unusually colorful for such a soiree. Make that off-colorful."*

"That's trumped up. That's nonsense," Noah insisted as he blanched.

"Not from what I've been hearing," Jack persisted. "She may be beautiful-- But she's got quite a mouth-- As the word of mouth goes."

"Jack," Noah roused and stood up from his desk just barely thwarting himself from grabbing hold of his baldy head and slamming it against the wall. "Don't!" he snapped as he shook his finger at him. "You can say anything else to me. But not that."

"Well I will say this much," Jack fired right back. "Whether you know it or not, you were lucky this time. Oliver Wilton detests Liz Warton and probably was thrilled by this item. But... And it's a very big but. In the future, be careful who she's bad mouthing. This sort of thing can backfire on you and set off a megaton."

"IT'S ONE OF THE MOST DISGUSTING things that's ever happened to me," she told Noah that night after the item appeared. "I only died dozens of times today thinking someone in my office might be after seeing it. Thanks be to god, they don't read the gossips. I must say, it's some profession."

"Does that include me as well?" he snapped.

"Whatever you make of it yourself." She gave it right back.

"You know I don't write crap like that. I never have, and I never will."

"Oh Noah," she sighed. "I'm never going to take to the likes of this city. Sometimes I think I'd best be packin' me bags and going back home."

He blanched and then held her tightly insisting: "Not without me. There's no way I'd ever let that happen, Nora. It would ruin both our lives. This is all going to work out the way we want it."

12

IT WAS A STRONG BLOW to the gut. One that not only rendered him breathless but for numerous seconds unable to regain the breathing process. Late Saturday morning, the end of February. Awakening, making love. Then Noah pulled on his robe and went into the hall to collect the mail before starting breakfast. He opened the box, and there it was. He had forgotten. Perhaps in defense, perhaps out of fear. *The New Yorker.* There was the letter. Much sooner than he had expected. God, it was truth time again. It was going to be a rejection. It had to be. He knew he'd been disillusioning himself. Just as he had before. He couldn't bear this. The icy drafts of the hall swept round him chilling him to the bone as he opened the envelope.

"Oh my god. My god, my god." He threw open the apartment door and roared: "Nora! Nora, look at this!"

Frightened. Not knowing what to expect, she rushed to the door, pulling her robe on while knocking over water and turpentine-filled tins of paintbrushes as she went. Noah handed her the letter. "They bought them?" she gasped with delight.

"They bought one anyway," Noah answered in shock, still trying to make himself believe. "One thousand dollars for *Children of Fortune.* Amazing since they can take a year to accept one now days."

"That's terrific," she cheered throwing her arms around him. "I knew this would happen."

Noah was so excited he couldn't eat breakfast. Again and again, he stared at the check in disbelief. Finally he laughed, and once he had, he couldn't stop. He was a real writer after all. Someone or ones of importance thought so...and more important had drawn up a check to prove it. No Mason curse after all.

"It's real," he said, holding out the check to gaze at it. "That makes me real. For the first time. You gave me this chance, you know."

"I just gave you a boot up the backside. See what that can do for you?"

"Indeed. Now I believe it can happen. All of it's going to come. I can reach right out and-- I'll finish my novel again. I will for certain. And just wait till they see it."

"Thanks be to god," she cheered. "That's the best news I've heard since I arrived. I'm only high as the flippin' stars. I'm so proud of you. Ah they'll all be wanting more of your work now," she continued enthusing. "They've just discovered a great new writer."

He grinned and let himself drift with her thought. Even more, he let himself drift among the heavens for the next few days. But unfortunately a larger envelope arrived back from *The New Yorker*. This one containing the upstate story and a rejection slip. "Well, I'm not going to get upset," he told her. "The time may not be right for the upstate piece. Or it just may not be right for them. Or-- maybe I'm not quite ready for that yet."

"You are. I know that with all my heart. And I know I'll be proven right once you go through that novel again."

"Maybe so. But no matter what we're on our way now."

"HOW CAN YOU HELP but jump for joy," Noah thrilled, literally lifting her and leaping into the air. It was early March and Nora had just received word from Winsor de Caine that they had sold one of her landscapes for nine hundred dollars.

"It's only the first one," she answered modestly. "I suppose I'm just being practical."

"Let yourself go. It's going to be great. And it's just the beginning." They were both talented artists; and as such, the world would be theirs. And waves of thrills overtook him. He had to do something now, something that would equate them with the world they so deserved as true artists. The desire had been with him for such a long time. Now he would act.

"WHY ARE WE GOING IN HERE?" Nora asked, as Noah led her up a lofty staircase to a splendid red brick and gray stone Greek Revival townhouse on Gramercy Park South. Fenced off in black enameled iron and with enormous high windows, the structure was a monument to the city's 19th-century Beaux-Arts days, when it was said Stanford White had considerable say in its design.

"This is our new home."

"What? You have to be jokin' me?" she gasped, stopping dead in her tracks and gripping one of the mighty metal banisters.

"You know I don't kid about this sort of thing."

"Right enough. But you said we were going out to eat."

"That's true. On the first floor. I have it carefully arranged. It really is all ours now."

"I don't believe this. I just don't believe this." But he simply looked at her and smiled. "Will you, for the love of god, tell me this is a dream I'm after having?" she asked as her shock prevailed.

"It isn't. You'll see." He laughed and finished leading her up the outside steps, pausing to unlock the massive temple-like doors, which with a boom sprang closed behind them causing her to jump. He laughed again and then led her up three hulking marble steps, through another set of double doors and into a towering hallway. Their apartment was to the left while other dwellings were aloft and off a spectacular dark wood staircase. He proceeded to unlock their equally imposing, though single, hardwood door and beaming stood back to let her enter. Inside everything was gleaming white, and there was a high, high ceiling and three vast multi-paned windows overlooking the park. Centered in the area paralleling the door was a well-preserved mahogany rectangular dining table with an immense carved pedestal and sprouting legs. On either side were three equally handsome mahogany curved-back chairs and at each end was a similar armchair.

"I bought this set from the old tenants for only four hundred dollars. I'm so happy; it was some of the money I made from my story. And it's Empire," he prided. "They told me at least some of the chairs were original Duncan Phyfe's, but at that price I can't believe it." In the center of the table was an over-sized glittering Waterford crystal vase filled with yellow roses. "Carole Dawson gave it to us as a housewarming gift. But I couldn't tell you about it, or it would have ruined the surprise."

"You're telling me everybody knew about this but me?" Nora asked, still in a state of shock.

"No. Only Carole. She knows the owner, and that's how I got the apartment."

"God Noah, it's only beautiful." Her mouth opened when she noticed the crystal chandelier that hung over the table.

"Isn't that something else. It came with the apartment. That was one of the major selling points."

For an instant, Nora thought of the Georgian mews townhouse in Joyce's *The Dead*. The vision conjured from the rare elegant side of Dublin life--one that goaded her considering Noah's attraction. Then she was remembering what he had said the night of the Capote ball at Carole Dawson's about dying for these things. She found she couldn't thwart these thoughts, even if she tried. But then in the dimming light of early evening Noah began opening a bottle of champagne from an ice bucket set atop a brilliant, small oval walnut table that was crowned with a gray-veined white marble.

"This is said to be the best champagne you can buy," he said, pouring the pale amber fizz from the clear bottle into Waterford glasses. "It's Roederer's Cristal. Its liquid is supposed to fire the soul." As they clinked glasses, he added: "And the body as well, let's hope."

She took a brief sip. "And what will it do for our

cottage in Ireland?" she asked, trying to fight back the anger over what she now considered to be his bewitchery.

"What?" He jumped, nearly dropping the glass.

"Well this wouldn't quite look like our quaint little Irish cottage high above the sea. Would it now?"

"What do you mean?"

"*Fine and proud and whitewashed be*?" she asked as she stared him down.

"Ah come on. Give us a chance."

I am really nasty I know, she told herself. Just stop for now. His eyes are so innocent. Oh god, I love his eyes. I could only die for him.

"You know we had to have something better than that dump."

"Ah Noah, all we need is a roof over us for now. Queens would have done us. After all, it was the first place we were together."

"Yes, but we couldn't stay there forever. We have to have a better existence until we can have the best."

"But the rent for the likes of this. What must it be?"

"Well, let's see the rest first."

"The rest," she gasped. "There's more?"

"Of course," he answered with trepidation. "This is only the living room and the dining room." Then he laughed and tried to make light of it. "Where did you think we'd cook--and more important sleep?" His eyes glinted at the thought of the latter. Then he took her arm. "Come on, let's stroll around. It's ours now, you know."

At the back behind the dining area was yet another spacious set of high windows overlooking small richly landscaped gardens that were attached to the back of a group of 19th Street townhouses. Twilight crept through the panes and sent blue shadows to focus on an area to the right where doors led to the bedroom and the bath. "I think the bedroom's going to be a bit pinchy once we get the furniture in," he said and then grinned. "But that won't stop us from carrying on like wild things."

"It's fine," Nora replied, attempting to share his enthusiasm. But the underlying annoyance and the edgy feeling of being led astray was not going away. And it intensified when he led her from the bedroom to the stairwell at the left. "The kitchen is downstairs."

"Downstairs!" And this time she did gasp again.

The stairs pitched forward leading them back to the front of the building under their living room. "Don't be disappointed, Nora. We don't have the whole floor. There's a boiler for the building behind this.

She actually felt a slight relief. If they had any more space they'd probably be on their way to the slammer for owing so much. If they weren't already.

"I think it's a nice kitchen," he enthused. And surely it was, she thought. There was a grand big range, sink and working area. Plenty of cabinets for storage. And there was room enough for a table and chairs. Even though they were barred, and wisely so, two fine big windows overlooked the street and let in plenty of light. Directly in front was their own fenced off garden broad enough to contain huge cement planters of dwarf conifers and several ornate jardinieres ready for planting. To the side, there was even another outside entrance door protected by a giant wrought iron gate. When Noah mistook Nora's shock for disappointment over the kitchen, he quickly added: "They're going to install a new dishwasher, too."

"Ah Noah," she started, unable to contain herself and about to take him to task again.

"Don't worry. That's free. It goes with the apartment." And at this point, he went to the refrigerator and removed two what looked to be fine china dinner plates in a lovely blue-and-white pattern. Each was laden with a selection of fresh fruits and assorted cheeses. "Look, I did dinner for us. Would you just grab a couple of those mats and napkins on the counter. There's silver in the drawer there and cheese crackers in the cupboard." Then he bounded up the stairs. How could she give out after all of this, she thought.

She mellowed over the delightful dinner, surely aided by more glasses of the Roederer and the now whispery softness of his voice.

"I thought we could have our living room over there by the windows. And the dining room right here. I think that's the way it was before, judging from the placement of that chandelier. And you see that way both areas can share the fireplace."

"Fireplace!" She turned around quickly and saw a gleaming carved white marble one with a mantle. "Heavenly god." It took her breath away. "I didn't even notice it until now."

"I would have had a roaring fire going for you, but they wouldn't let me. They have to clean the flue first."

He had more than made up for the lack of a fire by magically producing candles flickering from antique pewter holders. It would be enough to beguile the knickers off a saint, she thought.

"I only bought two place settings of the Wedgwood and the silver to see if you liked them first," he interjected halfway through the meal, realizing something was bothering her.

"They're only gorgeous," she said, attempting to quell the little waves of anger that began rising once again. She thought of what her granny used to say--you may as well be hanged for thieving a sheep as a lamb. "The Waterford's lovely, too," she sighed, holding her half-filled glass up to catch the candlelight. It flickered and shimmered, and when she realized it was drawing her hypnotically, she quickly sat it down.

"I only bought two of them as well," he offered, trying to soften the blow he now felt he must have delivered by not involving her in the first place. "We have to start somewhere. And they can be used as water glasses, too. If-- If you don't like them for wine—that is."

"Well, I should think so."

"Nora, you're unhappy about this, aren't you?"

"No. I don't think unhappy is the word. Mystified...maybe. No. Yes. I wish you had told me about it before. I knew nothing of your-- I mean Carole Dawson knew. I thought all along we were tucking in, rolling up our sleeves as it were to do something else."

"Oh, I wanted so to surprise you. I can't say how much that meant."

"Well, that you rightly achieved."

"So you don't like it?" he asked, crushed to the bone.

"Yes, I like it. I'd have to be daft not to. But it takes us off course. Way off course."

"Not that much, you'll see."

"Ah Noah, how in god's name are we going to come up with the where-with-all for all of this? Now I ask you, how?" Her mind was already racing to the thousand-dollar-a-month mark.

"That's another great part of the surprise. Carole collected on a favor for our benefit and we've got this fabulous rent."

"Really?" She brightened. But she couldn't believe it could possibly be that good, since they were only paying ninety-eight dollars and forty cents a month now.

"Would you believe four hundred and fifty?"

"Four hundred and fifty," she repeated alternately sighing and gasping. There was relief and fear. Thanks be to god, and oh for the love of god, she thought.

"And the best thing about it is that I wangled a three-year lease. And there's more--." When he saw her face go pale, he stopped himself "Well I mean—well we don't have to keep it that long. We could get rid of it at any time." What he was going to tell her was that Carole had insisted the owners add a clause of renew-ability to the lease offering them three more years at the same price. But he feared she might think he had given up on their Irish dream and not understand that it would only be sensible to retain a place in New York while they lived in Ireland. "But anyway at that rate," he continued. "I mean they could have easily gotten seven, eight, maybe even a thousand for it. They owed Carole a favor and that was that."

"What does she want out of it?"

"Nothing. She thinks the world of us, and she just wants to see us do well as she said that night at Bonwit's. That's the way she is. A really fine person."

"Still it's going to mean a huge change for us. Three-- Over three---four times what we're having to pay now."

"But look at what we've got in comparison. We can do it. I'm going to get another raise soon. And I'm going to ask for a big one. Then I'm on my way to finishing my novel again. And you've got your paintings. Why the light alone is reason enough for us to be here. That northern light," he said gesturing to the windows. "Not only is it perfect but I should think essential to your work. And don't think I didn't think of that when I went after this. I don't know how you could do anything in that dungeon-like light in Queens."

"Well, I made do in that windowless room in Ireland, right enough."

"I know, god love you. But with your talent you should have nothing but the best conditions. And that aside, just look at this place and all the things we can do with it. We couldn't turn it down. I mean this is really us."

"I suppose you're right for the time being," she conceded, but not very forcefully. "I just keep thinking of our cottage and wishing we were putting all our money towards that dream."

"We'll have it. We will. And it won't be that far away. You'll see. All it takes is determination. And that we've got in abundance."

"I love you, Noah." She leaned over and kissed him. "When do we move in?"

"At the end of the month because they're still putting the finishing touches to it," he answered, gazing into her shining eyes that held so much love for him. "I just wish we had a bed here now," he whispered.

"Oh, do you now? Well, that's never stopped you before, ya big goballoon ya."

He stood and lifted her into his arms. "This'll be the christening then," he replied in a whisper. As they kissed, he moved her over to the wall where he dimmed down the lights of the chandelier. And then the place literally transformed into a pure paradise from the onrush of ecstasy as they made love in the flickering candlelight glows with the pale blue wash of Gramercy Park lamplight coming through the big windows.

13

IT WAS SUNDAY. A gorgeous Sunday. March 26, 1967. Easter. After having spent most of the previous day and night packing their belongings and readying their furniture, they made several trips from dawn's early light in a U-Haul between Queens and Gramercy Park South. When it was over late that morning, Noah took one look around and shuddered. "It's worse than I'd imagined. The furniture is horrible. I wished it had fallen to bits while we were dragging it in here. Then I could have left it in the street."

"Don't be daft. It'll do just fine."

"Are you joking me? I hope none of the neighbors saw us. Look at it compared to our Empire dining set. And somehow it doesn't quite make it with that chandelier either."

"Noah, we've got a great apartment. That'll have to do."

"I guess you're right. But I don't have to like it."

After they'd had a quick shower and changed their clothes, they rushed off to Easter Mass at the nearby Epiphany Church and then on to Central Park where he along with a number of Wilton Press photographers had been assigned to cover the *Be-In* in Sheep Meadow. Oliver and much of the staff were abuzz over Flower Children and the effect the burgeoning youth movement might have on fashion and society.

With the aroma of pot and incense, the sitar music of the Ravi Shankar imitators, the thousands of hippies pelting flowers, chanting, shouting, cheering—*love*, and everywhere the screaming psychedelic colors of the times, Noah decried: "The only influence they're going to have is negative."

"Ah Noah, relax and enjoy it," Nora said. "It's grand all the same how they can be so free. They've come away from everything just to be at one with the joy of life. Going after the real values. It's the new freedom as you once called it."

"Hardly. They don't know how to handle freedom. Painted faces, shabby clothes. Bodies reeking to high heaven. I mean there's got to be some economics to all this or it won't work. Like where do they eat? Where do they live? I doubt if some of them even have hovels."

"Ah but it's their spirit that's so great," Nora insisted as an exuberant crowd passed by raising a tie-dyed banner on high with the words: *We proclaim a permanent state of happiness* and singing in full voice the Beatles *Love Me Do* while they cast flowers their way. "That's the spirit we have to have when we move to Ireland."

"Spirit yes. But—I'm a good few years older than they are. Remember I was born in the Depression. I know it has to be grounded," he professed as he looked back over the sea of youthful crazies and pondered their misspent dream.

"Well we're going to have our house," Nora assured. "We'll be able to eat. And I'd venture to say, we'd have the where-with-all to buy the soap to wash ourselves." But then she stopped herself. "But that won't be enough for you, will it Noah?"

"Well I'd say I might need a bit more." He looked at her, laughed and chucked her under the chin, trying to take away the sharpness of her query. Then he bent and snatched up a cluster of pink azalea blossoms flecked with deep brown.

"Sh-sh-shh," he insisted attempting to soothe away her fret as he put his arm around her and gently tucked the cluster into her long silky brown hair. Slowly he brushed his lips along the soft milky pinkness of her cheek. "You're only gorgeous," he whispered. "Now let's go back home, pop our champagne and have our own *be-in*."

THE NEXT MONTH PASSED as if in another of their beautiful dreams. Noah had but one overnight out-of-town assignment and just a sprinkling of major evening events which he attended alone but left at the earliest possible opportunity. So most evenings they were together in their 19th-century apartment across from the enchanting little park with its stately English elms. Noah worked furiously, happily on his novel, while Nora continued to paint.

During this time she began adding to Noah's LP collection. "I always thought that the music created a good bit of a spark to the work. That is when I could tune in on it with my wireless at home. See what you'd be thinking of it Noah." And so the instrumental likes of Debussy, Rossini, Shubert, Chopin, Handel, Vivaldi, Mozart and Brahms wafted through the apartment at her prompting and just as she'd said it did add fuel to the artistic flames.

"How do you manage so often to summon musical metaphors that match my work when you haven't read any of my new stuff yet?' Noah asked one afternoon.

"Ah don't you know I can see what you're at over there. Just a glance up from my work to your face and your hands. They excite me so much. I'd never be after getting these emotions into my bare bones sketches if you weren't there circulating them."

"Really? My hands is it?" he asked as he lifted them from the typewriter and began rubbing them together. "Supposing I were to come over there and let them roam over you for a while. Would they not excite you and your work all the more?"

"Well I suppose it would do no harm to give them a go."

And after a splendid round of lovemaking, she breathlessly managed the words. "Oh Noah, it's only magic what you do to me." Then after their breathing had normalized, she leaned on her elbow and with her other arm stroked his face and his now disheveled hair. "I think I'm after assimilating everything you are and do into my art. But I'd be wrong if I didn't open the very truth to you. I'm only robbing you of that sensitivity and passion you're creating. There's the times like now I feel the guilt of it. I could never achieve the degree of perception that's coming to me now."

"Ah hold on here Nora. I think you've gone daft being around me. You've got it all backwards. I look at you and take all that stuff away. I'm the thief here. You're the wonder-maker."

"Ah sure. Well I know what I know." And she smiled. "Back to work now."

IT WASN'T LONG after that one Saturday morning, she looked up from her work and said: "It's finished."

He immediately jumped up from his writing, came over to her easel and was startled. Instead of a landscape, there was this portrait of a strikingly handsome young man at a typewriter. "Who is he?"

"You, ya eejit. Who'd you think he was?"

"Me?" He was astounded. "I don't look that good. Come on now, you've got some other dude on the side you're not telling me about."

Then he looked at it some more. "Me? Is it really me?" He felt tingly all over. What struck him first was the youthful assurance and the tenderness. "Wow," he exclaimed after he caught his breath. Then foolishly he couldn't resist teasing her. "I wonder if other women see me like this?"

She caught the twinkle in his eyes. It touched that nerve that set off the fury. "How could you think such a thing?" she snapped bitterly. "There's no other woman who sees you like I do, who knows you and loves you as deeply as I do."

"I didn't say there was," he quickly defended, ready to kick himself.

"Damn! Now you've bloody well ruined it," she raged as she jumped up, snatched a landscape canvas from the floor and pitched it over the portrait. "Damn, I'm going to feckin' well destroy it."

"Don't you dare. How could you feel that way? I was only kidding."

"If kidding is wishful thinking."

"Do not start that caustic turn of phrase stuff again. How could I spend my time longing for other women when I literally consume every free moment making love to you?"

"Maybe so. But-- Damn you, Noah, I'm just not able for that kind of tease. Not when it comes to you. Sometimes I get so scared that something might happen. That--"

"Don't be so bloody serious. Don't take away from this beautiful moment." He uncovered the portrait again. "All you should feel now is the enormous pleasure that you finished a great piece."

When she still looked glum, he insisted: "Come on out of that now." Then he began tickling her. "Oh no. Not that," she cried out as the two of them stumbled over water jars and tins of brushes and fell to the floor atop a spattered canvas drop cloth scented with the sensuous earthy odor of wet paints. "Stop," she gasped.

"Not till you're happy," he insisted, straddling her and continuing until the tears came, and they both burst into endless fits of laughter. "I love to hear you laugh," he said when they finally gained control. "Oh god, I love everything about you."

When he looked up, the morning clouds above Gramercy Park parted spilling dazzling sun rays down through the budding trees, in past the windows and across the portrait allowing its colors to lift from the canvas and affording the figure a free and separate existence. "It's a magnificent portrait, Nora. Truly it is."

After he got up, he walked over and studied it in the dazzling sunlight. Studied it as though it must be someone else. "My god, it's uncanny when you look this closely at it. You really did capture what a writer is. What he goes through. You can see into his mind and find the words there...the thoughts he's using. All the light and the dark shadings. The true depths he's experiencing." He looked down at the eagerness of the hands and realized that they really were his hands. Looked back at the face and yes identified the youth as his. But even through its complexity and strong masculine quality, there was a gentle purity rising from it that he thought must have been misread. A perfect goodness that maybe she wanted, needed. For the moment it frightened him, though at first he didn't know why. But then the penny dropped. It was a way he would never be.

EVEN THOUGH SHE REFUSED to ever sell it, Noah worked to convince her that since it was her first portrait she must show it to the people at the gallery. And they were more in awe than she could have ever imagined. "Oh my," the usually hard-boiled Julian said as his eyes brightened. Then after a moment of thought, he continued. "Some artists can paint, but they can't draw. Others can draw but they can't paint. Not only can you do both, but with equal presence and grandeur. You really do have something here. A special grace accorded so few."

By now Julian's associates, sensing the thrill of a new work, had gathered and were nodding in agreement. "It certainly adds a new dimension to your career," Julian continued. "All I can say is you must do more portraits Nora and do them soon."

"I thought maybe I was chancing it a bit," Nora admitted.

"No. You took the risk of working with a subject on a broad scale, and you brought out so many varying depths of character. *This* is an achievement." Then he sat the portrait aside and turned to her. "You know Nora, what I like most about your work is its basis. You know the rules. Well, every true artist has to. But you aren't bound by them. You aren't afraid to break them to achieve what you feel. And that's an ability even some of the most successful artists don't have. They're often masters of technique, but they're also slaves to it. You've passed them. You've learned the most important lesson."

Even though Nora was adrift among the stars, she refused to leave without Noah's portrait. Since they were certain it would fetch top dollars, they were tempted to show it immediately. But she tricked them by saying she thought it would be more important if the portrait were included in her show. They agreed. Since the show was now scheduled for October, she'd be able to do another portrait or two, maybe even another of Noah, and then that would take the pressure off her putting this one out for sale.

Later when she was in the apartment, two words came back to her...your career. It couldn't be. Surely it couldn't, she thought, then pondered, then went and looked in the bathroom mirror. A warm red glow, not a flush, greeted her as involuntarily her breath caught from the sheer wonder of what was happening to her.

14

ON ONE OF THOSE heady warm days of early May, days of budding green leaves and dogwood blossoms in Gramercy Park, an editor from *The New Yorker* called

Noah at *FCD* to let him know. "It'll be in the next edition" and said that an advance copy had been mailed to him at his new home address. He was in seventh heaven waiting for it. It was the accomplishment of his lifetime thus far. To see his story on its pages, to see his name there, too. The thrill he felt the day his fingers finally touched the cover of the issue with its Ilonka Karaz's floral art was indescribable. He went on to the contents. His title, his name. Page 28. When he got there and saw the first words, tears came to his eyes. He was that happy. Other than the day he met Nora, this was the most momentous moment of his life. He had undeniable evidence of his skill to write. And now surely his novel would follow.

Buoyed by that thrill, he rushed to Altman's and purchased a ruby brooch for Nora. Then he went into the office and phoned a friend on *Interior Design Connoisseur*, one of the Wilton sister publications, for names of a few places where he might obtain good deals on furniture and rugs that would be worthy of their Greek Revival habitat. She gave him the name of a great place that because of his Wilton connection would offer him a sizeable price reduction and the chance to pay off the balance in installments.

"DAMN YOU! I wish you could at least bother yourself to tell me about your bloody highfalutin' plans before they're fait accompli," Nora aghast snapped fiercely, ready to eat the face off him that bright Saturday morning as these giants alighted from their vast lorry and began moving in all this furniture and taking away their old.

"It's just a few things. I wish they could have been finer."

"Just a few things! You wish they could have been finer!" Her rage along with her hurt was building by the moment. Already she'd noted a Mission style sofa and settee, a window seat, several upholstered armchairs and tea tables. And it was nowhere near over yet. "Will this be going on all day?" she asked, terrified of the answer.

He looked at her with such sad eyes and asked the usual question: "Don't you like it?"

She seethed and didn't answer.

"Why are you getting your knickers in a knot?"

"*Jaysas*, Mary and Joseph," she bellowed. "The cost, Noah."

"It's not all that bad," he winced as in came a parade of inlaid rosewood bedside tables and bureaus followed by a magnificent matching rosewood Empire sleigh bed and then the restored 19th-century full size ingrain carpets and the Shaker area rugs. Next in line was a massive Empire wardrobe that even stunned him. He'd forgotten he purchased it.

These were pieces that weren't that different from some of the princely items adorning the pricey Dublin antique shops off Stephen's Green, she thought as she continued to seethe. "Do you realize we're paying almost four times the amount of rent we were in Queens? And now all this."

"Well most of them are only reproductions of the Empire period," he inserted, hoping it would calm her. "I mean even the Mission furniture is reproduced and--"

"Excuse me sir," one of the movers called in from the entry door. "Would you mind unlocking the downstairs door so we can bring in the kitchen set and the hutch. Those early American pine and butternut pieces are bitches to lift."

"Noah, if I could get that chandelier down from the ceiling I'd bloody well crown you with it."

"Ah come on, Nora. Just look at these things. They're beautiful."

"They're hardly things. Don't try to play them down now. It's just not right, it's not." And she started to cry, and it was breaking his heart to see her hurt.

"Oh don't. Don't worry." And as he put his arms around her, he added: "I got a really good discount—I-I mean because I work for Wilton and--"

She heaved him away. "I thought we were supposed to be saving our money."

"Don't do this, Nora. We've got to have furniture."

"We had furniture."

"Yeah, Salvation Army chic. That's where I had to get it you know."

"It was good enough. What for the love of god are we going to do with all these yokes when we move to Ireland? If we still are, that is." Then she added even more snidely: "Give them away?"

"Of course not. We'll take them with us. We can have them shipped."

"Ah don't be daft. These enormous pieces? Whatever happened to our idea of a simple little cottage with basic Irish Sugan furniture?"

"Well-- We'll sell the stuff then. Those that aren't antiques are fine reproductions." Then he busied himself emptying out the drawers of their old bureaus before the men snatched them out the door.

"Excuse me, miss," one of the movers signaled. "Could you make way for the sideboard?" Nora enraged stood aside as the crew proceeded to haul in a gigantic two-story hand-carved mahogany Victorian buffet complete with supporting colonnades. Then she walked into the bedroom as more tears came. Noah followed her. "That's a reproduction, too. Look we'll pay it off a little at a time. And we'll still save money for Ireland. You'll see. We've practically got four jobs between us now."

"It's thousands of dollars, Noah. It has to be."

"Okay, let's just be calm. It's not thousands. But I was wrong. I admit. I should have told you. I wanted us to have this. To be like this."

"Oh Noah, how could you? Damn you." And she pounded his chest in rage.

He grabbed her fists. "Wait now. Just hear me out. Stop. We'll keep it for a couple of days. We'll think about it from all angles. And if on Monday we feel it's wrong to keep it, we'll just send it back."

"And sit on the floor? They're after carting off all our old stuff."

"Oh they'll still have it on Monday. They can send it back."

She brightened a little, then blew her nose and dried her eyes.

"I'll arrange it with the cleaning lady."

"What cleaning lady?" she gasped.

"Why I hired one last week. Just for a short time so we can get everything spic and span. I'm sure I told you," he said matter-of-factly. And so much for the brightness.

She sighed and shook her head. "You're incorrigible. I don't know what to make of this." Suddenly she felt a wave of hopelessness combine with her anger, and she could take no more. She burst out the door, down the steps and proceeded to run. By the time he caught her, she had reached Irving Place. "Stop! Let me go," she cried, attempting to pull away from him. "You're so caught up in what you want, you'll never miss me."

"Are you all right, miss?" a big burly guy in a body-hugging T-shirt called out as he flashed Noah a murderous glare.

Realizing the show they were making of themselves, she calmed herself. "Yes. Yes, it's all right."

"I'm sorry. I really mean it. I was completely off base. I just got so excited about it all. But we'll decide this together. I promise. It's not too late."

She said nothing, just stared over at the park gate and wondered if it weren't more important to him than she.

"Look, I'll tell you what," he said, turning her to him, then tilting her chin and looking into her eyes. "The men will be gone soon. We'll get ourselves together. We'll go down the street to Pete's for brunch and take things calmly. You'll see. It'll all come right. Please? Please give me a chance."

"I guess."

AT PETE'S, the old 19th Century tavern hearkening to O'Henry days, in the middle of eggs Benedict, with the Turtles *Happy Together* playing in the background, he handed her a tiny box.

"What's this?"

"It's for your pretty yellow sweater. No your gorgeous yellow sweater." And he ran his fingers along her cheek. "Careful, don't drop it in the Benedict."

When she saw the rubies, she was stunned yet again. "Oh god Noah, what is it with you?"

"Oh I-- I paid for it with cash. I-I mean money I saved up."

"But-- What's the occasion? The soften-the-blow day?"

"N-a-a-w. You can't believe that." Her thought stung him. "I bought it because the rubies reminded me of the flush of your skin when I kissed you on the cliffs of Aran."

"Ah Noah." The tears came this time because once again he had touched her heart.

"YOU KNOW MY DAD always wanted to get mama beautiful things," he said later that afternoon as they strolled the gravel paths of the park under the breezy rich green of the English elms. "But he never could. He never had money."

"That was so important to them, wasn't it?"

"Yes. They only came close to it once. And then the chance was gone." He sighed as he reflected. "I guess that's why I am what I am."

"I don't need that to be happy," she practically pleaded from exasperation. "When will you realize, I just need you?"

"I *do* realize it. But god it gives me such pleasure to live here," he exclaimed, gesturing to the 19th-century townhouses that surrounded them. "To have a key to this private park and be able to open the gate for you. You have to know how much--"

His face was ecstatic. He was so absolutely sincere that she shivered.

They sat on a bench, and he put his arm around her and pondered. "I guess I want to give you all the happiness my mother never had."

"You did that the day I met you."

"It's just that I saw her all those years. That I need to prevent that somehow. And that I need to prove I'm deserving of you. That I love you that much."

"But--"

Before she could finish, the ruby brooch suddenly caught the sun of the late afternoon, blinding them. "God, it's beautiful on you."

DESPITE THE FUROR she had created over the furniture, to Nora one true factor loomed from the situation and that was his love for her and how captivated she was by it. It made the whole issue begin to blur. It also made her realize just how much she needed him. It couldn't have been clearer than that next Friday evening when Tim accepted Noah's invitation for dinner in their apartment. Even though she did take pity when he spoke of his long ago lost love, as the hours stretched by, she so wished that he would be gone just so she could be alone with Noah.

And on Saturday after several morning bouts of passion, he made her feelings of need even more apparent. "You know something," he said, as still in bed they nibbled on the buttery-scented croissants he'd dashed out to retrieve from the Gramercy Park Pastry Shop. "I'd like us to get married right now."

"What?" Her heart leapt from the joy. "But I thought we were going to wait until September and do it in Dublin."

"Nope. I want us to do everything we can to bind our love as soon as possible."

"Why? Do you think I might be makin' off with

another fella?"

"No, but these vows are important. I don't want to flaunt this or mess it up the way my friends seem to have done. Tim. And now Janet, the one you never got to meet, called me from California the other day. She's pretty miserable. She had twins you know, and now her husband Russell's so busy with his work she never sees him. So what I'm hearing now is—do something and keep on doing it, to keep it going."

"I don't know why we couldn't." Nora was beaming. "You mean here?"

"Yeah. Over in Epiphany. Now that we've completed those eejity marriage classes. It would be just the two of us. And no big *do* as you'd call it."

"Ah god that would be only magic. Avoiding all that family madness. And the money alone. But Noah, wouldn't you're mother be upset?"

"No. She'd be overjoyed for us. And it would be our vows, just us and the priest. And a photograper, because we'd want pictures of course."

"Ah Noah, I love you only to distraction for this. Let's do it soon."

15

THE AZALEAS WERE IN BLOOM. Bright pinks and salmons against the dazzling lawns of the Southampton estates that late May. Already the sun had warmed the sands and the North Atlantic waters to near early summer temperatures. It was Memorial Day weekend, and Noah had been dispatched to cover the earliest blossoms of the Hamptons social scene. He had taken Nora along. This was the first such event she had attended with him in a very long time. Purposely so. And as such she approached it with considerable trepidation. They had driven out in a rented BMW (well it had to match the surroundings Noah insisted) and were staying at Gurney's in Montauk. The distance between the Hamptons and their lodging had been planned just so they would have the excuse of escaping those soirees come early evening.

From the very first cocktail party, Noah knew something was radically wrong. The shoulders weren't just cold. They were icy. Where these people had once gushed over him, now they were polite, just barely polite.

"Why did they invite you, if they were going to act like this?" Nora asked.

"I don't know. It baffles me," Noah shrugged. But it was obvious to Nora he couldn't shrug off the hurt he felt. This both pained and angered her as the old feelings flooded back. God, what is in him that makes him give a fiddler's damn?

The thought stayed with her as she strolled into the gleaming mahogany library of the Finch estate while Noah attempted to mend fences in the gardens where most of the guests had ensconced themselves. Here she could be alone and not be subjected to all his abhorrent pandering.

Pandering that once again made her feel things unraveling.

To escape her thoughts, she took down an old rusty red volume of poetry and flipped through it. Without conscious plan, she paused at the Yeats section and slowly turned the pages until her eyes caught and held on one of the lines--*paced upon the mountains...* Suddenly drops of moisture fell on the page, startling her. Where did they come from? When she realized, she quickly put the book back and dried her eyes.

"I do believe we've met before, my dear," Lady Augusta Donnelly--American wasp by birth, Lady through marriage to British royalty and heiress to multimillions in brewing and electronics--spoke as she came to Nora's side. "Fortunately those were far more pleasant circumstances."

"Well, it's pleasant to meet you again Lady Augusta." And Nora held out her hand, remembering that the first time Noah had introduced her she had insisted on being called Augusta because she was so fond of them or so she had said.

This time Lady Donnelly ignored Nora's hand. "I wish I could say the same. Sadly, I can't."

"Oh. What's wrong? Why do you say this?"

"I see your husband--" And she peered over her spectacles at Nora. "Boyfriend-- Whatever. Has turned into a common guttersnipe."

"Lady Donnelly," Nora exclaimed, her voice rising. "I don't take kindly to your words. Now you'd best be telling me what all this is about."

"That story in *The New Yorker* was quite the piece. After we've taken him under our wings, he tears us asunder."

"I do believe you're overreacting. He wasn't writing about any specific person or people. It was only a piece of fiction."

"Why he portrayed us all as a collection of the most despicable sort. Riding the charity circuit for all its worth, I believe he put it. Using it to forward our goals without the least concern for the poor, the needy. Heartless. Ruthless beyond belief. Weren't those his words? Why he even made contractual thieves out of some of us as though we were part of some despicable ethnic mob. Anyway, it's all too sordid to be repeated. It was without a doubt the worst piece of rubbish I've read in years. I think *The New Yorker* was dotty for publishing such poor writing. It certainly debased itself with that issue. But then I suppose nothing is sacred these days."

"Well certainly you're right about one thing, Lady Donnelly. It wasn't good writing. But it was great writing. And obviously you aren't able to tell the difference between that and pure trash," she snarled to the top of her lungs. Then as she followed Lady Donnelly out into the cocktail hall, something gave way in her. For the first time at one of these gatherings anger vanished, and she succumbed to a mixture of hopelessness and the most unbearable sadness. It was as if some force had robbed an important part of her spirit, and she found herself sobbing in front of the shocked hostess Amanda Finch. "Heartless is right," she managed to roar at Lady Donnelly in conclusion and then hurried across the marble hall looking for a way out.

Noah, who had heard the explosion all the way out in the gardens, told his photographer to take over and hastily apologized to the still stunned Amanda Finch as he rushed after Nora while speechless guests looked on. "Come on, let's get out of here," he said, and they quickly walked through the open French doors and onto the blazing green lawn where they made their escape.

IN THE CAR, after she calmed down and explained what happened, she asked: "Do you not think they set you up for this?"

"No. The invitations for these things came in way before the story appeared. Oliver Wilton said there was a bit of a ruffle over it. But nothing like this. He was even gleeful about it. I don't think he knew people were this upset. Jesus, what am I going to do now, lose my friggin' job?" If only I hadn't brought her, maybe I could have contained the whole thing, he thought. God, it couldn't have been a more emotional scene if she'd tried.

"I wish you hadn't been so distraught," he finally said, unable to contain himself as he drove around the area in vain. "You should have ignored her."

"Don't you be after blaming me for this, Noah."

"I'm not blaming you. I just wish you hadn't been so damned emotional that's all."

"How could I be anything but with the things she was after saying about you?"

"Well, obviously things are bad enough, and this doesn't make them look any better."

"Look any better! All you ever worry about are how things look."

"No. But practically every other time you go to something with me, there's some sort of a disturbance. It just pisses me off. Why don't you do me a personal fucking favor for a change and control yourself."

"Oh that's just glorious, that is. So I'm the sow's ear after all." And with that, she opened the door, preparing to jump out. Noah slammed on the brakes and the car careened up onto the curb in front of Saks on Main Street, causing passersby to leap out of the way and police to hasten to the vehicle. Fortunately Noah hadn't had anything to drink, and the officers believed his story of the door malfunctioning and springing open.

"Do you realize you could have been killed--and a few others as well?" Noah said after they'd calmed their nerves and were mobile again.

"Don't you mean--we could have been arrested. And that it might have made the papers? And so what if I had been killed, you wouldn't have to be worrying about my rampant emotions anymore."

"Jesus Christ, Nora, we're getting married in a month. What do I have to do to prove to you I love you?"

"Take a stand."

"IT WAS A GREAT STORY, NOAH," Carole delighted as they lunched at one of the prime tables in La Caravelle's status alley. It was several days after that weekend of aloof Southampton parties (the remainder of which he attended alone while Nora remained at Gurney's). "Superb really. I particularly delighted in it." And she laughed then bit her bottom lip as she grew serious. "But I must say I had such fear when I was reading it knowing it was yours. Because no matter how brilliant the writing, I knew you had no idea what you were up against." Then she looked around the room as did Noah noting a number of surreptitious glances from social luminaries at neighboring tables. "The trick is," she continued, "to be like me and not care what any of them think. But it's too soon. You can't afford that now. Not with the kind of money you're getting from a *New Yorker* short story anyway."

"But I honestly don't understand what all the fuss is about. I mean I didn't portray any of these people so they could recognize themselves. Or so anyone else could," Noah stressed and then took a deep drink of the Petrus Bordeaux they had ordered. By now he could feel the heat from those nearby who were most certainly whispering of him.

"Keep smiling and don't let them realize you're even aware of them anymore." Then she leaned forward adjusting her silverware and the water and wine glasses as she quietly insisted: "Don't you see, what you did is almost worse. They're all reading themselves into it now. *And* they're imagining you might do even more."

"Well it's just a work of fiction."

"Yes but you went for their jugular."

"I had no idea." Even though he was smiling, the tension was overtaking him.

Leaning closer, she put her elbows on the table and pressing her slim hands against her cheeks stressed in a whisper: "Charity is the be all and end all of their social existence. As you rightly dramatized, it has nothing to do with the cause and everything to do with their egos and their pocketbooks. I don't mean to be an alarmist, but quite frankly if you dump on those, they're going to turn viperous." Then she too pursued the Petrus and a waiter quickly topped their glasses.

"Well I guess you have a point," Noah sighed trying hopelessly to quell his panic. "But Oliver seems to be amused by the whole thing."

"Of course he is. It fits right in with his power wielding at the moment. You know he's a Yalie--Skull and Bones. There's always something more in his mind than what you see. And there's always the possibility that he can switch and play another card."

"As long as he doesn't play me."

"He is playing you."

"Well what if it backfires. Couldn't all these angry people go into attack mode? Try to disrupt advertising? That sort of thing?"

"Oh I doubt if they'll stage a full-scale range war. I

mean it could be a decided negative for the so-called compassionate *regals* to show their true selves. Dripping blood as it were."

"Well then?"

"As long as Oliver seems to be on your side, they can't give you the instant coup de grace as they most likely wish they could. But. And it's a big one. They can get you in little ways and slowly twist you into great pain. I've seen it done before so I know. Through looks and glances, whispers and falsehoods. Through little acts that result in big losses. Seriously it may not sound like much but it could get to someone as kind hearted as you. Call it underhanded corrosion of the spirit. I think if you've let yourself, you've already sensed some of this." As their waiters set forth a *mousse de brochet havraise* for Carole and a *coq au vin* for Noah, he slipped into stunned silence.

"Now you're really scaring me," he said when they were gone.

"Oh Noah, can't you see how this city runs on charity balls, stunning gowns and lavish jewels? Don't forget the magnitude of that enterprise for one moment."

He shivered. "I guess I should take this pretty seriously."

"Well don't let it plow you under. They'd love that. But what I think you should do, since you're such a superb writer, is to work on that novel you told me about. Get that published and under your belt so you establish yourself as a serious novelist. Meanwhile save all this society material until then, instead of parceling out these short fictional episodes. That way you can fire away with both guns, knowing it will really bolster your career rather than sabotage it. Why I can even get an agent to help you through all that."

"I think I have one, and I'm even working in the direction you suggest."

"Keep at it then. And meanwhile I'll just continue saying wonderful things about you whenever and wherever. But I think I can do even more or at least imply such. You see when it comes to charity they know I'm true blue and most of them are as phony as their smiles. So they better watch out. You see I can get away with anything my friend."

"Oh that would be more than I could ever hope for."

"Well consider it done. But I did want to say something else as well," she continued on rather cautiously as she collected her knife and fork and broke into her mousse with its streams of creamy white sauce.

Noah ignoring his food just looked at her for a few seconds. "I think I know what that might be." And he sighed.

"Yes I think so." And she rested her silver on her plate and looked directly at him. "Noah you might want to warn her. She's a truly lovely girl and a brilliant talent. Certainly you know, she's on her way, just as you are, to becoming a famous artist. But you don't want to compound the situation making it look like the two of you are in cahoots, hell-bent as it were on debunking these people. Even though from what I can see she's spot-on when she speaks out, she may be too outspoken for the moment from what people are saying. It might be better to wait till she's got the money and the fame. Then she can say anything she wants, and they'll have no choice but to pass it off as colorful eccentricity."

"Yes," he chuckled for the first time in days. "I'm certain you're right."

"I want to see you two make it. I want to see that it can be done. Because with all my money, I couldn't prove it could happen."

"Oh I'm sorry. You've got your own problems."

"Yes. And they aren't getting any better." She sighed. "But-- I'll survive." She nodded and laughed and drank some more Petrus. "I just want to make certain you do."

EVEN WITH THE PASSING OF TIME, the whole *New Yorker* issue didn't fade. Other gossip gurus thrilled with keeping it alive in their columns. So much attention was paid to it that an editor at *The New Yorker* kept calling for more pieces of the same ilk. Noah could only imagine how elated he would have been had he been free to comply.

"Well I think all this brouhaha is a great circulation builder. An enormous plus for your column," Murphs said as she came out of the *FCD* ladies room early one evening. She had changed into a mercury crepe Galanos dress that all but swept the floor, one she had selected at Bloomingdale's for some big Seventh Avenue celebration of fashions at the Waldorf.

"I think Oliver is absolutely gleeful over the idea that the BPs feel they're on the spot," she went on. "They hate you on the one hand but on the other they have to accept you or else you could just ignore them in *FCD*. Then again you could write something more condemning about them, this time using their real names, something that they couldn't disprove. And they would consider that a fate worse than death by torture."

"Yeah, but it's all so dicey. I could also lose my job."

"Noah, you've got to stop being so timorous. Do you realize in this short period of time you've gained more power with that column than Suzy in the *Daily News.*"

"No I guess I didn't." He stopped to think for a moment. "Still in all, before this happened it was a wonderful feeling being in such favor and having them treat me as if I were one of them. Not because I wanted to be. That's the last thing I'd ever want. But god, I could imagine I was wealthy then. I *did* imagine I was wealthy then."

DURING THE NEXT DAYS, Noah not only longed for the return of this imagination but worried about suffering even greater losses.

"*Ah* wanted to see how all of this commotion would

play out dear boy, before *ah* commented on it," Oliver Wilton quickly replied after Noah finally approached him at the reception area of his office.

"What's that Oliver?"

"Why your risqué little *New Yawka* short story of *cauze*. You sly devil."

"But Oliver," he immediately defended. "I'm sure, as you went to Yale, you can understand how a writer such as myself would long to be accepted by the *New Yorker*."

"Well of *cause ah* can Noah. *Aham* rather envious myself, but nonetheless thrilled that one of *ahwa* writer's work has appeared on those pages."

"I meant no offense. I want you to know that."

"Well *ah* wouldn't mind if you had. All the better for *ahwa* paper as it were. The more *ahwa* readers are startled the better. Bedazzled might be a more apropos word. My only concern here is that we not lose you. And *ah* mean not lose you in any way. That all your effort is directed toward the thrill of *ahwa* paper. Now if you could manage both without any—disruptions—well how *mahvelous* that would be. Perfect, in fact. But should there be too many distractions—well—that would prove rather baneful indeed." With that he returned to his inner office, leaving Noah—though anxious--with a sense of some relief.

16

CHOPIN NOCTURNES DRIFTED through the airy modernist Epiphany Church just off Gramercy Park that Saturday in June when they exchanged their vows in a private ceremony. But they were scarcely aware of the music. Everything seemed muted and distant, even the open altar that Noah had arranged to be laden with violets. He, so dapper in a new Brooks Brothers suit with his hair that little bit ruffled, had recovered the full bloom of innocent youth, after coming to terms with the *New Yorker* episode--at least for the time being. And Nora in a mauve dress of crepe de chine that he'd helped her select at Saks looked positively ravishing, that along with the soft glow of her face stirred his blood. The photographer, a workmate of Noah's from Wilton Press, snapped away and kept whispering how beautiful they looked. He along with the pianist would be their necessary witnesses.

And then there were words.

"for better or for worse"

"for richer for poorer"

"in sickness and in health"

"to love and to cherish"

Cherish, Noah thought. The only word he really heard. What a beautiful word. Our word. He felt so passionate about it that he persuaded the priest to allow its inclusion in the strictness of the vows.

When following a brief Mass, after they had kissed,

they turned around to find three people in one of the pews at the back of the church. "S-u-r-p-r-i-s-e," they all called in unison.

"I don't believe it," Noah gasped to Tim, Russell and Janet as Nora looked on in stunned silence. "Oh this is great, just great," he called out as he took Nora's hand, stepped down from the altar and walked toward them. "How on earth did you know?"

"Oh I have my ways," Tim insisted.

After they'd all hugged and kissed, Noah introduced Nora to Russell and Janet his college friends now living in California. Then they went out into the gushing sunshine for more photographs. "Smile," Noah muttered under his breath to Nora. After the others came over for a group photo, Tim told them he had arranged for a little champagne reception at the Gramercy Park Hotel.

"Why did you do this?" Nora snapped in a whisper as she and Noah went back into the church to present the pianist, the photographer and the priest with a monetary gift for doing them the favor of a private ceremony. "You said we'd be alone and the vows would mean that much more."

"I know, and I meant it. I'm as surprised as you are. Look, I'll make it up to you. I will. Just don't say anything. They're my best friends. They meant well. After the champagne, we'll still have most of the day."

She didn't comment. She just looked over at the violets that now seemed more wilted than muted.

"TO NORA AND NOAH," Tim toasted as they all lifted their glasses. "*Fortunati ambo.* Or for those who don't speak the language—you happy pair."

"Don't tell us you're back on that mumbo jumbo. You sound like you swallowed a dictionary," Russell quipped. "Let's drink before the champagne goes flat."

"All right. *Gaudeamus igitur.* Or for the ignoramus here—let's be joyful. Just look at them. May you always have what you've got now." Then they all hugged and kissed some more as a waiter trotted in with a giant elegantly wrapped box—a collective gift from the three. It contained an enormous pedestal wine cooler, an aperitif decanter and glasses and an ornate oval rose vase, all of glittering antique Waterford crystal.

Both were stunned, and Nora felt a wave of guilt for having such angry thoughts. "Thank you. It's way too much," they both said unison. "It's enough that you came, but to do all this," Noah continued.

"We wouldn't have missed it for the world," Janet said. "The minute Tim told me, I said to Russell: No matter what work you've got planned or how important it is, you're not doing it this weekend. It worked. I arranged it with the twins' nanny and we're here."

"I haven't had a day off in six weeks. I'm with Warners now, you know," Russell said scarcely containing the boast. "We're just about to do a wrap on this great new project *Bullitt* with Steve McQueen."

"Nora, don't ever let this happen to you and Noah. At least insist on your weekends," Janet warned. "Before this we never wanted to be apart. But now, work and money have taken over." For the moment her big green eyes seemed to reflect her growing sadness. Noah glanced at Tim and realized they were both thinking the same thing. The foster homes and all the bad feelings had returned. Noah remembered a flash of conversation he'd overheard when they were college lovers.

-Oh Jan., I was so fortunate. What they did to me was bad enough. But I could kill them for what they did to you. For all those years of it."

-Well thank god it only comes back to me when I'm away from you. Then it's hell again."

"Well once I get established things will change." Russell broke the brief silence.

Janet sighed and snipped sarcastically: "Yeah and you'll let go of your new social life too?" Then she took a deep drink of her champagne. "Oh I'm sorry," she suddenly exclaimed. "I'm sounding like the voice of doom. Forgive me."

"Nothing to forgive," Tim insisted. "Don't I wish I had somebody who wanted me around that much. As you see I'm alone again. My latest flew off to Sardinia."

Then out of the blue and aided by the champagne, Nora suddenly chirped her true belief: "Tim, if you had any more women racing after you, you'd be going for your tea. Why from what I already gather you've a rag on every bush."

They all laughed hysterically, especially Noah.

"*A rag on every bush*? Where in god's name?" And he shook his head. "Don't you just love her, the way she puts things?" Tim said. "I try to muster some sympathy, and she reduces everyone to stitches over it."

"Oh poor Tim," Janet said, reaching over to hug him. "We care about you. We're just going to have to find somebody for you who can take it, that's all."

"Take what?" Tim asked puzzling.

"All your joie de vivre," Noah clowned.

"Oh, is that what they call the old *membrum virile* these days," Russell added.

"Hah," Janet smirked at her husband. "I thought you'd all but forgotten what that was." And suddenly there was an awkward silence until Tim quickly attempted to cover the slur jokingly adding: "Well I guess I'm just a *monstrum horrendum* when it comes down to it."

"Oh I think you must be *monstrum* alright. But there's nothing horrendous about it when it comes to the women," Noah followed through with a hearty laugh. "It's just that they're always the wrong ones."

"Ah well," Tim sighed. "*The fault dear Brutus—* But you never know what might arise between lust and hope."

"Yeah we know what'll rise alright," Noah added

bemusing everyone. But then he felt badly for continuing to make Tim the brunt of the jest. Tim with his glistening strawberry hair that was now even longer but still perfectly stylish seemed to have slipped for the moment with his blue-green eyes dimming. This sent Noah's mind's eye suddenly flashing back to his college room in Ithaca when Tim stood staring out the window at a straight fall of late autumn rain.

-My old man wanted me to go to Harvard like he did and stick it straight through law school so he could show me off to his peers like some goddam hotshot trophy. All I wanted to do was write. But I was scared shitless of him. He used to beat me when I was a kid, you know. Broke my goddam arm once. Always made me feel like such useless crap."

-How'd you bust out?"

-There was this girl. She was a little older than I was. She was already in college. She helped me see what I really could be. She helped me stand up to that bastard. We became lovers, and god I loved her so much. Jesus god, I would have died for her. So I made up my mind. Screw Harvard. I'd make it on my own without my father's bread."

-So you're here and alone. So what happened?"

-It got all screwed up. Fatally screwed up. And I do mean fatal."

With that Noah remembered how Tim suddenly rushed out of the place and how he had chased after him.

When he caught up at surging Cascadilla Creek, it was raining so hard he could scarcely make out that Tim was crying. But he knew he was.

-I'm sorry, pal. I didn't mean to dump on you. It's just that sometimes it sneaks back up and hurts like fuckin' hell what happened. I never knew anybody I could tell this to before." Then he completely blew it and started sobbing. Noah remembered how he had put his arm around him until he had gained some control.

-It's lost. It's gone forever, pal."

"And money," Russell was saying as Noah snapped back to reality from the pop of another champagne cork. "I'm going to have my own production company, and we'll have it then like we've never had it before."

"Well I have it, but I don't have anything else," Tim said.

"Except that play that David Merrick was so anxious for you to revise," Noah reminded him.

"Yes—if and when. Time and the agency seems to be squashing that too."

And the silent pause started Noah thinking of boundaries being crossed into territories from which it might be impossible to return, of loses that couldn't be retrieved. He looked at them and realized their fate and promised himself on this his wedding day that the same would not happen to them.

"Noah, are you all right?" Nora asked while the

others were gobbling the rest of the hors d'oeuvres.

"Oh yes, I'm sorry, Nora. I was just thinking of the old days with these guys." Then he leaned forward and gave her a long kiss on the mouth.

"Wow! Hold on actionwise," Tim said. "We've all got to partake of the wedding feast before we let you go off and get into *voluptates corporis.* I hope it's all right. I reserved The Hayloft at The Coach House for us. I know how much you said you guys like the place."

"Well--" said Noah knowing they had long since reserved a table for two at The Four Seasons and that Nora would not be happy. But what could he do.

"THAT WAS AN ABSOLUTELY GREAT WEDDING FEAST," Noah told Tim later that evening after they'd all left the restaurant. Mellowed out on superb wine, they were strolling past the Washington Square fountain headed toward Fifth Avenue. "I really wish you'd let me at least help to pay for it. It was so expensive."

"I agree wholeheartedly that I should at least pay for some of it." Russell said.

"Not another word moneywise," Tim insisted. "It was worth every penny to have us together on such a fantastic occasion."

"Well then at least come over to our apartment for a drink."

Now he's really gone and done it, Nora raged to

herself. Blast him.

"You must be joking, buddy," Tim said. "We'd be the real coitus interruptus. What are we going to do, sit around watching the two of you do it and give you pointers maybe. Easy. Slowly, slowly. A little up and to the right. Now speed it up. Faster. Faster. *Perge! Perge! Perge!!*" Everyone was tumbling about in gales of laughter, even Nora had to laugh. "That's it, pal. You're almost there. *Plus! Plus!* Faster. Faster. You're on the verge. *Hui! Hui!* Pow. Over the top. Red lights."

"All right, enough," Noah called out. "The offer still stands. We'd love to have you."

"Well, don't bother to consider me," Nora said bearly grinning.

"That's right, Nora," Janet finally jumped in. "Stick up for your rights. And start tonight. There's no better time. Now Noah you go off with her and behave yourself. No. Better still, you go off and don't behave yourself." With that, they all laughed again, and Noah could have leapt for joy. She had saved the moment from Nora's cold remark.

After the final hugs and kisses as they waited for their signaled taxis, there was a brief moment of silence tarnished by fading smiles. It was one that revealed the depths of loneliness of the three dear, and now he thought lost, friends who stood before him.

"AND SO MUCH FOR THAT," Nora said when

they were at long last alone and safely ensconced in their taxi home.

"Don't start. How you could have said that at the end and embarrassed me so?"

"Oh that's a grand one. Do you realize for one moment how hard I tried, Noah? I was so good until you canceled our reservations at The Four Seasons."

"I know you were. And that was brilliant."

"Even after that, I forced myself to be decent through the dinner."

"You were great. I just wish you could have held out for--" And he began to put his arm around her. She pushed him away.

"You really provoked me, Noah. And after all I'd gone along with."

"Okay. You've made your point. I know. I said I'd make it up to you."

"How can you make up the one day, the very most important day of our lives? Now it's gone forever. We can never be after having it again."

"It's not gone. We've still got the best part ahead of us. You'll see."

"Yes. And you were going to ruin that. I can't believe you invited them over yet."

"Oh for god's sake, I had to ask them. Russell and Janet came all the way from California. And look at all they spent on us. And the gifts yet."

"But it's our wedding night." She sighed in

exasperation. "Noah, I think you really wanted them to come home with us."

"Of course. I was happy to see them. They're my friends."

"Make that best friends. And I'd say as such that makes them one better than me."

"I can't believe you're saying this. Nora, the world wasn't made just for the two of us. It was obviously planned for other people to be in as well. And we're damn fortunate to know some who really care about us."

With that the taxi drew up to their building. They got out and as they started to climb the steps, he stopped and took hold of her. "Let's end this right here, so that when we go inside we can create a beautiful evening of memories that will live on through the years."

She tried as they went in, tried to let her mind go blank, because she really wanted this. But she couldn't.

"Now stop. Just stop," he said pushing her against the living room wall and attempting to kiss away the tears. When it didn't work, he whispered: "There's only one way to put an end to this." He tossed aside his jacket and tie and proceeded to peel off his shirt. Then he unzipped the back of her dress, slid it down over her shoulders to her waist and hastily yanked away her bra. He pulled her to him and began rubbing his chest against her aroused breasts as he gave her a long deep kiss.

When they finally broke apart to gasp for breath, Noah panted: "Now stay there. Just stay there." And quickly he darted off to switch on the hi-fi, softly filling the room with orchestral versions of Gershwin love songs. He looked over at her, his eyes shining. Then he turned back to the player, lifted the needle and dropped it at the band containing *Our Love Is Here To Stay*.

He came back to her and snapped off the chandelier lights. Then he took her in his arms, held his face against her velvety neck and traced his tongue up over her cheek, across her earlobe and into her ear, causing her to shiver. "Cherish," he whispered. "I cherish you." His hand moved down, lifted the hem of her dress, loosened her panties and slid under them so that he could part the wetness and sink two stroking fingers well up into her.

"O-h-h-h," she gasped and hurried to pull down his trouser zipper and the front of his briefs. She took hold of his hot arching erection and began to squeeze and tug at it to the swell of the music. Then in the wash of starlight, moon white coming from the windows, they swayed until they finally cried out. And the sweet agony of their cries melded with the music and the night white light to form an exquisite tapestry.

"Forever,"he whispered. *"And a day."*

17

DURING THE MONTH that followed, Noah was able to lose himself in their lovemaking and his fictional endeavors. They provided escape from his sense of loss--the nurturing sense of wealth that the society world had once imparted and that he so savored. Even though they needed him, they had pulled back that little bit to subtract. It would all come around once more he kept telling himself. Only this time he wouldn't need them. The playing field would change yet again and he would actually be moneyed.

One night when Nora returned from work, he greeted her at the door. "We have another reason to celebrate."

"We do? I have one, too."

"You do?"

"Yes, but you go first."

"No, you."

"No."

"You're not pregnant?" He froze.

"No." And she hated that reaction of his. But this time she was too excited to let it bother her.

"W-h-e-e-e-y-o-u."

"Now come on, tell me for the love of god."

"I called in sick, and I stayed home all day. And--" He paused for dramatic effect. "I finished the book."

"The whole thing?"

"The whole thing."

"Oh, thanks be to god. That's only brilliant." She started jumping up and down.

"But wait," he said stopping them. "What's yours?"

"The gallery. They sold... Two more of my

paintings," she cheered. Eight hundred and fifty dollars. Each!"

"Yaaah! Yippee!" he roared. "We're making it."

"IT'S A BEAUTIFUL BOOK, NOAH," Nora said early the next morning after she sat up all night reading it. Only a faint silver streak of dawn seeped in through the split in the drapes as Noah stirred and awakened. "You really did it. I have such empathy for the characters. I can feel their presence as if they were alive. You did that. You got right in there with them. And that ending is only too moving. I could scarcely bear it."

"You really mean that?"

"Yes. I'd never say it if it weren't that way, don't you know. I'm so thrilled with you. This is one of the happiest mornings of my life. Right up there with the one in Boston after you first made love to me." She hugged him and looked into his eyes, as the light of joy flooded the room.

TWO DAYS LATER, Noah called Jason Blackwell, one of the country's leading literary agents, who resided at William Morris. Noah had first met the stylish, middle-aged and independently wealthy Blackwell while covering the posh ski resorts of St. Moritz and had renewed his acquaintance numerous times at BP gatherings.

"Of course, I want to see your manuscript. Have you shown it to any other agents?"

'No. You asked me to show it to you first."

"Well yes. I'm most anxious. Especially after that sensational *New Yorker* story. I must tell you that shows true promise. It was satin. Pure satin, I tell you. But with a powerful bite"

For a moment, Noah trembled. God, he's thinking it's going to be more of the same. I've aspired to a *Last Picture Show* of sorts and he's anticipating an acerbic version of *Breakfast At Tiffany's*. But then he instantly stopped himself. He had that much confidence in this version of his novel to feel certain it would make it, that any agent worth his salt would see this.

"Okay. I'll send it over today."

"Terrific. It will take a couple of weeks to get to it, because I'm a bit backlogged."

Noah hung up and felt delightful chills rise up his spine and encircle his brain.

18

IT WAS DUSK WHEN THEY ARRIVED at Le Bourget for the first leg of their long awaited honeymoon that September of 1967. Because of Nora's Aer Lingus connection they were accorded free tickets to Shannon where they transferred to a flight to France. As their taxi sped into Paris, the lights came sprinkling on, bathing the city, accentuating all its romantic hues.

They stayed at the Hotel San Regis at 12 Rue Jean-Goujon on the Right Bank. Noah had chosen it for them, as he had Paris. Although very romantic, the place had the elegance of a grand hotel with its marble lobby and its lavish 17th and 18th-century antiques. Carole had suggested it, and Noah was delighted, especially with the suite. They filled it with a passion and rapture that made everything around them even more radiant than it already was. Nora wanted them to stroll about the city so Noah could absorb the feel of the writers' haunts. But he insisted on the Grand Galerie at the Louvre and the Musee du Jeu de Paume and Orangerie for Nora's sake.

Hours passed before they moved on to the Tuileries, which by then were catching the spread of a salmon sunset. They strolled through the gardens, paused to kiss as Noah whispered a line from Joyce's poetry: *"Play on, invisible harps, unto love."* The flowers, the fountains, the long gravely paths and the cool lawns all came together in a watery bleed that absorbed them.

STANDING ON THE DECK of the *Naomh Eanna* on its way to the Aran Islands, watching the glittering roll of silvery green waves, they held each other and once again felt the fusion of their souls. This was after a few mercifully quick days in Dublin, when Nora felt her family was swallowing Noah once again while ignoring her.

On Inishmore, a jarvey's horse cart jaunted them to Breda's manor house where they had first met. And that afternoon, they walked down to Kilmurvey Strand and the dazzling sea. It was another of those forever days befalling the Arans and western Ireland, crystal halcyon days when time stopped. Days so clear you could see all the way across the vast sweep of sea to the mauve hills of Connemara.

"I just wish we had the time to find something here this year."

"Sure what could we do. We've scarcely any money available."

"No, but to settle on an area, explore the possibilities. I'd love it here."

"Ah sure it's so remote Noah. How could you ever manage it?"

"I wish you'd stop talking like that. It's exciting me all over again. There's so much beauty here it causes a lovely pain, an ache that-- that you can't bear to lose," he went on gazing out over the sea as if to absorb it all and wish it into eternity. "Sometimes I wonder if any of us can fully appreciate it. Can ever live up to it. Can ever be worthy—God it just sets me ablaze with the desire to write as I know it does you to paint. If not right here, somewhere in this country." These were the words she so wanted to hear. But as she watched his eyes go misty, she realized he had drifted to another plane. Soon she wondered if he weren't doubting himself so she chanced: "What of New York, Noah?"

"What?" he asked in puzzlement after he'd pulled himself back.

"When you're here, it's as if New York doesn't exist."

"Well it doesn't. When I'm here, I want to get the most out of this existence that I possibly can. It's the same there. Getting the very most you can wherever you are."

"Of course, you realize you can't be after having both."

"What do you mean? Can't have both? Ah Nora, don't be settling on that philosophy. You can have both. And even then some. No one's going to stop us."

"Then we must be about to be making history. How can anyone live in two places at the same time?"

"Not at the exact same moment. But during the same time period--yes!" When she shook her head in utter amazement, he continued. "It's just a matter of living part of the year there and part of the year here. And--living life to the fullest in each place."

Nora just stared at him.

"What? What's wrong?" he asked.

"Nothing."

"There is. There has to be."

"Only that half the dream has just washed out to sea."

"Where are you getting that from?"

"I guess it all fits together though," she went on struggling to speak. "I'm an eejit for not having guessed.

No. That's not so. I'm a bloody fool. I kept sweeping it away from me mind. Hiding it from my own eyes yet. And for so long."

"What in god's name?"

"All the way back to when I first came to America. To the night of Truman's ball, when we were at Carole's dinner party. Those words keep coming back: *Wouldn't you just die for these things?* And everything that's happened since has proven it."

"Why do I suddenly feel you think I've betrayed you?"

"Noah, I've shared things all my life. And I've had quite enough of it. Our dream was to be alone in the world together. The cottage beside the sea. Since then you've gone off and concocted your own version of that dream and it's developed a bleedin' wanderlust. My fear is that some part of you will always want to be the darling of the beautiful people."

"No. You haven't a clue after all this time. Forget the feckin' beautiful people. They aren't so beautiful. All I want is *money*. Because money will set us free."

"Noah, it will never set us free. We have our freedom now."

"Oh but we're going to have so much more. The cottage is only the beginning."

two

ON A CRISP OCTOBER afternoon, they returned to Gramercy Park. Scarcely able to contain himself, Noah had allowed his imagination free reign. Before yielding to the inevitable cascade of accolades, he insisted they seize upon the glory of the moment and go for an exhilarating stroll through their park. Passing the bronze statue of Edwin Booth, it became the symbol of the fame that would soon be his. As they drifted hand in hand, down past them tumbled gust-hurled waves of fan and pear-shaped leaves, skittering over their feet and across the darkening lanes to collect in voluminous banks beside the black-iron fencings. They were not the same as the spiky fall leaves of what now seemed his distant yearning youth, leaves rendering their life's blood. Instead these were golden luminescent heralds, the like of which he had never seen. Leaves as beacons that lit their path with blinding, ecstatic light.

2

"YES, I DID HAVE A READ of your manuscript, Noah,"
Jason Blackwell told Noah when he phoned him the next
morning.

"And what did you think?"

"Well, I certainly feel you're a real writer. No question."

"But?" Noah asked as his blood turned cold.

"My initial reaction is that even with such beautiful
writing I question whether this is the vehicle to launch your
career as a novelist."

"How do you mean?" Noah felt nauseous.

"I'm not saying it's not publishable. But it's such a
personal novel and so rural. It would have been better if
you'd waited to do this as a third or fourth project. Once
your fictional work and your name is really known, then
this sort of thing, which is more of a memoir, could be
important."

"A memoir? So you wonder if you can sell it then?" By
now he could feel his face blanche from the shock and
depression. He only hoped everyone else at the office was
too busy to notice.

"Well I'm willing to give it a try." By now Noah was
only hearing bits of what he was saying.

--sometimes fads and trends. You never know—

--some editors might be interested but--

"Then I won't get much out of it regardless," Noah

finally picked up as he stared at a late payment notice from the antique furniture shop. It had arrived on his desk while he was away.

--publishing is all businessmen today—no Maxwell Perkins anymore

-- not a major money maker if that's what you're getting at

Shit, he thought. Shit, shit. Automatically he wadded up the bill and tossed it into the basket. Panic was rising and beads of sweat were sprouting on his forehead.

"But I have to tell you there's great hope here." Suddenly Noah perked and was listening to his every word again. "Yet I'd be remiss not to say, it would have been an enormous plus for your career, if you had developed that *New Yorker* short story into a novel. That would have been a blockbuster. One that would have set the publishing world and the public on its ear. You could still do it."

"And just shelve this one?"

"It's a credible scenario. I mean if you're worried about losing your job it might be well worth it. What's important here is that the market is literally crying out for a masked expose. Very few have access to these people who have the cognizance and can write as well as you can."

"But I haven't experienced enough of that world yet to do a whole book."

"Well you will have soon enough. Another six months and some copious notes and you could plow right through one. And I predict it would be a gold mine."

"Aren't you forgetting that Capote's thinking along those lines. I thought he'd already signed a contract with Random House."

"Oh he'll never come through for them. In the end he'll see those people mean too much to him."

"So what you're really saying is that you don't want to try to sell this property."

"No. I'll try. I believe the book is honest. The style is rich." But his words came with little enthusiasm.

"Well at least it's something, maybe."

"Maybe is right. And it's a big maybe. But keep in mind what I told you. You can do it. I know you can."

"Sure."

"WELL AT LEAST I'VE GOT FOUR COPIES of this manuscript, so we'll be in great shape if there's a paper shortage," Noah said as he sat in his wing chair in front of their dwindling fire and wolfed down a rare second martini.

"Oh Noah, don't be like this. Sure you don't know that it won't sell. He was just being cautious, that's all."

"Cautious! Some caution. He even trotted out the standard--there are no more Maxwell Perkins--speech that every college freshman gets, as though I were some thick eejit. Nora, the bloody thing is going to fuck out on me again."

"Well now, I don't believe that for one minute. That book is just too good. And if he does come back and says he can't sell it, don't you dare stand there and take it. You go show it to someone else, because one thing would be certain. He would be wrong. Very wrong."

"Oh Nora, I think maybe you believe too much in me."

"No. There's no such thing."

As he sat solemnly a Louis MacNeice verse suddenly sprung to mind. *Sunlight on the garden...hardens...and grows cold.*

"Look, let's just go to bed so we can be together," she said coming up behind his chair to massage his shoulders. "That'll make it right."

"Yeah."

3

"MY DEAR, YOUR WORK IS ABSOLUTELY MARVELOUS. Just the sheer energy of its beauty would be enough. But you capture an infinite quality that I haven't seen before...at least not in this age," Jeffrey Allingwood, one of the decade's leading art curators, delighted to Nora on that November night of her opening at the Winsor de Caine. He was one of the early arrivals and professed: "I'd heard some strong rumors about this showing. The art world is so small and gossipy, you know. But this is really quite amazing. And I never give an artist my first impressions at an opening. Never."

As Noah stood watching from a distance, he thought *amazing* was really the right word. Not only was there a sizeable collection amassed from Dublin but of late came an outpouring of landscape oils composed from her early prelim sketches. As if this weren't enough, she'd pulled together several vivid portraits of Gramercy Park characters along with an array of richly colored floral watercolors.

While Jeffrey Allingwood, dressed in elegant bespoke clothing and with perfectly groomed silver hair, gushed away, Noah thought--the decision-maker. Sort of the Bennett Cerf of the art world. He even looked like Bennett Cerf. Would that he were, Noah's mind raced. And would that he were saying those things about my work. God, fuck. There I've gone and done it. I bloody well hate myself for thinking this way. And so he slipped away for another scotch-and-soda.

When he returned from the bar, the gallery was bustling with art devotees, all encircling Nora, lavishing their praise. Nora, with her lustrous long brown hair held in place by a pearl enamel headband, wore a sapphire chiffon dress that seductively caressed her knees. She had accented it at the throat by the single rope of snowy pearls interspersed with inky drops of lapis lazuli that he had once purchased for her at Saks. As such though unduly nervous, she was more glamorous than anyone in the room. God, she was only vibrant, he thought. And then he felt a severe pang of jealousy that she was away from him and amidst the chic crowd. He guessed that was the way she felt when she attended all those lavish parties with him. Well, tit for tat.

When her panic began to ease, Nora became dazzled in a way she'd never thought possible. *Yes it is true, I could never be attracted to this lot, but god I could be a good bit more than partial to their flahulach words of praise.* And reaping heaps of it was Noah's portrait which Julian and the rest of the Winsor staff insisted she include because they were certain it would astound the critics. Fighting against this, she finally gave in when they promised to honor her plea not to sell it under any circumstance.

"How are you doing?" she asked Noah when the crowd finally parted so she could join him for a moment.

"Fine. Great," he replied grinning and struggling not to make it look like a put-on.

She glanced down at his drink. "What's got you onto that stuff?"

"Jesus, does it show?"

"No," she insisted but was bewildered. "It's just that I thought you really didn't care for spirits that much, and this champagne is only gorgeous."

"I'm sorry. I really am." And he scratched his forehead.

"No, it's all right. It's just that I think your uncomfortable being here. I don't want to see you unhappy. And I think you must be."

"No, no, I'm thrilled. I'm proud. I really am. It's well-- It's just that I feel I shouldn't be here. I-- I guess."

"Ah Noah, if you feel that way, then I shouldn't be here either."

"Don't be ridiculous." And his voice grew more intense. "I want you to be here. You should be. I'm sorry. I've no right to cause you bother. This is your evening."

"Take it easy pet," Nora whispered, taking his hand and holding it. "It'll come round. It will, don't you know."

WHILE NO ONE OF HIGHER EMINENCE than Jeffrey Allingwood appeared that night, the die had been cast. The faint flicker of a new star appeared in the eastern heavens of the art world. Word traveled fast. As Jeffrey had said--it's a small, gossipy world. Two days later, a *New York Times* art critic visited the gallery. And within a week, a brief, but electrifying review appeared.

It is very rare that even an established artist touches the core of existence in an entire collection of paintings. Well, Nora Mason reaches this enormous achievement in her very first showing. Indeed, the Winsor de Caine Gallery is most fortunate to have discovered such a prolific artist. Her Irish landscapes express the full range of life's poetry. There isn't an unmeaning brush stroke in her work, and the same can be said for her unusual portraits and watercolors. After all the Popism, Minimalism and the Happenings of these Sixties, isn't it a joy to see what life is really all about once again? This is the new direction of art. And Nora Mason is most definitely someone to watch closely.

Noah read the review to her over their breakfast table

in the kitchen, and although she was thrilled, she subdued her feelings. If only the *Times* would be writing of Noah's novel in the same manner, she thought. Then they'd both be over the moon. How painful it has to be for him now. After all, he's toiled so dutifully for his craft. It just isn't right, sure it's not.

Within a week, five more of her paintings sold, including two to Jeffrey Allingwood. Altogether she netted nearly four thousand dollars. Already the directors of the Winsor de Caine, who were being touted for advancing the cause of women artists through Nora, set about planning a late April or early May showing of her work. At the same time, they requested that she increase her output of portraits and watercolors. She was on the verge of telling Noah when Jason Blackwell called and told him Simon & Schuster had just rejected his novel. "But I'll keep trying," Blackwell said.

HE WAS STILL TRYING as Christmas approached that year. By now Noah's panic was on a par with his debts. Of course Nora knew they existed, but as to the amounts, he kept them hidden. Now he would have to deal with Christmas. Gifts for Nora, gifts for his mother. Nora insisted that they "go easy this year. A few gifts for your mother, right enough, but only one for me. A small one."

"That's a good idea," he agreed, much to her relief. But small to Noah meant small in size. Tiffany size.

What would he do? I've got to try to hold back on

these charges at least until something happens with that goddamn book or at least until I get a raise. But then the solution struck him. It wouldn't be so bad if he took a low interest bank loan. He could easily get one with his job. So off he went to First National City and borrowed two thousand dollars. Then on to Tiffany's for a delicate white gold necklace embedded with a sprinkle of blue sapphires for Nora and next to Bloomingdale's for a few select pieces of Limoges for his mother. She had once so admired them in a magazine and had marveled at how they would look in her one treasured piece of furniture, a Victorian china cabinet. And so went over half the loan.

As for Nora once she'd purchased a few inexpensive gifts for her family, she wanted to do something grand for Noah, not only because he was always choosing such gorgeous items for her but because she knew how lofty it would make him feel. So she took the money from her last sale, went to Brooks and bought him a classic double-breasted camel hair topcoat and matching color cashmere turtleneck. Just imagining how they would look on him was rousing her till she felt herself flush.

On Christmas Eve a ferocious upstate blizzard resulted in the cancellation of their flight and the holiday at his mother's. So next to their tree and by the roaring fire, they exchanged gifts. "I might have known," she sighed at the sight of the glittery sapphires.

"So might I," he delighted.

"God you are only gorgeous in those," she gasped. "I

want to tear everything off you."

"Please do. Just don't rip them." And that on-going, luscious love bout wiped out all of his angst and set them blissfully aglow at least for the time being.

4

"WHERE'S YOUR CHARMING WIFE," called Mark Lowellsworth, a kingpin of business and finance magazines, who like Oliver Wilton had recently inherited a publishing empire from his old money family and was becoming a well-known art connoisseur.

"Yes, didn't you bring her along Noah?" pursued Sid Rudell, one of Wall Street's leading new and youthful brokerage wheeler-dealers.

"No," said Noah as they boarded the January junket flight to the Bahamas to herald the opening of the Paradise Island Hotel and Casino organized by Serge Obolensky, former Russian prince and husband of Alice Astor, now bon vivant and publicist extraordinaire. He was herding over four hundred of the world's most beautiful people from Europe and down from the United States on no less than three chartered jets. And Noah was assigned coverage for *FCD.* "She's pretty swamped with work these days," Noah added of Nora.

"I should say after that fantastic review in the *Times,*" Lowellsworth went on. "I nipped in to see her work at the Winsor and let me tell you it's something else."

When he thought Noah was out of earshot or maybe when he thought he was still within earshot, he whispered to Sid Rudell: "Maybe he thought she'd swamp him too, if he brought her along. Too bad such a talent is married to that blasphemer."

As Noah sank in his seat, he realized that Mark and Sid were just two among many of the super-rich who were pressing his buttons a little more forcefully each time they met him. Just as Carole had said they would.

God what wouldn't I do to be wealthy right now, he thought. Then I wouldn't give a damn. Not a good goddamn about any of them. They're such empty fools. But what he couldn't bear was how they were exuding that special aura that buoyed them above all others—that rara avis of freedoms that only money imparts. Damn I must have it or at least feel I have it. Only a few months ago, when they made me part of their world, the scent was like osmosis. But now even in their midst there's this impermeable wall, he thought. And how unbearable it is to live without such precious oxygen once you've inhaled it. I can only imagine it tantamount to losing some indispensable drug, the unendurable pain of withdrawal.

SATURDAY NIGHT BOASTED the big dress dance at the faux-lavish hotel, set afloat on seas of Piper-Heidsieck. There was the Meyer Davis band for the old folks and a rock group dressed in tin foil for the young. "You're looking marvelous," everyone cried over the music to everyone else. The women sent themselves into ecstasies, gasping their usual clichés: "Darling, your dress is sensational." "It's stunning." "It's absolutely gloriously you." But few had brightened to the occasion more than Noah. He had filed his column via phone, air expressed the film from a hired photographer and then taken some sun that afternoon. As he did, a crowd of European BP--who by now were avid *FCD* overseas subscribers--had swirled around him, charming him with their lavish attention. Perhaps they hadn't heard of his *New Yorker* escapade. But no, better just think that it was the beginning of a new acceptance--a renewal, a reinstatement. This heady thought had reconnected him with such a supply of great exhilaration that it transported him to the bar for an early start on the champagne. By the time the party began, he was blissfully high. As he drifted over to a less crowded bar for more high, the rock band punched out the Monkees latest *Daydreamer Believer*. My life is not just daydreams, he told himself. It does have substance. It will surface as a reality and become golden. It will. It just has to.

He collected a fresh glass of froth, downed it and thought of heightening his euphoria with a little roulette. Just as he was about to head off to the casino, a voice bubbled seductively from behind: "It's a beautiful evening, Noah." When he turned, he immediately recognized the woman in the silky pink, slip-strap gown. She was the overly familiar whorish heiress Gloria Hamilton Collins. Before she would have turned his stomach, but tonight it was different. Being as high strata moneyed as she was, he convinced himself she was a sort of spokesperson welcoming him back into the American BP fold. His lifeline as it were. "Beautiful," he agreed savoring an even greater rejuvenating buzz.

"It seems so tragic to be drinking champagne inside on a night like this," she whispered as she tossed her flow of long blonde hair over her shoulder. Then she licked her frosted lips, sipped some more and smiled seductively. But even though she was most likely in her late thirties such wiles could scarcely conceal her overly calculated glamour, probably siphoned from numerous makeovers. It was at this point that part of his brain suddenly came to life looming the warning to elude her but the champagne was swiftly fighting it.

"Let's go outside. It's too warm in here anyway." With that she reached behind the bar, grabbed an unopened magnum of the Piper and began pulling him toward an exit.

"No I don't think so," he struggled in defense. "I should be in here catching more stuff for my column."

"Oh come on. We won't stay long. Besides I'm sure there's others of us out there. And that would be part of your story too."

So they walked out flutes and bottle in hand and, after they kicked off their shoes with Noah stumbling out of his, they continued down the beach until the sounds of party mixed and were finally drowned by the lap of waves. Still all along, caution kept returning--*lamb to the slaughter.*

"Look we probably should be heading back."

"We just got out here. Drink some more champagne before we go." And she poured him a goodly amount from the newly opened bottle which hastened to douse the lamb analogy and led him back to savoring the thoughts of money and well-being and that sumptuous dream. As his vision was drawn skyward to the opalescent galaxies, he began to lose his balance. "I think I'm getting a bit tipsy."

"No. Take off that formal jacket," she whispered anchoring the magnum and their flutes in the sand. Then she slid it over his shoulders and down his back. "And you look like you're strangling to death in that tie." She gave the bow a pull until it came undone. Then she opened his collar button. Suddenly the gust of sea breezes made him feel so sensuous and otherworldly.

"Once I used to take off all my clothes and walk along the edge of the sea sipping champagne. You catch moonbeams in your glass. Then you drink them," she sighed as she refilled their glasses. "They're magical you know. They make the connection between the gods and goddesses. Aphrodite and Apollo."

Noah coasted along with the drift of her words and the wash of champagne.

"My first husband taught me to do that on the Cote d'Azur. Then when we got tipsy, we'd pour champagne all over each other's naked bodies and make outrageous love."

"Where'd he go anyway?" Noah vaguely remembered

asking.

"Who knows. Someone so wild and sublime. But the rich don't appreciate what they've got. At least not in time. They're always looking for something more. Fearful of impending tedium, I guess. How mad I was to lose all that fire. I want to have it again, I say."

As Noah stumbled backwards and dropped his newly retrieved glass, she grabbed him by the arms. Then to his disbelief he realized she had already progressed to peeling off his shirt and was now trying to rid him of his trousers. "No we can't do this," he insisted as he attempted fighting his way out of his trance while she proceeded to slide the straps from her shoulders and let the silky material fall away from her fully aroused breasts. She stood there beckoning him in the nude except for a skimpy pair of panties she was about to remove. And somehow in this lunacy he had been reduced to his boxers while suddenly realizing a rapidly growing erection.

"Ummm, what have we here?" a voice cleaved the tender night air. "A society heiress doing relief work for the needy?"

"Jesus Christ," Noah gasped still struggling to gain some control.

Gloria scrambled to pull on her dress. "You ass. What are you doing here?"

"Why I was looking for you, dear wife," the voice went on. "These little social missions could be fraught with danger, you know."

"Shit," Noah muttered as he struggled to re-dress himself. "Maybe the whole thing is a nightmare. I so bloody wish."

"Oh, who have we here?" the voice continued. "Why it's the newspaper boy. What are you up to, gathering material for a special feature?"

"Shut up, Bruce. You're a fine one to talk," she said, grabbing his arm and pulling him away. From the moonlight, Noah through blurry vision could make out Bruce Collins, Gloria's womanizing racing car husband.

As Gloria continued to pull him up the beach, he turned and stared at Noah's boxers while shouting back: "What are you going to call this one Noah—Social Uprising?" Then he burst into laughter.

"S-h-u-t u-p," Gloria roared, whacking him on the back and then retrieving her shoes.

Noah at this point collapsed onto the sand relieved Bruce hadn't wasted him. But then the whole event struck him--and that was far worse. "Holy hell. What did I do? Jesus, help me."

He spent the entire night lying on the bed fully dressed asking himself over and over, how could I have gotten into this mess? Jesus. Bloody booze and money hunger did this. And then he kept seeing Nora's tormented face. "God, I love you. I love you so much. I didn't mean this. I just want to be with you. Always." What if she finds out? What if it ends up in the *Daily News*? I'll deny it. I'll say it was made up. But I can't lie to her. I never have. God, stop thinking this way. I've got to get up and file a column before I get fired on top of all this.

"I'M GOING TO TRY TO KEEP THIS QUIET," Carole Dawson told Noah when surprisingly she joined him on the flight back to New York.

"How do you know about it?" Noah asked in a state of total shock. He could feel all his blood draining as he froze in his seat.

"Oh I was the one who put an end to it all."

"What?" he gasped.

"Fortunately I flew in for the dinner last night as a favor to Serge and of course the opportunity to encourage more funds for my charities. I just happened to catch eye of you leaving with her. I would have had no hesitation in stopping you right in your tracks, but for the crowd I was with."

"Well certainly I should have acted on my apercu and stopped myself—instead of letting the champagne act for me." And he shook his head in disgust.

"Oh I could see she was seizing the opportunity. And she could have done incredible damage to you."

"But why? Just because she had the hots for me?"

"You know I don't like to use vulgar language, but when it comes to Gloria and her like, there's nothing else. She's a common slut resting on the laurels—and the cash flow—of the Hamilton family. The danger with her and her crowd is the undertow."

"What does that mean?"

"It has to do with their despicable nature. You know the only reason she and her kind were at that Newport party you covered was because John is well aware of their old money bloodlines. But of course he can't see that they're the dregs of that world." Then she suddenly added with a snap. "Or maybe by then he was becoming so dissolute he was attracted to it."

"But what does that have to do with me?"

"Everything," she replied looking directly at his eyes. "Oh Noah, you have to be so careful when it comes to people like that. Through all their glitz—the beauties are really the beasts." And she stopped to let that register before she went on. "I think of them as bored profligates. The whole crowd of them. Living for the next day's thrill—or havoc— or whatever. The wrecking crew. They take great glee in making mincemeat of others."

"But what do they want from it?"

"Spite. Malice might be a better word. They hate anyone with brilliance and vitality. So that's reason enough to knock you down a few pegs. But there's more. There's Nora with her talent. And then there's the sport of disrupting a very happy marriage and a truly beautiful couple. They love to get their claws into something like this, because they have nothing of the sort. They could never arrive at happiness if they tried. They don't even know what it is. So they're sorely jealous if they see someone they think has it."

"Well that's all pretty frightening and much worse than I'd ever imagined," he said as he shivered with the thought of what might still happen. He was almost too afraid to ask: "By the way, how did you put an end to last night's craziness?"

"As soon as I could break away from everyone, I went into the casino and had a word with Bruce Collins that out-and-out philandering stud. I told him in no uncertain terms that unless he went to the beach and snatched his wife away from her planned malefaction he would live to regret a number of his criminal wrongdoings. And I went on to mention fixing certain specific sporting events, and the names of those very much in the know who would back my words. So that's the reason he blustered right out to you. Then after their return I coldly confronted Gloria and told her point blank that unless she complied with my wish for complete silence, I would gladly reveal certain secrets that she unquestionably would not want known least she risk the strong possibility of family disownment. So I can tell you that was that."

"Wow—that just takes my breath away. I don't know how I can ever thank you enough for all your continued guidance and actions. Why would you do all this for me I'm such an idiotic fool?"

"Well you're not and don't think that way. It takes time to know all these people and where they're coming from. We were innocent like that once. You know I met John on his furlough when I was working for *Time* in the research department. It was during the early war years, and I came from the proverbial poor-as-a-church-mouse background. But that didn't bother him then. He was such a proud soldier. It was all that mattered. That and the fact that we were deeply in love. He was such a determined man. He saved something like half his battalion on the Italian front and was given the Bronze Star. Even though I was far removed from their sort, the Dawson family approved of our marriage because I had urged him not to re-enlist. Instead he became a partner and a lightening-rod in his family's architectural dynasty. A year later, we had a son and lived a life of pure happiness."

"Well what happened then?"

"You know our son was growing up in the same tenacious mold." And she paused and rather anxiously flicked her rope of pearls. Her eyes dimmed and Noah expected tears, but they didn't come. "Peter was his name. I don't speak it very often. He was our only child. You're a good bit older now than he was then, but you're the perfect image of him. Even as a boy he had the same *élan vital* that you have. Do you like sports?"

"Well yes. I like to swim and we ski a little."

"So did he. Well skiing more than a little." Her eyes, her whole demeanor darkened and she sat forward with her hands clasped. "He wanted to outdo everyone on the slopes. Of course, his father encouraged him. It was his joy to see him excel. He'd just turned eighteen. He had a girl who truly loved him as much as I once loved John, and certainly as much as you love Nora. Well, we'd all gone out to Sun Valley for the Christmas holidays. I didn't want us to go. I had all these ominous feelings. He took too many chances. He reveled in his father's war heroism stories and that just nourished his will to be valiant at all costs." She paused shaking her head and Noah could see the flicker of anger. "I should have done something instead of listening to John. But what good is *should have*?" And she fell silent as if she were trying to answer her question but then gave up. "We were skiing the lower slopes. But Peter insisted on doing the higher ones. He came down and wasn't prepared for the jump. He broke his neck." With that she paused and looked directly at Noah. "So you see, I want to protect you. The way I didn't--" Then this time her eyes did fill with tears.

"Oh Carole, I'm so sorry," he said. "What can I ever say?"

"Nothing," she replied as she pulled herself together. "It's just so special to have you around. Like a gift from god really. You can't imagine how happy we were in those days when Peter was alive. And what a brilliant mind he had with that wondrous spirit to match. Why he could have done anything, been anything. But at that age-- *a boy's will is the winds will* as Longfellow wrote. When he went everything changed."

Now he knew what it was that had marked her. The chilling horror of her agony came right through. "God, how horribly cruel."

"I often wonder if money might have been the poison,"

"How do you mean?"

"If we hadn't had it, we wouldn't have been going to Sun Valley. Certainly not in those days when it was only a playground for the wealthy snobs we abhorred. So you see what I'm saying—from everything it left us with nothing."

5

"GOD, I'M SO GLAD to be back," he said crushing her in his arms, trying to dispel all the horrors of the previous days through the return of their passion. But there was something wrong, it was more one-sided than he could ever remember. "What is it?" he said as he pulled away from their kiss and was caught up with the panic that somehow she might know.

"Nothing," she whispered, and her sadness was cutting. He stroked her face: "What?"

"Well—I'd have to be telling you. It's just becoming so unbearable, your being away like this. And now straight off you'll have to be going out again tonight."

"Oh," he sighed relief and shook his head. "No I don't. I figured an angle. I felt so miserable being away from you that when we landed at Kennedy I called Wilton and told them I had a bug and I couldn't cover that damn shit social thing tonight."

"You did?" she delighted. And lost in the return of her sunshine, he cupped her face and they began feverishly kissing and then stripping. "Wait," he said. "I've got to shower. I stink from the plane."

As he hopped into the tub, he hoped that the shower would cleanse him of the shame he hadn't shed. For a moment, he stood there letting the hiss of the spray tranquilize him. Then as he began shampooing, he heard the shower curtain slide open. "Poor fella, I want you to figure another angle as well," she whispered taking hold of his shoulders, and he could feel her breath skitter down his back followed by the heat of her lush breasts as they pressed against him.

"What's that?" he managed as she took his breath away.

She turned him around to face her and as always he was awed by her naked beauty. "I want you to figure a way you can angle that bold fat cock into me while we're standing here."

He smiled. "Easy," he said and lifted her onto it. "Now what?"

"Oh," she gasped. "Drive me crazy and never stop."

And that he did. But even this didn't take away his agonizing over the Saturday night crime. Somewhere in the middle of their rapture and without stopping, he said: "We have to make things right."

"WHAT DID YOU MEAN?" Nora asked when they finished toweling each other.

As he pulled on a fresh pair of boxers and she a silk robe, he said: "Well come on let's go sit down." Taking her by the hand, he led her into the living room. There with his arm around her, they sat on their Stickley sofa facing the park as he summoned determination. "You were right," he dived right in. "They are too much. And I am giving too much of myself to all that."

"Did something bad happen?" she asked already worrying for him.

"Well nothing good," he replied looking into her eyes. "I just realized how much I'm taking away from us. Somehow I have to fit the pieces back together."

"Well that could only be all the better for us," she said with some relief that such perception might finally be after catching hold of him. "You know I had this feeling while you were away. Well I've had it before. But it was stronger this time."

"What was it?" he asked driven by thoughts of second sight, sixth sense.

"Well god Noah, you know how I am. How completely fulfilled I am when you're inside me. When you're not, even though we're together like now, there's still some feeling of emptiness. I guess as a writer you would say—of being bereft."

"I do know that of you. And being away doesn't help." He squeezed her tighter.

"I guess it has something to do with the sense of loss that used to catch hold of me in my childhood. That bloody feeling when I was in bed in the dark. That they didn't care. I used to wonder if maybe they wished me dead. How could they not care if they loved me at all? But you see I started dreaming that crazy lunacy again. Except it wasn't lunacy.

But it shouldn't be coming to my mind anymore. Anyway I reached over in bed in my drowsy sleep and you weren't there and it all got doubly worse. I know you have to do these things, but I think I'm starting to go half mad when you're away now."

He hugged her and kissed her and snuggled her against him while he let himself realize that she was clairvoyant, that all of this was coming forth because she too sensed dangers were worsening. Oh god, he just wanted to go on making love and avoid facing this. "Maybe I should get out of Wilton and try for another job. *Harpers, Fortune, Esquire*," he said scarcely aware he was speaking aloud.

"Could you?" she asked brightening.

"I don't know." And he was struggling to hide his trepidation. "I'm only beginning to think about it. It could be a strong possibility though. Regardless I have to make some positive moves."

Then the phone rang jarring them from such thoughts. It was Jason Blackwell. "I thought maybe we were onto something at Morrow. One of the editors, albeit green, really liked your manuscript. That's why it took so long. It went to two other editors."

"And they didn't like it," Noah dejectedly finished Blackwell's statement.

"Well it was a nibble. So I guess I'll try again even though I'm doubtful of the outcome. But I truly hope you're working on that society project."

"MAYBE YOU SHOULD go ahead with that other book while he's trying to sell this one," Nora said the next evening as she worked developing sketches from some Polaroids she'd mustered the courage to take in the grimier, crime fringed areas of Time Square. They were of drug addled souls, despondent to the point of mindlessness. And this had been a daring challenge to explore new working areas for her spring show while at the same time escaping her sense of loss in the absence of Noah.

"You wouldn't mind? I mean knowing how you hate those people," Noah said as he sat drinking a scotch by their dimming fire with Simon & Garfunkel's *Sounds of Silence* playing in the background.

"Well no. Not if it would sell like he thinks it would."

"I probably have enough material by now to do it. But god it would take months and months and then he'd have to sell it before we saw any real money."

"But by then he could have sold this one and as you said you could go ahead and get work at one of those other magazines," she went on.

"But would I have the heart to start in on another whole book? I just got so depressed after hearing from him yesterday." Then he rose from the shadows of his wing chair and headed back to the bar table to collect another scotch, saying as he went: "And don't give me that things-will-happen-soon speech again. I just feel so bloody low." Then he looked over at Nora and saw how quickly, how positively she worked. There wasn't a moment's doubt or hesitation.

She knew exactly what she wanted to achieve. And she did it. Did it and got results. You could smell success in the scent of her oils.

"I wish you'd stop degrading yourself," she said as she put down her charcoal pencil and turned from her easel to look at him. "And that means drinking that shite that you hate. It's like you're trying to poison yourself. I know things are hard on you now. But you've got to be accepting the fact that it does take time."

He looked at her and his eyes smarted. "Couldn't prove it by you."

"That hurts. That really hurts." And tears sprang to her eyes.

"I'm sorry. I'm really sorry," he said as he poured more scotch into his tumbler and then took a deep drink. "Damn it all, I so want you to have reason to be proud of me," he suddenly blurted.

"I must be a right bloody failure in conveying my feelings," she snapped back drying her tears. "I couldn't be more proud of you if I tried."

"But how could you be proud of someone who isn't successful?"

"How do you measure success, Noah?"

"Money!" he roared in a complete state of rage as she jumped back from her work. She had never heard that tone from him, and it startled her.

THE WORD ECHOED through his sleep that night

and carried with him into the next day and right through the benefit luncheon at the St. Regis Roof. He thought of all those moneyed people as afterwards he wandered uptown. They really were little more than hollow bores emanating airs of pompous grandeur, he told himself once again. Why wouldn't he begin to put an end to this? Use all the material he was gathering by the day to write the book Jason so wanted while at the same time setting off to a *Newsweek*, a *New York* or whatever? Change is good, he kept telling himself. Maybe great.

Before he knew it, he had drifted into The Bar at the Sherry Netherland and was ordering a martini while clinging to such thoughts as he struggled for determination. But then he glanced down the length of the magnificent, near-empty bar. There he saw a man and a woman, probably in their early thirties, who were the personification of the golden couple. Tall, lean and lightly tanned with dreamy yet piercing eyes and well-groomed flaxen hair, they wore their elegant European suitings with the perfect degree of masculine and feminine nonchalance that effused the aura of immense wealth. He felt the blood rush through him the same as it did when he became sexually aroused. His brow began to sprout droplets while the yearning grew more powerful, more irresistible. He blinked and blinked again until the couple became the Masons—Noah and Nora. Now he knew he had to make the money, make the fame. God he loved her so much. But he didn't deserve her if he couldn't make them into what this couple represented. Suddenly he was in turmoil.

6

"SOMETHING'S GOING ON over at Random House. It's gone to a second editor," Jason Blackwell phoned to tell Noah at *FCD* two painfully long weeks later after he'd collected yet another rejection slip and more reminders of late amounts due on his furniture. "Now I don't want to get your hopes up. But I got a leak that the first editor really liked it. So start saying your prayers."

Noah's mind pounced on these words and drew them into his soul, nourishing it. The prayers were about to be answered, he thought as he hung up and crossed himself. So elated was he after these months of blight that on the spot he decided to do something positive that would intensify his high. And off he went to Bloomingdale's to refurnish some of his mother's house. "She'll be so thrilled with these pieces. Especially when she knows they came from this store," he exuded to the sales lady as he charged them on his Bloomingdale's plate.

After that, he zipped across town to Bonwit's men's department to charge a Cardin suit. Then he rushed around to Tiffany's for his most important purchase an engraved silver cuff bracelet — *Nora—Love, Noah. Forever*

Afterwards, to curb the few vexing thoughts and retain his joyous mood, he went home, wrote a three-hundred dollar check, a bit of a stretch--quite a bit of a stretch, as payment to--as of that morning--the now demanding furniture shop. For the first time, he'd snitched the money from their savings account, an account that now contained money from Nora's art sales as well. So what, he'd be paying it right back. Certainly before Nora ever found out.

And god he felt great again.

"NOAH, IT'S SO PRETTY. Why it's beautiful," his mother proclaimed when she called him at the office one early May morning.

"Do you really like it, mama?"

"Oh dear god yes. Thrilled!! It's the first time I've honestly felt good in this house. The sofa. And that dining room set. Coming from Bloomingdale's yet. Why it looks like it's right out of a movie, Noah. I could see all the neighbors watching it coming in from the truck, and they were turning green I can tell you."

Noah laughed with delight as he felt goose bumps. "That's wonderful, mama."

"But it must have cost you a whole pail of money."

He laughed again. "Just enjoy it, mama."

"What can I do to repay you? I'll have to. You can't afford all this"

"No. Just continue to be as happy as you are right now." Poor soul, he thought. That's all she's ever had of that dream that's haunted her so long.

Before he hung up, he suggested that she come to New

York for a visit that summer. "Then we'll all go off to Bloomingdale's on a shopping spree."

"Oh, I'd love that. Boy, won't the neighbors think I'm something."

"THERE'S SOMETHING WRONG HERE," Nora said when she opened the mail at the end of the month.

"What?" Noah asked.

"This bill from Bloomingdale's. I hope someone isn't after snitching our charge plate. One thousand fifty dollars for furniture and shipping fees."

"Oh-- No-- No, there's nothing wrong with that," he quickly replied praying there wasn't a statement of their savings account in the same mail. "I bought some things for my mother. I just forgot to tell you."

"How in bloody hell could you forget to tell me such a thing," she snipped, tossing the bill on the dining table.

"Well, I've been so busy. Well I mean I was going to tell you. I just-"

"Sure. Like always. I may as well be off on me holidays somewhere."

"What you're really saying is you resent my buying her these things."

"That most definitely is not what I'm after saying. I think it's only endearing that you would think of your mother. But you completely spin off and let opulence take you over."

"What did you think I was going to get her--

schlock?"

"Ah come now Noah. I'd chance with all your contacts at Wilton, you could have been finding some fine wholesale pieces."

"Well I did want her to know that it was the best. The least I could do is to lavish her a little."

"Lavish is a raging fever with you. It sends you into a bloody delirium."

"Well it looks as though my book is about to sell now. And I am going to be getting a hefty raise. So don't you think you're going a bit far over my mother's furniture?"

"It's not your mother's furniture that this is about," she insisted. "It's me. And how you keep losing me."

He could only understand a little of what she meant. But he wondered if the silver bracelet wouldn't be the cure all. Damn, why couldn't the engraving have been finished by now. Maybe he could do a little more sweet-talking in the meantime. But then the phone rang. A moment into listening to the voice, he felt the blood drain from him. "Okay," he managed to say. "When do you want to see me? Yes, I can make that. I'll see you then." He held the phone in his hand and sighed.

"What's wrong?" Nora asked.

"Jason Blackwell."

"What?"

"He wants to see me. Maybe they rejected it after all."

"Oh no. Why would he want to see you then?"

"To congratulate me. I'm sure," he answered

sarcastically as he looked at the bar table but then forced himself to turn away. His heart ached.

"I HAD A TALK WITH TWO of the Random House editors. I actually dropped by to see them," Jason Blackwell said as he leaned back in the burgundy leather swivel chair behind his vast Chippendale mahogany desk at William Morris. He puffed out cigar smoke that immediately joined forces with Noah's pitching stomach and the tom-toms in his head.

"They liked much of the book. And that's all to your credit."

"But?"

"They didn't like the ending. They don't buy it. Well at least two of them didn't."

"They don't buy the ending?"

"No." Then he wrinkled his tanned brow, and as he rolled up the sleeves of his crimson-striped dress shirt, he casually added: "Well the last quarter. Maybe even the last half of the manuscript."

"What do they think is wrong?"

"They don't think it carries enough of a dramatic punch for today's market. It really needs to explode and go somewhere. A seismic revelation or something. That's what they want. I was afraid of something like this."

"So that's that then."

"Not exactly," he said, running his manicured fingers through his slick black hair then leaning back and hooking a thumb under his suspenders. "If you change the ending and build dramatically enough toward it, they'll buy it."

"Well the whole idea of the situation is that everything happens slowly, almost imperceptibly but in the end it changes everything in overwhelming fashion. So obviously they didn't understand it. But you think I should change it their way?" Noah asked. By now his head was paining so much he thought it might explode. Even though Blackwell was in his forties, Noah would have gladly exchanged places with this dapper mogul just to be rid of his pain.

"I've come to the conclusion that these editors have hit on a real problem with the manuscript. I've also come to the conclusion that you should withdraw it and fix it," he insisted as he anxiously checked his appointment calendar.

"By rewriting half the book."

"That's right. Rather than having everyone reject it. Or-- Better still, put it aside for the time being and work on the society project," Blackwell beamed as he stood preparing to dismiss him. "You can do it. You're a real writer that's for sure. And no one can take your talent away from you."

WOULD THAT SOMEONE COULD, Noah thought as wandered down Third Avenue absorbing the day's gritty fog. "What a friggin' bust," he muttered. By the time he reached Molly Malone's Pub on the fringe of Gramercy

Park, he had abandoned all thoughts of returning to Wilton that day. Instead he wandered into the dark bar to the jukebox strains of the Beattles *Nowhere Man*. "Couldn't have timed it better," he muttered again as he collapsed on the corner barstool. Starting with a bloody Mary, he advanced to vodka martinis. In doing so, he managed to lose the headache but not the constant sting from the manuscript Blackwell had forced him to take away. At some point, he began to leaf through its pages, reading them at random, until he came to the conclusion that he was a lousy writer and that this was his real trouble. Then he put all the pages back into the box and laughed aloud. "God we can use them in the bathroom the same as they used to use pages of the Sears catalogs," he muttered some more and smirked. Then he noticed that people were watching him. But what the fuck? So he drank a little more and forgot all about them. But he couldn't forget about his Nora and the hurt he would feel having to tell her.

"I'M PRETTY WIPED OUT," he told her as he wove into the apartment reeking of spirits and obviously not knowing what time it was. Vaguely he was aware of a big fire going in the fireplace and the smell of good food, so he guessed it must be late. "I think I'm just going to bed," he said as he groped his way out of his trench coat. Then he kissed her on the cheek. "I'm just so sorry. It's been a rough day. You shouldn't have wasted time cooking."

"What did he say?"

"He gave me back my manuscript," he shrugged as he flung the bagged box on a chair. "If he's going to do anything with it, I've got to rewrite the thing."

"Why?"

"Why? It's not dramatic enough." He headed for the bathroom, leaned against the tank and let fire with a bursting long piss. "I think probably he wants some murders or something," he mumbled.

"Well that's damn eejity ridiculous," she insisted as she came in and stood behind him. "How could you let him get you into this morbid state. I'd pay no mind to anything he says. Just take it to another agent. I'm sure Carole with all her contacts could help you find one."

"God, I'd be mortified to ask her after Jason Blackwell turned it back. You can't get much better than William Morris for clout."

"What good is it if he doesn't appreciate your work? From the time you told me about him, I wondered if he was right for that book."

"But no one in the business appreciates it. Jesus, what a mess." As he finished his piss the misery hit him, he sank to the floor and began vomiting. She held his head until he finished. Then she sat him on the side of the tub, dampened a face cloth and pressed its coolness against his neck. "Why can't things go just fizzin' smoothly for me," he managed stopping just short of adding—*like they do for you.*

"They will," she whispered as she helped him into bed. "But only if you let them. You can't be doing the likes of this to yourself or nothing will get sorted out." After she helped pull off his clothes on the bed, she covered him and sat stroking his forehead. "You have to know how good you are, Noah. It's like I've always said." He suddenly grinned up at her and began to mimetic her words in unison: "You're a beautiful writer, and it won't be long before everyone's going to know it." His grin faded as his eyes closed and he felt himself go icy cold while Nora slipped in beside him to warm him.

"YOU KNOW YOUR REALLY DOING a very good job," one of the spruce eager-beaver Wilton vice-presidents told Noah when he approached him for a much overdue increment a few days later. Prompted by a notice from *FNCB* that his last bank loan repayment was overdue and a reminder from the furniture place that larger payments were expected, he felt he had no recourse. Unfortunately the vice president felt he had no recourse but to say: "As far as a raise goes right now, it doesn't play."

"You can't be serious," Noah pursued. "But I'm due one."

"Oh, we can muster a small one. But not the kind you're thinking of."

"No bonus?" And with that his whole body began to sweat.

The vp shook his head. "You see Noah, there's all this talk about a possible merger with the profits here being so high. There's a real push to keep those books going even higher. The Wiltons—especially Oliver-- think they could skyrocket if we weren't operating as a private company. So salaries are on the hold right now."

"Who's going to bite?"

"Well, this is strictly *entre nous*, of course. But there's strong talk of Champion Communications among others. Once that's established, if it is, you'll most likely be set for whatever you want. You're doing a really good job, really you are. You must know that."

"So what am I worth now?" Noah asked as cooly as possible.

"Twenty a week is all we can manage."

"T-w-e-n-t-y?" He may as well have said ten cents. "Are you sure you can afford it?" He sneered as thoughts of pilfering their savings account ran rampant.

"You know Oliver wanted to give you a huge raise to prove how confident he is in you, but all the advisors said don't give anyone anymore until we're going like lightning rods for the big stuff."

"And all you could muster is twenty dollars for me?"

" Oh come on Noah, things aren't that bad with you. You can hold out until negotiations right themselves. Besides look how well your lovely wife is doing."

"How do you know about that?" he asked aghast.

"Are you kidding me? Everybody's talking about your wife's brilliant work that's selling and approaching fortunes. "Oh but that reminds me, Oliver called from his Vineyard estate and is most anxious to cover her next opening. Not for your column bur for a big double-page spread as well."

"You must be joking."

"Not at all. I can assure you of that."

"But how can I cover my own wife's opening for the love of god? How awkward and embarrassing to say nothing of how unprofessional it would be."

"No way. Don't be so sensitive. It's not like you're covering a clothing line or a designer's boutique. This is the high-minded art world we're speaking of. And it would be so romantic. You're covering your wife's showing. She's really going to be a star, you know. Oliver thinks *famous* beyond words. What a coup this is."

"Oh yes, and so very romantic."

And now he realized that Oliver was getting his power jollies by shifting figures on the playing field and pulling all the strings. Skull and Bones indeed.

7

"IT'S ALMOST AS IF SHE'S CREATED these as an homage to Cezanne or Pissarro. And in some moodier ways even Carot. Completely unique, of course. But I can't help but feel they have the same degree of profundity." So went the prelude of praise at Nora's second opening at the Winsor de Caine in early June of 1968. This one was a black-tie event no less where accolades from the gathering crowds soon built to a crescendo, echoing through Noah's mind.

 -Lucid, enormous truths."

 -Spectacular élan."

 -Wonderfully sensuous, intense. It's impossible to look away."

 -Timeless. Even her darkest portrayals are radiant."

 But this proved to be only a segment of the event. Off in another area of the gallery between gasps of surprise came raves over several dozen of her trenchant, extremely graphic city-wide sketches. *Realisme extraordinaire* cried a French enthusiast curator whose praise resounded over the many others.

 Noah began to wonder if this might never end, as he visually panned the scene then surreptitiously took swift notes. He prayed no one would realize what he was doing. It was such a humiliation, one that made him feel all the more the failure. As such he hadn't told Nora of his assignment, pretending to be there solely for support. As if she needed any support. Because of the accruing ego damage, he had told his photographer, who was still to arrive, to blend with the other society lens men and not let on that he was Noah's charge.

 All this had struck him like a thunderbolt. It wasn't just the embarrassment of the situation. It was the rising jealousy he could no longer curtail or even subdue, one that was only fostered by all these words. They were words of the like he had wanted to hear practically all his life. And with the jealousy came the waves of guilt. How unfair this was. He should be puffing pride over her right now, unable to contain himself.

"Yes she *is* going to be a major factor in the art world--and very soon." These came from the *Times* critic as he strongly agreed with a lady friend. "I haven't seen a one-person showing as stunning as this in years. Everything she's done is thoroughly convincing and most of it so powerful in intent." *Powerful in intent,* Noah so relished as he summoned a scotch-on-the-rocks and quickly downed it.

"Noah dear," a voice called from across the gallery, and Noah's knee-jerk reaction was to stash his notepad and pen. When he turned he realized it was Carole Dawson making her way to his side. "I want you to meet some of the art world's best. And I mean that in the truest manner. Then she led him over to a small group of influential connoisseurs and curators and introduced him. "Noah is one of my   dearest and most trustworthy friends. *And* a brilliant new artist in his own right."

"That's always nice to hear. Thank you," Noah grinned with delight.

"Well it's true. True of you and your lovely wife, Nora. And speaking of which--" she paused as she motioned her out of a crowd and over to them. Then for the next fifteen minutes after she introduced them they praised her work. As they prepared to leave, Carole hugged Nora. "I'm so proud of you. I can't tell you how happy I am. I've told everyone I know about your work. And I think the gallery has invited them all."

"Well that's all fair dues to you."

"No. Word is spreading fast that you're so amazingly gifted. And don't let anyone tell you anything to the contrary. The art world should be so fortunate." Before Nora could reply, she was swept into another gushing gathering and Carole and her art devotees began their departure. At the door, Carole whispered: "God bless you for that little aside in your column this week, Noah. It really knocked John asunder in the middle of our case-- which is where he belongs."

"Well I only told it the way it was. You know I'd never do it any other way."

"Oh I know you wouldn't. But still I must say I'm delighted."

Delighted, Noah thought. Delighted for Carole. Delighted for the art world. Delighted for Nora. Delighted for everyone. Oh let's have another horrid scotch to celebrate all this joy.

As the bartender's face became more and more familiar, waves of important personalities not just from the art world but from the entire spectrum of New York society began rolling into the gathering. Included were such varying types as Babe Paley, Governor Rockefeller, the Leland Haywards, the John Lindsays, the Averell Harrimans, Doris Duke, Audrey Hepburn, Colonel Oblensky and Andy Warhol. With the latter came rumors of a possible tidal wave that would sweep in a host of socialites including Jacqueline Kennedy and Princess Radziwell. One thing was certain, they all wanted nothing more than to be in on the thrill of discovery. As Noah made small talk with the many whose only interest as before was to curry favor for the *FCD* connection, he continued to conceal his other reason for being there. Until--

"Noah," cried another voice from the crowd. He looked to see a hand flailing the air. It belonged to an *FCD* photographer, but not the one originally assigned to him. In a loud voice, he called above the din: "Noah, do you know the types of shots you want for your layout?" Although Noah immediately silenced him and gave him discreet instructions, enough of the crowd had taken note and realized the demeaning reason for his presence.

"How perfectly charming to be assigned to do a feature on your wife," smirked one of the elite *swellegants*, which was the paper's latest chic phrase to describe the young crowd of haughty sophisticates. "Isn't it unusually charming?" But this was only the first and mild mannered remark compared to the pungent ones that would come. Most were made as very catty asides that he couldn't help but overhear. "Imagine being a reporter having to cover your wife's smash opening. Isn't it delicious." "Perfectly apropos."

"See what I mean," a male voice from behind whispered to Noah. When he turned around, he realized it was Jason Blackwell. "I just dropped by to see what everyone in town is talking about."

"And?"

"Well I don't know the art world that well, but your wife's work looks pretty damn fabulous to me."

"I only wish mine did."

"Oh come now, it's not that far off the mark. But I can see why you'd be depressed judging from what they're doing to you here. They're just trying to scare you away from the great writing you might do about them. So what I say is--do it. Rub their noses in it. That book will make you a star. That's success. True success. And it's great vengeance."

"Well you have to realize it could ruin me if it didn't work out."

"Yes. But more likely it could ruin them or their image and make heroes of us."

And that's all Blackwell wanted. He couldn't care less about anything else, Noah thought. God what a fuckin' mess and what a disgusting person.

The instant Blackwell disappeared, Noah grabbed another scotch. Just as he did Nora caught sight of him and her worried look was most obvious. Damn it to hell, I'm hurting her, and he struggled for control. But still more *swellegants* arrived and the nasty downplay continued until it became too debasing for him. Even the bartender began treating him begrudgingly. That's when he started thinking that there were bars where no one knew him-- where he could make believe he was an enormous success and no one could take the feeling away from him. So he disappeared in a flash.

Nora continued greeting new arrivals and accepting their praise, but once she noticed Noah was missing she could scarcely contain her worry. As soon as she could, which was well over two hours later, she rushed out, hailed a taxi and had it speed to their apartment. What would she do if he weren't there? Where would he be? She hadn't a clue. When she departed the taxi, she held her breath for an instant. Then she rushed up the steps and opened the main doors of their building. Instead of relief, she began raging at what she saw. For collapsed at the front door of their apartment was Noah, his chin slumped over his black tie and resting on his chest. Instead of gently trying to rouse him, she began pounding his body. "Wake up you effin' bastard, you," she roared in a low tone so as to keep the upstairs neighbors from hearing. "How dare you do this to me." When he didn't respond, she began shaking him.

"Oh ho ho," he finally mumbled and then grinned out of his stupor. "You've got the highfalutin world now."

"Get up and get into that house, ya bloody swine ya."

He obeyed, laughing and giggling all the way.

"Why couldn't you have been with me on this of all nights?"

"You were all the better off without me," he said as he crashed onto his wing chair by the fireside.

"Little thanks to you. And what were you doing

cringing round the place taking notes as though you were some sort of spy?"

"My job. You didn't know they insisted I cover this major New York event?"

"I can't believe that. You're having me on so you are."

"Well you'd better believe it."

"Oh god, Noah. They made you do that? How disgusting of them." And she could actually feel her heart ache for him. "You *should* get out of that bloody place."

"Well you're big news now. You're on your way."

"I don't want to be on my way. Not without you. God I was only ready to cut the bloody bollocks from you when I found you langers in the hall."

"I thought I was the perfect gentleman until I had to get out of there. It was all backfiring on me. And you were so caught up in everything as you should have been. No, as you most certainly deserved to be."

"Well I don't give a tinker's damn about all those people. Certainly I get pleasure out of painting and I do take delight from knowing people respond and like my work. But the most important thing in this whole looney world of yours is the two of us. If I can make the money to see our dreams come round that much sooner, then all the better."

"Don't you mean, if you can make the money to pay all my bills that much sooner, then all the better?"

"You're a bleedin' swine when you drink that shite. I

hope you know that."

"I hurt a lot tonight. I hate myself for it. I guess it has to come out."

"Well it has. You can be sure of that," she said sternly.

"So you want out?"

"No! Just the opposite. But what you don't realize is the more I want it, the more it's slowly eluding me."

"Oh if I were you, I'd really worry about things eluding me after tonight. Why you're one of the brightest lights out there now."

"By whose standard?"

"By theirs, Nora. They're the ones who count."

"To you I suppose that's so. But to me, you're the only one who matters."

"You haven't taken note of the devaluation." And then he was drifting off in the chair and didn't notice her tears. As he did, he muttered: "You did well tonight. Very well. And I'm so proud of you."

8

AND INDEED SHE HAD DONE VERY WELL. In the days and weeks to come brilliant reviews were to appear with scarcely a negative note amongst them. As for Noah, there were no such bright heralds. Only the opposite. Oliver Wilton flew into a quiet waspish rage following Noah's double-page spread and column covering the opening. "*Ah* could not believe that our *s-t-a-h* reporter could have been so very remiss in his coverage as to fail so miserably in bedazzling our readers while every other paper in this city was virtually ablaze with details. Why it's perfectly *obsurd* that we are caught with our very *d-r-a-w-z* down around our ankles. One would gather that we scavenged our material from a news service."

Noah sputtered something about his being too close to her and that it had been a mistake to let him cover it. "You *ah* one of the *fahnest* writers this city has to offer. To do so poorly—"

"Yes sir. But--"

"How could you have let such a *d-i-s-a-s-t-a* befall *awah* paper? This was a *majah* event for us." And with that he walked away with Noah sweating and still muttering "but--". Moments later, the spruce vp whom he had previously approached for a raise approached him. "I'd be very careful if I were you. That sizeable raise that you were in line for once the big merger takes place is beginning to look a little remote at this point. You might forever be stuck at your current mark."

That all occurred toward the end of the day sending Noah retreating on his own to various bars culminating a couple of hours later at Molly Malone's. But damn it, he told himself, I can't do this to Nora again, have another fast fade. So he left Molly's and his drink behind. When he arrived home, he found she had made them lobster salads— one of his favorites. Oh thank god, there's forgiveness in the air.

"I'm sorry," she said hugging him with great compassion.

"You're sorry. I positively hate myself. And now I can't even kiss you because I have booze on my breath again."

"Oh don't be a fool. Who would ever blame you?" And then they did kiss before she went on: "As if you haven't been through enough, you had to cover that bloody thing of mine."

"It wasn't a *thing* Nora. It was downright beautiful. I'm the *messer*, the fucker upper."

EVEN THROUGH THE GROWING GLOOM of the times, with much of the country despairing over the assassination of Robert Kennedy, Nora Mason was being hailed as one of the leading lights of the rapidly changing art world. Major dealers, seeing a swift rise in profitability, called to woo her into becoming a client. And literally more than a dozen of her paintings, along with some of her earliest Dublin efforts, sold at prices now escalating to the thousand-dollar bracket, thus far above what most female artists of the time were commanding.

When these copious sums began rolling in, Nora made a pact with herself. As guilty as she felt, she was determined not to let it be frittered away. Knowing that Noah was already pinching from their joint savings, she opened a separate account in her name only and put most of the painting money into it. This was the only way they would attain their dream of an Irish cottage.

IT WAS DURING THIS TIME that Noah decided to go forward digging his way out of his mess. Even though thoughts of wealth still possessed him, he'd renounce the rich who by now he had come to loathe with a passion. And this would remove him from that opulent world that continued distancing him from Nora. He called an editor at *Esquire* whom he had befriended during college days and had more recently met up with at several of the grand events he had been covering. It seemed perfect, the friend said. A fashion and features editor was about to resign and crossover to the newly formed *New York* magazine. So off Noah went for a few interviews and easily passed muster. In fact the powers seemed so thrilled that they offered him two hundred a week more than he was making now. God it appeared such a blessing. Pretty much a ten to six-er on a monthly with few evening and out-of-town assignments. Now he would have the time and courage to work up the society book with the notes he'd carefully kept. Then too he could reconsider what to do with his first novel. The money would help straighten his finances. And there was even an added bonus. *Esquire* had a fiction department. But most of all, this would mean so much to Nora. They would be happier than they'd ever been.

"OH GOD, I'M ONLY SO RELIEVED for you

Noah," Nora delighted. "You're out of that madness."

"Well not quite yet. The guy is holding on at *Esquire* for another month. But then it will come around they assured me. Oh but it's top secret until then. I don't want to get dumped out of Wilton, column and all, before it's *fait accompli.*"

It was true. In the days that followed, happiness rushed them and swept them high. Something was happening on Noah's front after the long blight following his *New Yorker* short story. And through it all, Nora's success continued to grow as other artists who were curious about her work began visiting the gallery and asking to meet her. Among them were such varied talents as the abstract expressionists Mark Rothko and Barnett Newman, composer Virgil Thomson, Dadist Man Ray, designer Cecil Beaton, Leonard Bernstein, sculptor-designer Isamu Noguchi, Tennessee Williams and one whom she greatly admired for achieving her own style and becoming a beacon for women's artists Georgia O'Keeffe.

All of them had such unusual yet striking personalities that she was tempted to throw a lasso over each and keep them as subjects. One of strangest of these was a rising young photographer Conrad Landis who literally terrified her when he suddenly appeared at the gallery while she was arranging some of her work early one morning. He was tall, lean to the point of gauntness and had the greenest eyes she'd ever seen. They weren't just green, they were maximum green. Darkly vivid viridian.

Such a color should have ignited a green fire, she thought. But the blaze if it had ever been there had been reduced to a dying ember. Eerily it was as if he were on the verge of expiring. And it wasn't just the eyes. The almost skeletal face was excessively ashen as if the flesh were being wasted from his high protruding cheekbones. Even the too-closely cropped black hair lacked any signs of life. All of this combined with his slight limp made *zombie* leap to her mind.

"Like I said," he began with a most grating voice and an icy, rough-as-sandpaper handshake. "I was told I should come by to look over your work before I went to Ireland." But they were words that seemed as if they had been recorded before he arrived. God, she panicked she was the only person in the gallery that early in the morning. There wasn't even a building guard. Why hadn't she latched the door?

After a deadly pause, as he stared at her and then glanced quickly around, he finally spoke again in that chilling harsh tone. "I'm going to be shooting this feature for *Life*, and I guess I don't know what I'm doing."

He laughed nervously and began backing away. At first it appeared as if he were attempting to position himself for a better view of her paintings, but then she thought he was sizing up the place or worse sizing her up. "Well you must know something if you're doing a feature for *Life*," she finally offered casually pretending to cover her fear.

"Yes, but you see I've never been to Ireland," he added as he accidentally backed into a gallery table, knocking over a phone and nearly toppling himself.

"Whoops. Be careful there," she said. "Are you all right?"

"Yes." And he laughed again as he fished and fumbled to put the phone back in its proper place, which somehow made her relax a little. "I guess I'm not used to civilization anymore."

"Where have you been that you'd be saying that?"

"Viet Nam. Two years in pics and mo pics."

"In what?"

"Pics and mo pics. That's even crazier than it sounds. It means pictures and motion pictures. I was an Army photographer."

"I'd say you had more than a bit of fortune to get out of there."

"Well my time was up," he said swift as a breeze, which was the complete opposite to the way he had been speaking. But somehow it still sounded recorded. "And now I'm off to Ireland."

"How did you hear about my work?"

"Oh I've got some stuff over at the Castelli Gallery. They're beginning to dabble a little in photography. When I told them about my *Life* assignment, they mentioned your paintings and said you might be able to help me."

"Well I don't know about that. I do know a little about Ireland though."

"Yeah, I can see that," he said as he relaxed a little and began to wander about looking at her work. His jeans and his denim jacket worn over a tie-dyed T-shirt were as faded as he was. But once or twice he did smile, and a faint light crossed his face. "They're empyreal," he finally pronounced with a similarly faint lightness of voice. But for the first time, his words sounded spontaneous.

"They're what?" she asked with a start.

"Oh it's not my word." he shrugged. "One of the guys in our platoon who thought of himself as a writer-- well he was. He used to talk about it as having to do with this realm of radiance. This highest heaven. This purest form of light and fire. That once we saw it we'd know that's what we'd want our lives to unite with. Never got a chance to find out though before he got his guts blown out. "

"Oh god," she said and shivered. "Well I think he must have been thinking of something more spiritual than these."

"Don't know. Don't know just what he meant." Then he went awkward again, chucked his hands in his pockets and stumbled a bit over the words. "Just that-- Just that I feel-- Well, I guess the composition of these lets you inside. And that's good. I mean, I like that-- I guess." He hesitated for a few seconds and then quickly added: "Hey I'm not one of those Namvets who blows dope. Bet you think I am."

"No. Not at all." Though in truth she didn't know what she thought of him, except for his weirdness.

"Yeah. Well I guess what I'm trying to say is that you wield a mean paint brush."

She laughed. "That sounds grand to me, right enough. Thanks very much."

Abruptly he asked: "Could we maybe go and have a cup of coffee? Just so I could take some notes on places in Ireland."

Even though she still felt very ill at ease, she thought this might be the best way to bring it all to an end. "That would be fine with me."

They left the gallery and headed east that gray early June morning. As they walked his limp seemed to grow more pronounced. "Don't know much about coffee shops up here. I live downtown so I frequent those dark scuzzy dens around St. Marks."

"That wouldn't sound to be very healthy."

"Guess you lose yourself better. It's too bright and bustling up here." Just then he accidentally crashed into a wave of pedestrians coming from the other direction. "See what I mean," he said after everyone recovered. Then he laughed a strange private laugh.

They went into a Mayflower Coffee Shop, sat in a small booth and while attempting to avoid his awkwardness she talked on and on of the varying places in Ireland until mercifully the waitress interrupted with their coffee and doughnuts. Conrad in an attempt to quickly shift his notebook and pen knocked the cups from her hand sending showers of steaming coffee down onto the table followed by the crashing cups. With only seconds to spare, they leapt to their feet to avoid being scalded. How in god's name can this man be a photographer, Nora puzzled as the waitress diligently mopped and cleared the mess.

"I wouldn't blame you if you didn't want to try again," Conrad offered after the waitress went off for more coffee and fresh doughnuts. Vainly he attempted to dry his notes with some paper napkins. Nora ignored him and went on about the people of Ireland and how they often varied according to the landscapes.

At one point, he abruptly put down his pen and said: "From what it sounds like to me, it might be a nice place to start my past."

"What?"

"Well I don't have one so--"

"Oh come now."

"No. One day it disappeared. Just like that. You've heard of people saying if only I could start over again. Well I'm one of the ones who can. I can begin at the beginning."

"I'd say that's a bit rash."

"It's not, you know. I'm serious." There was a slight tremor both in the eyes and near the cheekbones. It was almost unnoticeable, but there along with a few flashes of coldness that sent another stab of fear through her. Then everything in him shut down once again and he grew even paler. So *zombie* came back spooking her. And she couldn't wait to see the back of him. Even then she glanced over her shoulder to be sure he wasn't following her. That was when she caught the cold stare of him as he turned to look back at her. Was he menacing her? Was he stalking her?

"I ONCE TOLD YOU THAT you have a special grace accorded very few artists," Julian of Winsor de Caine told Nora when she returned to the gallery that afternoon for a meeting. "But you must start doing more with it."

"Well how would you mean that now?" she asked somewhat surprised by the tone of his insistence and still a bit stunned by the weirdness of her meeting with Conrad Landis.

"Oh it's not meant to be a criticism. You've got all the essential background. As I said you aren't afraid to break the rules to achieve what you want. But you must take more time to do that very thing."

"Well I'd have to tell you straight out, I'm taking all the time I can right now."

"That's just it. It's not enough. You could accomplish so much more."

"But how with another job yet."

"That's what I want to talk to you about. We or at least I strongly feel that you should be devoting your entire time and attention to this."

"Well now that's all very well and good, but--"

"Now hold on. Don't just write it off. You're on the verge of making big money. Do you know what it means for the art world to think you're convincing? Even the severest of critics. You can't ask for more than that. So don't you see, you have to take advantage of their passion and reap it while the sun shines."

"But quit my job? I need to know I'm getting that three thirty a week."

"Quite your job. Yes indeed. Look if it's a matter of a money crunch, we would be more than happy to offer you advances against future sales. And for me that's saying a lot. There's very few in the art business today who are willing to do that. But with you, we'd be crazy not to, because on the horizon I can see such growth in your talent."

"You have that much faith?"

"Yes. And that's the direction in art today. It's becoming big business, and I think we're going to be one of the forerunners. But we have to have the talent before we can get the business. And you're the talent. A fabulous glowing one."

ONCE MORE SHE LEFT Winsor de Caine as if on a cloud. Until only recently the acceptance of her work, of her person had been but a dream. But that was changing more swiftly than she could begin to contemplate. No sooner had she arrived home than a feature writer from the newly formed *New York* magazine called to say she wanted to do a feature. It would be a piece not only on her art but her lifestyle. "The sort of thing where we come into your home, talk to you and get some pictures. Get a feeling of what your world is really like."

She agreed and an interview was arranged three weeks hence. Her first reaction was to tell Noah. But then she thought differently. He was so elated these days. Wouldn't it sound like what the Americans called one-upmanship if she went on about this? No, let him continue to advance with the thrill of his soon-to-be new job and all his re-born plans for work on his books.

9

KATIE JOHNSON WAS A CHARMING black journalist. Young and with a delightful sense of humor, she immediately put Nora at ease. So much so that Nora was scarcely aware of her photographer taking pictures. They talked on in a chatty fashion for over an hour. At one point Katie asked her: "How do you accomplish all this and still hold down a full time job with Aer Lingus?

"Well that's changed now. I resigned my job there the other day so I'd be able to concentrate all my efforts on this. I know it's a bit of a gamble. But sure if you don't gamble on what you believe, what else are you going to do?"

It was at this point that the apartment door suddenly burst open and in came Noah. "Hi Nora, I didn't know you'd be home so early," he called out in a slightly louder voice than usual which was a pretty fair clue that he'd knocked back a few jars. When he came in, he just stared in surprise at the magazine people.

"Hi Noah," she cheered rushing over to hug him and cover. "I want you to meet these lovely people from *New York* magazine. They're doing a bit of an article on my work."

"Oh grand," he delighted but then muttered: "Nice of you to tell me, love."

"Yes. Katie Johnson, I'd like you to meet my husband."

"Noah Mason!" Katie exclaimed. "I know you from *FCD*. I never made the connection between you and Nora."

"Katie Johnson. It is you. I can't believe it. I thought I was mistaken at first." And he went over to kiss her on the cheek. "What a small world," he said in what Nora considered to be still too loud a voice. "We used to work together, Nora."

"It seems at one time or another, everybody in the writing business has worked for Wilton," Katie added.

"So dear Katie, you're interviewing my very talented wife. Isn't she wonderful?" And he went back to hugging Nora as the photographer took their picture.

"Noah please," Nora whispered in a pleading aside.

"What's this? Are you being shy of your talent again? Katie, she's so restrained you know."

"Oh, I know how restrained she is. But she has no reason to be. She's brilliant."

"I know. I keep telling her she's brilliant. Just brilliant. Of course, she really doesn't need me to tell her anymore. Half the city's telling her nowadays."

"Well she'll start believing it now that she's spending all her time at her calling instead of holding down an office job yet," Katie assured.

"Oh-- Will she now?" Noah said as he managed a frozen smirk.

"HOW COULD YOU HAVE DONE THIS TO ME? You've drink taken," Nora snapped when Katie and the photographer had gone. "Don't you think she could see that? I was so bloody embarrassed."

"Oh you were, were you? How do you think I felt? I didn't even know they were coming."

"I didn't want to put the damper on your joy of late. And what happened to it by the way? I haven't seen you with drink taken in days. And at this hour it's only shocking."

"I had a grand charity luncheon to cover for the Police Athletic League."

"And that's what you'd be offering for an excuse. I thought you were over that."

"I was." He paused, while walking over to the window and staring out at the park. "Until--" he sighed. "The fashion and features guy at *Esquire* decided not to resign after all. So that's out the window."

"Oh god Noah," she instantly sympathized. "Maybe they'd have something else for you."

"Well they don't," he snapped. "So I'll just keep

hanging on with my column while you continue to soar."

"And what would you be meaning by that now?"

"That you've become the silk purse after all," he let go turning back to her.

"I don't have to give answer to that," she said feeling her anger rise.

"Obviously you don't. Obviously you don't have to give answer to anything. Like quitting your job and not telling me for example."

"You'd better consider yourself damn lucky I haven't quit you."

"Oh maybe you'd damn well like to. Maybe you'd just not like to see me at all."

"Not when you're headin' off on the tare like this."

"Okay. So I will just go off then," he snipped as he prepared to leave.

"Oh grand! To what bar?"

"Dozens of them," he roared as he went out and slammed the door.

HE QUELLED HIS RAGE long enough to cross the park and check into the Gramercy Park Hotel for the night. Better to do it now than after hitting the bars, he thought. And hit them he did. He started at Molly Malone's and drifted through so many he couldn't remember them all. As he went, the alcohol fueled his anger causing him to mutter. How could she have kept all these things from me? She could have told me. Sure it was an excuse for her to lead her own private art world life and leave me by the wayside. She's so popular now my presence is no longer *de rigueur*. The failed writer. An asshole columnist isn't enough anymore. He squeezed his stemmed martini glass with such force it shattered cutting his hand. As he walked out into the street with darkness descending within and without, he grimaced. Maybe septicemia will set in. Then I won't have a writing problem.

"*WHAT OF THE HEART WITHOUT HER?*" he asked after he came up behind Noah, sat at the next barstool and put his arm around him. "*Nay, poor heart, Of thee what word remains ere speech be still?*" Noah looked up from his daze and nodded as Tim continued: "*A wayfarer by barren ways and chill, Steep ways and weary, without her thou art.*"

"Ah you're back with the Rossetti from Ithaca days again," Noah struggled while lifting his finger to shake at Tim and nearly upsetting his martini in so doing.

"I never really left him. You just didn't know that."

"Oh I find that hard to believe. Those words still passing your lips. Love's squanderer. Like the prodigal son--wasting your substance on riotous living."

"Partly true. But only partly."

They were in the Old Town Bar on East 18th Street. Just after Noah had left the glass-shattered bar, whatever that one was, he'd slipped into another anonymous place where he'd bummed an extra-large Band-Aid from a caring bartender and had phoned Tim to tell him of this mess and to suggest the Old Town. "I'm sorry, old pal," he slurred a little as he patted Tim on the back. "I didn't mean to interrupt your daily routine. Lascivious lout that thou art."

"I'm glad you did. Besides Tuesdaywise it's pretty vacuous these days. Babewise that is." Tim chuckled as he neatly draped his impeccable blazer over a neighboring bar stool. Through his now slightly blurred vision, Noah forced himself to a degree of sobriety by concentrating on Tim's appearance. Trendy as always, he wore a yellow Lacoste shirt, tan chinos and matching suede saddle shoes. He'd allowed his well-groomed strawberry hair to grow curly and even longer as the kingpin of his dynamic, youthful Madison Avenue agency.

Noah giggled as he realized if he weren't fairly pie-eyed he'd feel downright scruffy compared to spiffy Tim. Still in his now crumpled tan Brooks Brothers poplin with a large hardened blood spot on the knee, Noah was oozing sweat everywhere from all the booze. "Vacuous," he finally muttered. "That's a very un-Tim-like word for a very un-Tim-like fettle."

"Well then let's just call it a bust. A *pause* to put it in more upbeat ad lingo. *The pause that refreshes*. The old machinery that is."

"Don't give me that bull. I didn't think you ever paused. And as far as your machinery goes, I'd say it's getting more vigorous by the day."

"Well pal, you caught me off guard," he said as he

signaled the bartender for a draught beer. "And I'd say this is catching you off guard. What are you doing hanging out in this dark old-fashioned place? Looks like everybody's gone home--if they were ever here."

"Oh it's one of Wilton's many office haunts," he blurted.

"It's a haunt all right. But this certainly isn't very you."

"Oh, I don't want to be very me. It doesn't get me anywhere."

"Where do you want to be?"

"In the old swim."

"Well it seems that you're there all right." Tim laughed. "Be careful the way you choose your words tonight, buddy."

"Words. Ah words--"

"It didn't sell?"

"No, I've taken it back for changes. Back to work in progress. But the progress never seems to p-r-o-*gress*. If you get my drift."

"At least you've gone further than I have. I have to hand it to you. I'm so envious. All that writing I was doing once. Remember I even had Merrick interested that script. But all the richness of this world of mine kept me from even doing a revise."

"With that fantastic job of yours? I wouldn't start complaining. Look at this dipstick after all this time. Just a dumb ass society reporter."

"Not so dumb."

"Yeah? Everybody's making it but me." He'd decided not to tell him about the *Esquire* fiasco because in truth he'd come to the conclusion that they'd reconsidered realizing he was a shitty writer. This roused him to quickly finish his present martini and order another.

"Go easy on that stuff, pal. Look at you. You're gushing sweat. I've never seen you like this."

"I guess I'm not the dapper Dan today. But what the fuck. Who the hell cares?"

"I do, pal. I don't like that tone. This everybody's making it crap. What does that mean? Or more to the point, *who* does that mean?"

"Can't you guess?"

"Where is she?"

"Well as I told you on the phone, we had a bit of a tiff," he said shaking his head before progressing to a large swig of his new martini.

"She's doing pretty well, isn't she?"

"Yes, and it's bloody savaging me."

"I thought you wanted that for her."

"I do! Believe me. But me too, buddy. Me too."

"Well it doesn't necessarily happen in tandem like a mutual orgasm, you know. The problem with you is that you think everybody's better off than you are. Only now you're becoming unglued over it. In the old days I'd have said come on let's hit the circuit. Go off to Max's or Elaine's and really plug into some action. But you've already got it.

You've got the best any guy could want. And you're suffering? Well, 1 can't catch that drift no matter how you try to put it across."

"But you don't write books," Noah insisted as all this conversation was snapping him sober.

"The hell with the books. Life isn't a book, pal. Life is what you've got at home. Remember I almost had it once," he said as he let himself grow silent.

"Well you can still have it, if you'd try. How many times do we have to say it?"

"I'll tell you something. I wouldn't be here in this city if she were with me now. I'd be off in some country cabin writing my heart out. I know that. I've let myself be seduced by this life. But it's all a substitute. City, agency, money, women. Busy life, no time to think. Or remember— Except I do remember sometimes. Well lots of times."

"For godsakes, you've gone ahead and talked yourself into all this bullshit?"

"No, I did that long ago. I just never told you. But I think you need to hear it tonight. I don't know that I have a choice. But you do. Now damn well guard it."

"Yeah I have to, don't I?" Noah said in a sudden panic. But it didn't stop him from attempting to order another martini to cut the pain. When Tim insisted he had to leave, he suggested he drop Noah off at his apartment before he became even more sloshed. "Make amends now, buddy. Don't compound this." And then he laughed as he pulled him off the stool. "*Cuiusvis hominis est errare.* You remember?"

"Oh god, that wise old philosopher guy we had so much faith in at Ithaca. Am I too stoned to remember? Let's just see now." He struggled for the words as he struggled into his poplin jacket. "*N-u-l-l-i-u -s n-i-s-i* --- Oh fuck, I don't remember the rest. It was from that Cicero guy he loved so much."

"Well we all loved Cicero, too. Remember how we used to quote him all the time for the fun of it? Little did we know how true his words would become."

"Maybe so," Noah laughed as his giddiness pursued. "But what did he say? I can't quite get the words out."

."*Nullius nisi insipientis in errore perseverare*"

"You don't say," Noah replied as he reached back to the bar to snatch up the remainder of his martini.

"Any man is liable to err, only a fool persists in the error."

"You're right. I get your point."

"Then put that drink down before your arm's worn out and come along out of this funeral parlor. I want to deliver you to Nora in one piece. At the same time I want to advise you. *D-o-n-'t* take setbacks as final curtains."

"I DON'T LOOK THAT BAD. Not after last night," he muttered to himself as he splashed his face with cold water and peered into the mirror in the men's room at *FCD*. Even with the tom-toms booming in his head and a nagging rage over Nora still burning, no one would ever guess. After he'd left Tim the night before, he'd waited on the steps of his apartment until his taxi was out of sight. Then instead of going in he'd beaten a hasty retreat back to the Gramercy Park where after still more drinks he had spent the night in a dark hotel room. He remembered he couldn't decide whether it was that way because of the room or because his lights were going out. That morning he'd purchased the necessary grooming essentials—shaving cream, razor, deodorant, Lavoris and lots of peppermint LifeSavers and Bufferin--at the shop in the hotel lobby. Then he'd gone to his cleaners to pick up his suit and shirts, gone back to the hotel to change and had left his dirty clothes and extra shirts in a shopping bag with the porter. The only thing missing was clean underwear, so he wore none. But who would know? No. No one at the office would ever guess anything was amiss. I look quite all right, he reassured himself checking the image again in the men's room mirror. But do I? Then he recoiled in horror. I'm no Dorian Gray. But I just can't decline. It's all glowing youth here. Especially now that Champion Communications is perched to take over. Jesus, don't panic that'll make it worse. So to shake these thoughts, he quickly entered the editorial floor. On his desk a cup of black coffee awaited. It had become a daily courtesy from Murphs.

"You'd better drink that fast, before they call today's postmortem," she called out from her desk. "You do look a bit peaked, you know."

"God, does it show that much?" he asked choking on

the first swallow of the scalding beverage. "You should level with me."

"I've been trying to for weeks. But you won't let me. There were times when you seemed to be in pure anguish. Then you came out of it for while. Now you're back into it again. What *is* wrong with you, Noah? I mean my boyfriend Jimmy and I go through our traumatic moments. But I love him so much I'd literally die if we didn't get through them. And the way I see it, you're not?"

"No. No. Nora's upset that I'm upset. It's just this writing stuff. And it's snowballing," he shrugged. "But don't let it bother you. I'll get around it. And I'll make myself look good again. I'll have to."

"Well this really worries me. And I'm serious."

"Murphs, why are you always so concerned about me?"

"Because—" and she glanced away for a moment as if to collect herself. "You're the only one here I know of who isn't duplicitous. And you don't know how truly miraculous that is. Other than Jimmy, I don't know of anyone who's like that. But then I never did." And she smiled faintly.

"Okay, let's go everybody," called city editor Jack Warren, summoning the beginning of another postmortem and Noah's tom-toms. "It's follies time at 9 East Eleventh."

"I DON'T SEE YOUR LADY so often anymore, Mr. Mason," said Mario, the beefy, graying Latino bartender at the Gramercy Park, as he brought Noah a second martini after he had somehow managed to survive the nightmare of that workday. Amazing he figured since he'd been berated again for a benign colorless column with weak boring captions. And then there was the bitter reminder of the *Esquire* fiasco.

"Oh she's busy with her work these days," Noah managed as a brush aside. At this point he was still determined to register for another night at the hotel. Every time he'd verged on forgiving Nora, even in the light of what Tim had said, he would slide back into anger.

"A fine woman," Mario continued. "I love to hear her talk about the old country. She never forget her ruts. That I like about her. People they come to this city, they get a little money, they forget where they come from, who they are. But she--no. I see Ireland when she talk."

"Yes," Noah sighed.

"I used to think how good it would be to have a fine lady like her. A lady who always caring for you. Who worship you. Who worry for you," Mario mused, staring down the length of the bar. Then he caught himself. "Oh, I don't mean your lady herself, Mr. Mason. But to have a beautiful lady like that. The best there is. To be able to do things for her. To make her feel and look better than she already look." He sighed and his eyes dimmed. "It never come to me, I think."

"Oh it will someday, Mario. You'll see," Noah assured and then went back to think of the importance of his words. "Always caring--worrying. I guess I'm a pretty lucky man. Very lucky."

"You be that, Mr. Mason. Would you like another martini?"

"No. Not tonight, Mario. But I do want to thank you. And god bless you."

AFTER HE'D COLLECTED HIS SHOPPING BAG of clothes from the porter, he walked around the park and down Irving Place to a little newsstand that sold flowers. He picked out several bunches of yellow tulips that he bought along with a roll of Clorets. He munched on several of the latter to kill the gin smell.

Home. He could hear the kitchen radio playing. The Beatles *I Want To Be Your Man.* And he did. He sneaked down the stairs. Nora's back was to him as she stared at the kettle waiting for it to boil for her tea. He watched her for a moment, letting the sense of her beauty fill his being. It erased all the anger and made him realize how crazy he was for her and how crazy he had been for staying away on a bender. He put the flowers on the table, slipped up behind her and slid his arms around her as she jumped and screamed. When she realized it was Noah she sighed with relief as her worry fled. "Noah, thank god you're all right. I thought maybe you'd never come back."

"I know. I'm sorry. I'm sorry." He kissed her on the cheek and neck as his hands slid under her T-shirt to touch and rouse her nipples. She gasped and urgently moved around to press her body against his. Then they were kissing passionately and tearing off each other's clothes.

"Come on," Noah said, pulling her towards the stairs while trying to kick off his shoes and lose his pants at the same time. Even though by now they were seized by fits of laughter, he knew they'd never make the bed. So overcome were they that they fell against the steps, and he entered her with one long, swift thrust, filling her, making her come. Then as he moved in her, her orgasm continued. He could feel her vagina contracting around his penis stronger than he had ever remembered. When tears began to fill her eyes, he hesitated and then found he was tearing up as well. "No. Don't stop," she cried out, gripping his buttocks. "Don't leave me. Ever."

"No. Never. I love you so much."

"That's what I want to hear."

"THIS WON'T BE AFTER GOING AWAY, YOU KNOW," she said much later as they lay spent in bed.

"What do you mean?"

"Just because we went bonkers and made love like a pair of bleedin' savages. It's not going to whisk away everything that's happened."

"I'm sorry. I really am."

"And so am I. I should have told you those things. It's just that I love you so much I didn't want to hurt you. And I know too how bad it must feel for you to have lost the *Esquire* job. My heart only bleeds over it. But you left me and didn't come home for the whole effin' night. Where in the name of all that's holy were you?"

"I stayed at the Gramercy Park."

"How could you do that? Did you get too fluthered to walk around the park?"

"No. I just wanted to figure a way out of my anger and disappointment so things could come right."

"I was so bloody frightened when you didn't come back. I called your office the first thing this morning, and when I heard your voice I was so relieved. But I couldn't bring myself to say a word. So I rang off. I had to wait till you came back to me of your own accord. That you wanted to."

"Had to. I had no choice. I missed you that much." And he put his arm around her, kissed her and held her tightly.

"It was your portrait, you know. I had another look at it after you'd gone. I was raging with you until then. But that took it all away. That and all the hurt. Then I wanted you so much in that instant. Oh not just your body. Well that as well, I can tell you now. I think if you were to only touch a fingertip to me at that moment I would have had an orgasm so mighty it would have scared meself to blazes. But it was way more. When I looked at that portrait again I saw the strength and at the same time the gentleness of your soul. And there was such a powerful radiance and honesty. God it only captured me and drove me half mad with the passion."

"Captured what? Drove what?" he teased as he

looked at her.

"Ah don't you be being the smart aleck now. If there hadn't been you, there would never have been a portrait that exuded all those traits. And quite frankly I'd have my doubts and they'd be far from few that there'd be a painter now. But I just want to repeat one thing. I don't want to be a part of that world without you being present and accounted for. I always want you there just as you are in that portrait."

"But I don't know that I look like that anymore."

"You drift away from it from time to time right enough. But in your heart, I'm sure you're the exact same article. It's the substance of your being and that shouldn't go away. It's the rare quality you were given. You mustn't lose track of it. It's too precious."

"I do seem to have lost track of things all right. It's like Tim said--life is what you've got at home, and you always have to guard it. He was right."

"Tim?" she recoiled, pulling away. "When did he say that?"

"Last night."

"What?" she gasped as her anger instantly rose once more and she jumped out of bed. "I don't believe this. You saw him last night and told him about us?"

"Well, I had to talk to someone. I felt like I was coming apart."

"You fool," she roared pulling on her robe. "Don't you know all friends are bloody useless—always taking more than they give? Oh if I'd known you were doing that, I would have left. I have to tell you, I was certainly thinking about it."

"Well what stopped you then?"

"The thought that maybe you might need me, might want me. But obviously I was wrong. You're more than well taken care of by your so-called friend."

"Oh great. That's really rich. The way you say it, you'd think I was having an affair with him."

"Well aren't you? It doesn't have to be sexual to be intimate. Telling him those things. Sharing with him. And now you expect that we'll just go merrily rolling along."

"Look maybe we should call a truce."

"And what? Blithely ignore our problems--and let them destroy us? I can't surrender to that."

"And I can't surrender to you."

"Don't worry, I'm not going to force you," she said as she stared at him and realized that now there was a certain spiteful glint about the eyes that she'd never noticed until this moment.

"Where does that leave us?"

"Isn't it obvious?"

AFTER SHE'D PULLED ON SOME CLOTHES, she went off for a walk into the dimness of the muggy June evening. Rather than rage, she now felt devitalized. At some point, she drifted into a Twenty-Third Street coffee shop, nibbled on a sandwich, left and walked some more.

When she arrived back at the apartment, she found Noah nodding off in his Chippendale wing chair with her replacement--a martini--by his side. So she decided she would do her own thing as well. She drew the rollaway bed, the one they had purchased for the possibility of Mrs. Mason's visit, from the closet and set it up beside her worktable. Then she drew the curtains and went to bed.

When Noah awakened around midnight, he was so annoyed that he went to their bed without attempting to persuade her to join him. This was a portent of the distorted pattern of life to form for them. It was one in which they went their separate ways in the same apartment--cooking, sleeping, barely talking, except for him to insist on sleeping on the cot. God each wondered how this was happening to their once beautiful love--this sullenness, this festering that took them captive and advanced like a disease.

Those nights when he had no assignments, Noah hadn't the heart to work at his writing. Instead he would retreat into limbo behind a couple of martinis, while Nora worked at her easel trying never to glance his way.

As the days passed, he found himself struggling with his columns trying to make them lively, jovial, vibrant along with the touches of acidity that Oliver so loved. To stay on top of this, he finally killed the martinis. But nothing killed his disenchantment. So once again, this time without telling Nora, he began dropping queries through various trustworthy sources for editorial positions. He did get the calls and with each meeting, his excitement grew until as with *Esquire* he found there would be some sort of breakdown. God he so wanted to rush home with good news hoping to break their holding pattern.

He had begun to change once again, Nora felt. She caught herself watching him at night as he slept. There was no incessant snoring since he'd stopped drinking. Instead she would listen to the soft lull of his breathing. And oh how she wanted to cast off the burden of her clothes and only jump into the cot beside his naked body. But she couldn't let herself for a slew of reasons including the rage she still harbored for his sharing their secrets with Tim. So depression continued to rule.

Through all this pain as she worked, she found herself being drawn into her paintings and losing her overview. Something like a simple joyful landscape where lightness of tone should have predominated slipped into dark moody hues of gloom. Even the appearance of a grand and lengthy feature in *New York*, one that Noah noted with a warm smile was *fantastic*, didn't arrest her melancholy.

THE FINANCIAL CRUNCH, which until now Noah had kept at bay by paying the very minimum amounts on their bills, was beginning to reach its limit. While he never discussed this with Nora, he sensed that she sensed the full scope of the problem. It's surprising, he thought, when things really get rough the mind takes over to search for a solution. And sometimes in a flash it finds one.

It was a fluke. There was a partially open door to an

antique stock cabinet close by the rest rooms at the elegant *La Cote Basque* lunch bunch restaurant. And there was a stack of blank bright white customer checks with the slim perforated band at the bottom to be torn off and given as receipts to patrons who paid with cash. Before he knew what he was doing or why, he snatched a sizeable number of them and slipped them into one of the wide inside breast pockets of his suit coat.

It came to him in the taxi back to Wilton. Since there was no restaurant name on the receipt band, he could use them arbitrarily for his expense account, naming any restaurant and any amount within reason. In part it was normal for him to occasionally take a variety of BPs to chic luncheons. Indeed it was favored by the powers at Wilton in return for the luncheons lavished on one of their staff, especially their chief columnist. For all appearances he would do it more now and pretend he had paid. In the past he had always used a credit card receipt, but who said he couldn't change his method of payment. He would just have to remember to obliterate in subtle ways part of the number on the stub so that there could never be any detection in the Wilton accounts department.

At first he very slowly stepped up these charges on his expense account and as such was able to collect a few hundred extra dollars for each assault. It served them right for not paying him more. It also relieved him to no end that he would have this money when his mother visited them. But still worrying that even this might not be enough, he decided to nip another four hundred from their joint savings that he'd pay back as soon as he filed a few more of these loosely padded expense accounts. It was when he was checking the savings balance, he noted that it remained the same as it had after he'd clipped it months ago. Where was all the money going that Nora had made from her art? It certainly wasn't in their checking account. Was she secretly hiding it from him? He wondered with a flare of anger but given the distance between them he could hardly ask.

10

IN JULY, HE SENT HIS MOTHER her plane ticket. Besides keeping his promise to her, he thought her visit might break the stalemate between him and Nora.

"Could we not at least try to look the happily married couple?" he asked as they waited at LaGuardia for her flight to arrive shortly after noon of a Saturday.

"Well I'm willing to try, but I don't know if you can manage."

"For starters, we can share the same bed."

"Share only. And only while she's here."

"We couldn't go any further?"

"Well if you keep wavering back and forth, I just don't know."

"Oh, so it's all up to me?"

"I didn't say all. I just don't believe you're all for me. And I need that."

Thus they sat in silence until Mrs. Mason's flight arrived. After hugs and kisses, she scolded: "I didn't need a first class ticket, Noah."

"Oh yes you did, mama. This time traveling to New York I wanted you to do it in style. And likewise I want your stay to be in style. Not like it was in the Thirties."

"That sure wouldn't be hard."

"No, but I want it to be better than anything you ever imagined."

Nora shivered at the thoughts of what was to come. She told herself time and again that it wasn't jealousy that was embittering her. Sure she didn't mind him caring and doing for his mother, even though she'd done little to none of the same for her parents. After all, his mother was alone. But no, it was the lavish degree to which he would do it that would infuriate her. Errant extravagance run rampant, she told herself.

Though Mrs. Mason marveled at the grandness of their apartment, even she wondered if they had needed to go so far. "Although I might have wanted to I can tell you, I never in a million years would have dared to attempt all this."

"Oh come Nora," Noah jumped in quickly to change the topic. "We must take mama shopping right away. I think Bloomingdale's."

"No. You go along, and I'll be after getting the dinner while you're away," she insisted, concluding that if it was going to happen she'd rather not witness it.

At Bloomingdale's, Noah asked his mother to try on several designer dresses. Immediately they transformed her into an elegant sophisticated woman. Instinctively she changed the way she walked and carried herself. A graceful quality emerged that had never been nourished in previous times. Now she really was loftier than Joan Crawford. Noah grinned with delight as she admired herself in the mirror while caressing the fabric.

"I feel like a million dollars in these clothes," she said and laughed.

"You look that way too, mama."

"Just imagine what my friends at the flower society would say if I showed up wearing these," she delighted. But then she started examining the price tags. "Oh Noah! These are too expensive. Much too expensive," she gasped loudly.

"Mama hush. Don't be looking at the prices." Noah whispered. "You've wanted to look like this all your life. Now you finally do. And this time you won't have to put them back on the rack."

"But the cost! No. I can't let you do this. Not even one of them. This has to stop, especially after that furniture you bought me and all the other expenses you must have."

She started to put the dresses back, but Noah, who couldn't bear it, struggled them away from her and gave them to the sales girl. He would have it no other way. "She'll take them all and wear the one she has on," he said, asking the girl to clip away the tags. As he produced his Bloomingdale's charge, he thrilled at the thought of having given his mother the sumptuousness she had pined for all these years. He felt that in some way he was justifying his existence, proving that someone in her life had been worthwhile. Now if only he could tell her he had sold his novel. How proud she would be. Then he would have the success that eluded his father and all the Masons.

When he glanced over at the sales girl, she was skimming through a list on a white sheet of paper instead of processing his charge. The panic struck him. "I'm sorry Mr. Mason," she said as she motioned him over to her counter. "You're name and number are on this list. Did you fail to make a payment?"

"Oh yes, I did," he whispered, hoping his mother wouldn't hear. "You see I accidentally put the bill away with my paid bills, and I only discovered my error the other day. But I did mail in a payment then. I guess about three days ago."

"Well I must call billing before I can charge these."

"Is something wrong?" Mrs. Mason asked as she came over to him.

"No. No. No, mama," Noah insisted as he felt the perspiration sprout on his forehead and palms. "Nothing at all. So miss, I'd rather pay cash than bother with all that." But when his mother still looked worried, he scrambled to say: "There's some mix up in their charge records." It was true that he had made a payment, but it had been a month late. Would he have a cash shortage now while his mother was here, he panicked. If he did, he'd just have to withdraw more from their savings or use his charges. Thank god, he almost sighed aloud, his American Express bill had been paid on time.

"Well let me give you some money toward this," his mother said when he took out his wallet.

"You will not," he insisted in a strong voice as waves of embarrassment overtook him and his pride dwindled. He would have done anything to avoid this. He only prayed that he had covered it well enough.

LATE THAT AFTERNOON, after they'd arrived back from their shopping spree and much to their surprise, the doorbell rang. "Hello Noah," the immediately recognizable voice cheered over the intercom. It was Murphs. "I'm sorry," she bubbled after Noah went to escort her inside. "I hope this isn't a bad time for you. Nora please forgive me for interrupting and looking so sloppy yet," Murphs went on alluding to her bell-bottom jeans, sandals and rust colored T-shirt, which actually made her look like she should have been in a Hamptons what-they-were-wearing layout.

"Ah you're fine," Nora insisted.

"Yes, you look terrific," Noah insisted. "Come, I want you to meet my mother. Then I'll get us all a drink."

"No. No. I have to go and meet Jimmy. You know he just passed his bar exam. But I do want to meet your mother. That's why I barged in. I have a little something for her," she said shaking a shopping bag. "And I wasn't sure how long she'd be here."

Noah led her into the living room and introduced them. "Oh Mrs. Mason," Murphs thrilled as she took her hand then hugged her and smiled. "I am really so happy for this chance. Now I can see why Noah is such a special person," she marveled with delight as she smiled some more. Finally she said: "Oh, I brought a special little gift in honor of your visit. I was afraid of the size, but now I can see I chose right. Here."

Slightly stunned, Mrs. Mason took the Bergdorf shopping bag, reached inside and pulled out a tissue wrapped pink cashmere cardigan. "Oh my," she gasped. " Why I don't know what to say. It's just b-e-a-u-t-f-u-l." And she sighed in amazement as Murphs grinned with joy. After Mrs. Mason tried it on, she stroked its arms. "Why it's so soft and grand. I always dreamed of having a cashmere sweater. And a pink one too. Oh my, oh my. You people down here are too free with your spondulics." And they all laughed. "Well I'm serious. I just can't accept this." And she attempted to take it off.

"Oh yes you can, Mrs. Mason. It would break my heart if you didn't. I knew you'd like it. And I thought it would keep you warm on those wintry western New York nights." Then she hugged her again, and this time she kissed her and looked as if tears might come. "Well I have to be going. I can't keep Jimmy waiting." And just like that she breezed away with Noah once again amazed and wondering of her benevolence.

AS THE WEEK PROGRESSED, they took his mother to the theater to see *Mame* which she loved and *Hair* which she did not. ("What's the world coming to?") Then it was on to the Rainbow Room. There they glided down the sweeping staircase to the grand piano accompaniment of *Stairway To The Stars*. At a stunning window banquet, they savored a fine supper, while the orchestra played music from the Twenties and Thirties. Noah danced with his mother on the slowly revolving floor as the lights of the city spun round them and twinkled in the background. "This music sure brings back memories," she said wistfully. And Noah realized she must be recalling that night in the Pennsylvania ballroom when his father danced with Mae Murray and she with Ramon Novarro, who had called her 'the prettiest woman in the room'. But then suddenly she uttered a small gasp as the orchestra struck a whispery melancholic tune. "I can't *believe* they're playing this. Your father and I used to listen to it so much. I don't think I've heard it since the Depression."

By the time the male vocalist had finished the long prelude, Noah began to recall that it was in a Thirties film he'd caught a few years back at the old re-run house the New Yorker on Broadway. The song was *The Street of Dreams*. And as his mother heard it now, she could scarcely suppress her wistfulness.

"Oh mama, why do I feel this is so wrong, you hearing this?"

"S-h-h-h, just listen," she softly whispered as she stroked his face.

And then the vocalist went into the refrain as they continued their slow dance.

> *Love laughs at a king,*
> *Kings don't mean a thing*
> On the *street* of dreams.
> *Dreams broken in two*
> *Can be made like new*
> *On the street of dreams.*
>
> *Gold, silver and gold,*
> *All you can hold*
> *Is waiting in the moonbeams;*
> *Poor, no one is poor*
> *Long as love is sure*
> *On the street of dreams.*

"Oh we listened to that so much in those days, I can tell you. Trying to believe that at least something could come around again."

"Don't be sad, mama. You're remembering too much."

"Yes, I suppose I am."

As the vocalist finished his reprise, mama looked directly at Noah. "But it's also making me worry all over again."

"Worry? But what about?" And they both lingered in the middle of the dance floor.

"You and Nora."

"Us? But why?"

"I may be wrong. And I'm not butting in. But you don't seem the same."

"In what way?" Noah asked feigning surprise while suddenly longing for a good stiff drink.

"Just the little things. You don't hold hands like you used to. You don't talk as much or exchange smiles. It's just this silence. Why you haven't even asked her to dance this evening. Oh, I don't know. But they do say, it's the little things."

"Oh mama, I don't think there's anything to worry about. It's probably just that we've been married for a while now." And the desire for the drink become more urgent.

"True. Maybe."

SO THE DAYS SPUN OUT, and Noah became increasingly anxious to do things for his mother, rushing her about the city as though he were frantically racing to meet a deadline. He was also desperately trying to cover what his mother was beginning to see.

"Oh Noah, I'm exhausted," she said finally. "Couldn't we just stay home and take a rest?"

"We were planning on taking you to '21' for dinner and then on to the Music Hall."

"God Noah, we've seen and done enough. And your

poor mother," Nora snapped. "Could we not just stay here tonight? There's some chops in the fridge. And I could make a salad. Or is that beneath you?"

"I suppose it's okay," Noah conceded with annoyance. "I'll get us another drink."

"Oh no, not for me," Noah's mother insisted. "I'm too tired as it is."

"Yes, I think it's time we gave or systems a rest," Nora added as she fired an icy glare at Noah.

"Well suit yourselves. But I think I'll have another." And he headed for the bar table.

"I'll just go down and start the dinner so," Nora said.

"I'll come along and help you," Mrs. Mason told her.

As they went, Noah finished making his drink. Then he went over and put on the soundtrack from *The Graduate*. As *Scarborough Fair* drifted through the apartment, he tried to relax to it. Instead he was growing tense thinking of his writing and the Mason curse. He finished that drink and made another. It wasn't helping. He felt trapped by these thoughts. To escape, he called out to Nora: "I think I'll go out for a bottle of good wine for the dinner." Realizing she hadn't heard him, he went to the kitchen stairs and started down. It was at that point that he heard his mother and Nora talking.

"I think something's bothering him," his mother was saying.

"What do you mean, Mrs. Mason?"

"He seems so wound up."

"Well, I think he's a bit anxious about his work," she replied trying to sound as casual as possible.

"Is something wrong with his job? Is he short of money?"

"No. Not that. It's his books. That's what he really wants to do, and I think he's impatient with himself."

"That must be very hard on the both of you."

"Yes. It can be. I've sold some of my work as you know, and he's still waiting and longing. And that's not easy. Not on him."

"I'll say not. And there's another thing I'm worried about--"

"What's that?'

"Is he drinking a lot?"

"Oh a little I guess," she answered quickly while busying herself seasoning the lamb chops.

"Well maybe more than a little. I'd be concerned, Nora. I don't mean to interfere, but watch that he doesn't get to out of hand. And you know I say this because there may be good reason. I'm not trying to scare you, but I was pretty certain his father became an alcoholic."

Noah quickly and quietly went back upstairs and sat in his wing chair in a shaken state. He hadn't wanted his mother to see anything wrong. Least not this. And now from the day she arrived and with that messy incident at Bloomingdale's, things had gone wrong. He was so embarrassed and horrified. To be related to his father and his failures. All his years in New York had been spent trying to rise above this. He had to rise above it. He was quaking inside.

TWO DAYS LATER, when Nora was at the gallery discussing plans for her next showing, Noah accompanied his mother back to LaGuardia. On that humid rainy afternoon, the taxi took a different route out Queens Boulevard past the enormous Calvary Cemetery. His mother looked out at it, and suddenly tears flooded her eyes.

"Mama, what's wrong?"

"Nothing. Nothing." And she quickly wiped her tears.

"Is it me?"

"No. Not you. Just--."

"Sure?"

"Yes. Though I am worried about you."

"Nora and I will be fine. Believe me."

"Not just that. But you're--"

"What?"

"Less--calm. There's nothing easy going anymore."

"That sounds ominous, mama. What does that mean?"

"I know you love Ireland, Noah. Did you and Nora ever make any more plans about finding a cottage there?"

"Oh we still think of it. And I certainly want to do it. Just to have one. I guess probably I've been waiting till-"

"Thinking, wanting, waiting. I don't think that's

enough. Doing I think is the right thing."

"Really?"

"Yes, for now at least. I think it would bring you two closer together again."

"But we are together."

"Now just listen to me. You're not together. I don't care what you say. And that's sad, a lovely couple like you. Take some time. Maybe even a year. You're young. You can do it. You won't lose out. I would think you could sublet that beautiful apartment of yours at a good rate. I've read in the papers of that being done a lot down here. And if you wanted, you could sell a few pieces of that grand furniture. I don't know how you afforded it to begin with, but antiques bring in a lot of money these days. Then I was thinking once you're in Ireland along with Nora's beautiful painting, couldn't you write those articles and stories you used to do so well and send them to publishers here to keep you going? At the same time you could be working on your books." Then she stopped and sighed: "I just wish that you hadn't spent all that on me. I feel bad now. That has to have been a terrible strain on you. And I was so wrong to have accepted it."

"Oh mama, you don't know how much and how long I've wanted to buy things for you." And the hurt was overwhelming him.

"Well I do know. And it's too much. Now you've got to stop and think of yourself and Nora. Just to be able to get away from everything that's gotten hold of you."

"What's this? What's gotten hold of me?"

"Whatever's got your spirit." She looked at him for a long time and neither spoke. "Oh Noah, you and Nora can do it," she finally encouraged, taking his arm and squeezing it. "You have the life that we never had. Look at how far you've come already. Don't lose it, because you might never get it back again. Love has to be sure, Noah."

"But Ireland, mama. What if I never wrote anything that sold? What if--?"

"What if--" she sighed. "Noah, it's not Ireland I'm talking about. It's not writing books that sell either. And it's not paintings. I know how much money means, believe me. But with your education and ability, you can always get another good job when you need to. No, what I'm talking about is you. You and your lovely Nora. And not letting go. That's what it's all about, Noah. Not letting go. Holding on to what you've got while you reach out. Now you mark my words. We didn't learn that soon enough. If you don't, there'll come a day when like your youth your chance will be gone. Then no matter how much you reach out, it will be too late. You'll have lost your claim."

At the airport when they were saying goodbye, she took his hand and looked into his eyes one last time. "Noah, I envy you so much. I hope you realize that--and what it means."

11 I'VE GOT TO DO SOMETHING, he told himself on the way back to Gramercy Park in the taxi that day. Stop drinking, start writing again. And more. Much more. Get our lives together. The more he thought about it the more fearful he became. Things were spinning out of control. Mama's words played over his mind, stinging it again and again. *Like your youth, your chance will be gone. You'll have lost--.* God. Could this be? But how soon? Things are going. They have been. Once again turmoil began to take possession. Feckin' fight it. No bloody curse is going to take me. Break the chain. Yes. Think about sex. Think about how great it is with her. How long it's been. How long since I've seen the creamy flush about her neck and breasts, watched the nipples grow erect, reached down to the engorged hollow and felt the silky wetness flowing there. God that should be enough to break any debilitating chain.

"Could we rollaway for now?" he asked Nora.

She looked at him with a still cold expression but said nothing.

"I'm serious." he insisted taking her by the shoulders. She pulled away, but he continued. "I'm determined to reverse things for us. To pull out of this and go forward. I'm going to push ahead with the writing and give it all that's in me. And I'm going to cut way back on the bottle. Cut it out altogether for the time being."

"It sounds to be a bold enough start all the same." Even though she felt the first bit of delight she'd known in weeks, there was something there that said don't be a flippin' eejit.

"Yes, you're right," he insisted and went on with so much power it startled her. "But it is only a start. And I mean this. We have to make things better for each other. At least I have to make things better for you, so that we are together. Really together again. I was thinking about Ireland. Well, the truth is mama was thinking about Ireland. She feels that no matter what we should go ahead with the cottage there. But not just that. She thinks we should forget all this and really go ahead and try it for maybe a year."

"And you agree?" She was so amazed she could scarcely ask the question.

"Yes, I agree," he replied with even greater affirmation. "For us, I agree. Go after it. But this time, really go after it. We can always come back. Whereas if we keep this madness up. If *I* keep this madness up-- Well, we can't go anywhere but apart."

"Noah, I wouldn't have put those words together as well as that. But-- Well if you're ready to stand behind them like that-- Well what can I say?"

He sighed with great relief. "The problem, the holdup as I see it is the cottage."

"I wouldn't say so. Just let me work on that detail for a while. I'll carry that burden. You've enough to be carrying with the rest."

"Well it would help for starters--if we could be

together again."

They looked at each other and saw the pain their separation had caused. It dispelled the negatives as their passion surfaced. Then they were in each other's arms and within seconds undressing and uniting in the sheer bliss of ecstasy once again. After so long, it was so good that they both felt it had to be the answer to everything. And it was—for a time.

12

"NOAH, WHAT'S GOT YOU SO JITTERY LATELY?" Murphs asked when sweating he knocked over his mug of pencils one morning a few weeks later.

"I don't know," he said as he set to work picking them up. "I've been up every night working on these fiction pieces. I think they're just wiping me out."

"Patience please, Noah. Don't get back the way you were going. It isn't worth it, you know. Look why don't you take a few days off? Take advantage of the sick days."

"I never thought of that. But it would be difficult with my column right now."

"Is that one of the things that's bothering you? Why advertising and circulation has never been higher, and it's your column that's a very strong part of that. Oliver may be barking at you all the time. But you notice he isn't biting. You should know that every so often he goes through these obsessive spells of macabre delight over being the puppeteer. Now just stop in your tracks and let me suggest something that might help. My boyfriend Jimmy can get you some great Acapulco gold for nothing. We smoked a little the other night after we saw *Bonnie and Clyde*. It really was mind expanding, you know. And so relaxing and sensual. Wow, I couldn't believe it."

"Somehow I don't think smoking suits me." And he laughed a little as a release.

"Well, you need to do something to cool that's for sure. Take mother's advice."

And she was right, he had thought about it, had been forced to think about it, time and again since he'd stopped drinking. The return to lovemaking had mellowed him at first. But as the days went by he noticed a shifting in mood. A tension of sorts. Nora noticed it too and so worried it signaled yet another setback.

When the clamoring grew more intense, he had to do something. One of the Wilton artists was always professing the wonders of Valium. She was a very attractive but no nonsense woman. "I've been around," her voice boomed, and he could believe it. "But I've never taken anything as good as this. Just take one every morning. It's the best fix you'll ever have. Here, take one. It's a very low dosage. Only two milligrams. Because you don't want it to interrupt your love life. That's for sure."

He floated through the day. Yet he accomplished so much. Far more than he ever had. Nothing got to him. He drifted home as in a dream. After dinner, he did what he considered to be some good writing, then followed it up with some terrific love making. God, this is truly a wonder drug, he thought. Even though Nora delighted in his seemingly boundless energy and calm demeanor, he didn't tell her of the drug, because he didn't want to admit he needed anything that desperately.

But the first thing the next morning, he phoned his doctor's secretary. "I really need to see Dr. DiCarlo. I mean like right away."

"He's got a full calendar today and tomorrow. But is it an emergency?"

"Oh-- Well—Yes! Yes, it's an emergency." He couldn't believe he was saying this. But he was. And yes, he guessed it really was--an emergency.

DURING THE MUGGY WEEKS TO COME, Noah thanked god for the Wilton art lady. She had turned his life around from the bummer it had become. Nora was so thankful for this reversal that she never asked him how he'd achieved it, she just prayed it wouldn't fade away. Once again their evenings were spent working in harmony accompanied by classical music. And it was as if by magic he was doing unbelievable amounts of writing. Even when he was off on assignments, speeding to the Hamptons, flying to Nantucket, producing columns that Oliver began praising once again, he was able to hold all anxieties in check. With the aid of only one mild Valium a day.

If it's this great, what would it be like if I took some

time off? Like Murphs said--take advantage of those sick days. So he did. And how wonderful those days were. He made great strides with both his society novel and the rewrite of his first born. How much he would accomplish if he had this time ad infinitum. Then he thought of Ireland and their cottage, which he knew Nora was working to find. Oh how great that would be. He wasn't the only one dreaming such dreams, he told himself for greater reassurance. It seemed everyone who was young and spirited in the summer of 1968 was thinking of riding the waves of change. America was thoroughly disenchanted with itself. *Hey, hey LBJ. How many kids did you kill today?* And it was all punctuated by the television coverage of the Democratic Convention and the savage beatings of the peace demonstrators in the sweltering heat of that Chicago August.

13

"I HAVE A SURPRISE FOR YOU, PET," Nora called out one night when he arrived home. Then she jumped up from her easel, took off her apron and rushed over to hug him.

"What? You sound so elated."

"I am elated. You remember that married couple that I worked with in Dublin? Helen and Martin Doherty."

"Sure."

"Well Helen's grandmother lives in the Rosses of

Donegal. She has a house on this promontory high above the Gweedore River just where it flows into the sea. And Helen tells me it's away from everything. Oh Noah, it sounds only breathtaking. It's surrounded by the sea, and there's this lovely mountain called Errigal in the background. She says there's heather and all the lovely little wild flowers and the big sky with the stars tumbling out of the heavens to greet you and the wind lashing in off the sea and--"

"So?"

"Well that's the great news I'm after trying to tell you," she replied as she snatched up the opened letter from the dining table. "I called Helen about three weeks ago thinking I'd chance it. I didn't say anything to you because I didn't want to be falsely raising your hopes. And-- Listen to this. The granny was only delighted. She said to Helen-- sure what would I be doing with all the land I've got here? I may as well be selling some of it."

"And?" he asked as his excitement rose.

"I just received this letter from Helen today. The granny is more than willing to do the deed. She'll sell us a parcel of land for almost nothing. She said she'd be only that grateful for the company. Oh Noah, we could have a cottage built there. It would be only beautiful. Just look at these pictures Helen sent." And she pulled a group from the envelope.

Noah looked at them for a very long time and felt the tingle of new life. High on a hill, just above the sea. Just as he had once dreamed. "It's so beautiful it makes me ache."

"And those lovely strands. Oh just to be there together." And she put her arms around him and squeezed him.

"Yeah, but wait. What do we do about the cottage?"

"Helen asked about that for us," Nora quickened to add as she opened up the letter. "And she says here that the construction of a fine snug cottage would cost about two thousand quid or thereabouts complete with the conveniences. Of course we'd have to put the bit more with it for the land. But we couldn't ask for a better lot than that, Noah."

"That's a little over five thousand dollars. I hope we can pay it off along. Or better still, I've been thinking about this. Maybe we should take a bank loan." He meant another loan, but he hadn't told her about the first. "And then I'll insist again on Wilton giving me a raise," he added, wondering if he dared.

"Ah don't be daft, Noah. That's all we're short of. The last thing we need is to be doing something more on the never-never." He noticed the kindness of the word *we*.

He blinked and she could see his hurt.

"I'm sorry I didn't mean that to be rude. But it's just that we've got to be practical now, if we're going to go ahead and make this move. Besides we don't need to take a loan. We have the money for the cottage."

"You're kidding. Where is it?" he asked while

feeling haunted by all the money he still owed.

"I opened a special account. Well--" she hesitated but then told him. "I've been putting away a good sum of money I'm after making on the painting just for this. I wanted it to be a surprise."

"Shock me is more like it." And he fell silent. Where had he heard that before? It was exactly the way she felt when he surprised her with this apartment. Only now she had the wherewithal to do the surprising, and he didn't. He hadn't even been able to pay off his surprises, which had been his big surprise. But this? It was the answer to a dream. And now it doesn't come without pain. Unbelievable pain. This does hurt. Hurt-- It cuts to the bone. Not to be in charge. And her own secret savings account yet. He looked back at the pictures he still held in his hand to try to cover his fierce range of emotions.

"Well, what do you think?" she asked anxiously.

"Jesus, the scenery is beautiful."

AND HE KEPT THIS IN MIND during the weeks to come, as he took some additional sick days and wrote about thirty more pages of his society novel advancing it to the halfway point. Then he shifted gears and once again finished another rewrite of his upstate work and sent it off to Jason Blackwell incorporating the changes that Random House seemed to want. "Well I don't like it as well as the last version. I thought that was perfect. But I could be wrong," Nora said. "As a matter of fact, I probably am. I most likely misled you before. And that was wrong of me. After all, he knows the market."

"Let's hope."

BUT HOPE CAME sooner than he had ever expected. Two days after he'd mailed the revised manuscript to Jason Blackwell, he received a call from a chief editor at Doubleday. It seemed that recently she had lunch with one of the Random House editors who Blackwell had said was interested in his book before the company rejected it. Well now it came to pass that she was more than just interested in it. She and another Random House editor loved it. "When I heard about this piece I thought it would be absolutely perfect for us. If it's as good as Rose Carlen says it is, I think Random House is absolutely daft not to have jumped on it," Marie McCloud professed to Noah. "Of course now that I've heard about it, I want to read it right away. Do you have an agent?"

"Well I don't know if I want to talk about that. He had me do a whole rewrite, and I don't know if I'm comfortable about what he's made me make it into."

"Who?"

"Jason Blackwell, if you must know. He kind of dropped it though."

"Jason Blackwell! I think he's far too polished and up-market for this sort of book. Look, *don't* send me the rewrite. I want to see what Rose Carlen saw. And I want to see it right away. We can worry about an agent later."

"I certainly will send it right away. My wife and I are all set to go to Ireland for a few weeks. I hope that won't be a problem."

"Absolutely not. Go and enjoy it. I'll see you when you get back. But I want to tell you I'm getting quite thrilled about this project, because I know I can trust Rose Carlen."

ONCE MORE NOAH SAVORED the return of hope. Before that call he truly did believe things had been locked in place forever. Now that had changed. And other things had changed along with it. He forgot about the alcohol and the Valium, even the opulence. Heavenly god, it was such a release at last. Maybe now it would happen.

14

OH DARK DARK BLUE SKIES
Sun
Cloud shadows tumbling down craggy
        green hills to the sea
The rush of water, the whisper of pure air
Flowers dancing in full bloom
Nora in bloom

As they drove up the coastline from Shannon, alone with the sweep of cold water lakes mixed with purple mountains, deep green valleys and stretches of marbly green sea, they thrilled to this now seemingly alien beauty.

It took two wonderful days to get to the Rosses in Donegal. You could reach the Aran Islands far more quickly. But this county at the northwestern-most reach of the Republic seemed like a country unto itself. An unspoiled frontier land, Noah thought. And his mind would not stop writing.

FOR A QUARTER OF A MILE, their rented Ford Escort bumped up and down a narrow dirt road flanked by giant furze hedges until it arrived at an oblong gray house, starkly set out on a hill that faced the stormy estuary which led down to the turbulent North Atlantic. It looked like the beginning of the world. Just seeing it was cause for rejoicing.

A short woman dressed all in black and with white and gray sprinkled hair pulled back in a bun scurried to door as a child would. From Helen's description, Nora knew this was her granny *Mhathair*, or mother as everyone who didn't speak Gaelic called her.

"*Wahl, wahl, wahl,* would that be Noah and Nora now?" *Mhathair* asked excitedly as she came out to the drive path to greet them.

"Yes, it's us," Nora laughed. As she went to shake *Mhathair*'s hand and kiss her, she glimpsed the sea again and was awestruck.

Behind *Mhathair* was her bachelor son Hughie, who looked to be at least in his mid-fifties. He was so quiet and stiffly reserved, like the schoolmaster he was, until he spoke. "Welcome. You are welcome indeed," he said warmly and beamed with delight.

"And surely you took so long in the coming that we thought you'd never be coming at all," *Mhathair* went on.

"How did you find the journey?" Hughie asked and sucked on his pipe as he tried to light it with a stick match.

"Long. It's a lot further than we thought," Noah said, and then his eyes became captivated by the seascape.

"*Wahl* now just," agreed *Mhathair*. "But what are we doing standing out here talking at all? Hughie, you'll be having them think we'd be wanting to send them away."

"*Nil son deabhadh*," Hughie said to *Mhathair*. She threw her hands into the air, shook her head and then pushed him into the house, saying: "*Dia linn!*"

Nora laughed because she understood the Irish from the courses she had been required to take in school--Hughie saying that sure there was no hurry and *Mhathair* out of frustration gasping--*god bless us.*

So they went into *Mhathair*'s kitchen. "*Sui isteach*," she said, pointing to the two chairs by the turf fire. "If only I had the English to be talking to you the right way," she went on as she made the tea in a fine old blackened pot. "But I'll just have to be teaching you the Irish." And she laughed. It was true they were in the heart of the Donegal Gaeltacht, but nevertheless, these people spoke perfectly understandable English.

"*Wahl, wahl, wahl,* you'll be hungry now that your journey's over. Hughie, take down the bread and the biscuits," *Mhathair* ordered as she began to set out the cups and plates.

"*Mhathair*, do not put food out for us," Nora insisted. "We've had plenty to eat."

"Ah, you'll take the cup of tea in your hand now, you will and the bit of bread and butter to go with it."

"That would be grand all the same, sure it would," Nora said, realizing if they didn't it would offend her.

"*Ta aran baile againn*," Hughie said to *Mhathair*.

"Oh Hughie, no. Don't put out my bread. Take down the shop bread. They would be wanting that," *Mhathair* insisted.

"Do not," Nora said aghast. "We can have shop bread every day of the week, but we can't get the home bread." Noah grinned broadly, and Nora delighted that he was taking to them.

Mhathair's eyes danced with glee over the bread. "*Wahl, wahl*," she said.

Nora got up and took the teapot from her. "You sit, *Mhathair*. I'll pour it."

"Ah, *wahl* now just. I would want it that way," she agreed readily, as though she were relieved from the fretting that she might do something wrong. Then she sat in a tiny wooden child's chair by the fire. If it weren't for her snowy gray hair, she could have been a child. "And do you like this part of the world?" she asked Noah earnestly.

"Yes, I like it very much." He sighed as he listened to the wind whistle round the house snuggling it.

"And you would be the one that would be spending

your days writing, if you were to live here?" Hughie asked.

"Yes." His heart leapt. If only it can be. It has to be.

"*Wahl, wahl, wahl,*" she said, rubbing her hands together and marveling with her big dark eyes. "Isn't that a fine work now."

"Ah, it's a good place for a man with a pen to be," Hughie added as he sat by the cooker.

"And do you think you could be liking it enough here?" *Mhathair* asked them.

"Yes. Oh yes," Noah said.

"Do you have to ask?" Nora added beaming.

"*Wahl*, we would be in a happy way to see you stay"

"Indeed we would," said Hughie, and it was clear to Noah and Nora that they were already relishing having nearby neighbors.

After they ate, Hughie took them on a tour of the land, which consisted of about ten acres. It was just as Helen had described it. There was craggy Errigal Mountain in the distance And then nearer, the rugged fields of rock and mauve and white heather broken by the occasional watery green stretch of field, and always, always the vast sea. When you sat on the bank of the wide estuary on a still evening such as this had become, you could hear the voices of the people on the other side speaking in the lyrical chant of the Irish. Cows exchanged moos back and forth across the river, and the setting sun laid a deep purple swath across the water. They sat there for a long time without speaking. Noah kept closing his eyes, carving images on his mind--images he wanted to be lasting. Oh yes. Lasting. And the Yeats came to him then. *An evening full of the linnet's wings.*

"Hughie, this is where I would like to build a house," he said abruptly, knowing he was speaking for the two of them. Nora was joyous.

"And a fine place it would make," Hughie concluded.

Before they left Donegal, *Mhathair* and Hughie agreed to sell them a good few promontory acres at the very reasonable price of a few hundred pounds. They signed the papers one morning in the solicitor's office in the nearby town of Dungloe. That afternoon, they met with a builder Hughie had recommended. By the next evening they had worked out all the details. A small, fully equipped cottage would cost them two thousand pounds. And Noah amazed even himself by truly believing that in this case small would be perfect. The bargain was struck.

The next morning after Mass in Irish at the little tin-roofed church of Meenaneal high in the jagged hills above the local town of Crolly, they rested against a stone pasture wall savoring the crisp bite of the wind as it whipped the cloud clusters.

"It certainly bolsters the spirit," Noah insisted as he put his arm around her. "Imagine having this every day to push you onwards."

"The *ould* boot in the butt," Nora added and they both laughed and she kissed and squeezed him. "You couldn't deny that god's hand is in this landscape, right enough."

YES, THIS HAD ALL HAPPENED as if in a dream, Noah thought on the Aer Lingus flight back to New York. He guessed it had been the flight of dreams. But one thought did keep niggling him. It was all Nora's doing. And god, he wished it had been his, that he was at the helm.

As jubilant as Nora was with this accomplishment, she felt the need to pray constantly for their new life—that nothing would impede it. Through all her lingering fears, she kept telling herself that the enemy was all but gone at last.

End of Part One

The second and final part of *Craving* will be published shortly.

Don Fullington is a freelance writer who has covered a wide variety of subjects from business, social culture, politics and fashion in newspapers and magazines in the US and abroad. He has also had books published on travel including *The Connoisseur's Guide To Ireland* (Henry Holt, New York and Aurum Press,UK). He and his wife live near their families in New York and the northeast.